tasteofhome

EVERYDAY
slow
cooker 2009
& ONE DISH RECIPES

Preparing Wholesome, Home-Style Suppers Has Never Been Easier!

With the busy schedules and activity-packed days of people everywhere, recipes that require less time, preparation and cleanup have never been more popular. You'll be delighted with the dishes featured in Taste of Home Everyday Slow Cooker & One Dish Recipes because they deliver down-home goodness every time.

Inside you'll find more than 350 recipes and tips that offer convenience when it comes to setting a satisfying meal on the table. If your days are too hectic for a home-cooked dinner, breathe a sigh of relief because this book offers a variety of delicious, no-fuss dinners.

To make searching for recipes easier, the book is divided into three main sections: Slow Cookers, Stovetop Suppers and Oven Entrees. It's like having 3 books in 1! Each section is broken into chapters, such as Beef & Ground Beef, Poultry, Pork, Soup & Sandwiches and more.

Slow Cookers. Here's a chance to discover the wonderful benefits of this simple kitchen appliance. Its convenience is unmatched because you don't have to be at home while your favorite meal simmers to mouthwatering perfection—just set it and forget it! Slow cookers are also economical, because they turn affordable cuts of meat, such as beef stew meat or chicken thighs, into tender and delectable sensations.

The variety of dishes in the Slow Cooker section ranges from tantalizing appetizers to comforting entrees. You'll even find scrumptious side dishes that are perfect for potlucks, as well as recipes for chill-chasing beverages and decadent desserts. Plus, this book features 50 brand-new, never-before-published slow cooker recipes!

To get the best out of your slow cooker, refer to Slow Cooking 101 on page 240. This four-page section offers tips and hints so that every slow cooker recipe you create turns out perfect.

Stovetop Suppers. This section is full of one-pot meals you can throw together in a snap. Quick, easy and family-friendly, they require little cleanup because they usually take advantage of a single skillet or Dutch oven. These super-easy dinners are sure to satisfy.

Oven Entrees. If hearty one-dish dinners are what you have in mind, then check out the final section of this heartwarming cookbook. You'll enjoy tasty casseroles, such as baked pastas, as well as beef and pork roasts, potpies, pizzas and so much more. These meal-in-one sensations make fantastic family fare, and they are especially well suited for potlucks, church suppers, banquets and other covered-dish dinners.

If you're looking for a break from meat-and-potato items, check out the Fish & Seafood chapters of the Stovetop Suppers and the Oven Entrees sections. You'll find interesting and unique recipes that offer wholesome yet change-of-pace choices for dinner.

You can prepare every one of the recipes in this beautiful Everyday Slow Cooker & One Dish Recipes cookbook with confidence because every recipe has been tested for accuracy and flavor by the Taste of Home Test Kitchen. Recipes on the light side include Nutrition Facts and Diabetic Exchanges and are marked with an asterisk so you can find them easily.

So, set your slow cooker, grab your favorite skillet or preheat your oven and get ready to dig in! After one bite, you'll realize just how easy it is to make satisfying dinner-table memories every day of the week.

©2009 Reiman Media Group, Inc.
5400 S. 60th St., Greendale WI 53129
All rights reserved.

Taste of Home is a registered trademark of The Reader's Digest Association, Inc.

SENIOR VICE PRESIDENT, EDITOR IN CHIEF: Catherine Cassidy
VICE PRESIDENT, EXECUTIVE EDITOR/BOOKS: Heidi Reuter Lloyd
CREATIVE DIRECTOR: Ardyth Cope
FOOD DIRECTOR: Diane Werner RD
SENIOR EDITOR/BOOKS: Mark Hagen
EDITOR: Krista Lanphier
ART DIRECTOR: Gretchen Trautman
CONTENT PRODUCTION SUPERVISOR: Julie Wagner
DESIGN LAYOUT ARTISTS: Nancy Novak, Catherine Fletcher
PROOFREADER: Linne Bruskewitz
RECIPE ASSET SYSTEMS: Coleen Martin, Sue A. Jurack
PREMEDIA SUPERVISOR: Scott Berger
RECIPE TESTING AND EDITING: Taste of Home Test Kitchen
FOOD PHOTOGRAPHY: Reiman Photo Studio
GRAPHIC DESIGN ASSOCIATE: Heather Miller
EDITORIAL ASSISTANT: Barb Czysz
COVER PHOTO PHOTOGRAPHER: Dan Roberts
COVER FOOD STYLIST: Jennifer Janz
COVER SET STYLIST: Jennifer Bradley Vent

CHIEF MARKETING OFFICER: Lisa Karpinski
VICE PRESIDENT/BOOK MARKETING: Dan Fink
CREATIVE DIRECTOR/CREATIVE MARKETING: Jim Palmen

The Reader's Digest Association, Inc.
PRESIDENT AND CHIEF EXECUTIVE OFFICER: Mary G. Berner
PRESIDENT, FOOD & ENTERTAINING: Suzanne M. Grimes
PRESIDENT, CONSUMER MARKETING: Dawn Zier

FRONT COVER: Slow Cooker Lasagna (p. 31).

BACK COVER, LEFT TO RIGHT: Creamy Tarragon Chicken (p. 56), Beef Fried Rice (p. 119) and Wild Rice Chicken Dinner (p. 194).

International Standard Book Number (10): 0-89821-658-3

International Standard Book Number (13): 978-0-89821-658-5

International Standard Serial Number: 1944-6382

Timeless Recipes from Trusted Home Cooks® is a registered trademark of Reiman Media Group, Inc.

Printed in U.S.A.

For other Taste of Home books and products, visit ShopTasteofHome.com.

table of contents

SLOW COOKER

Soups & Sandwiches

15

20

23

Soups and sandwiches will never go out of style. Slow-cooked soups simmer for hours and are just the ticket for chasing away the chills. And a slow cooker turns meat into tender fillings for robust sandwiches. It's easy to create a hearty lunch or casual family supper with the specialties in this chapter.

Great Northern Bean Chili

Italian Venison Sandwiches

Andrew Henson
MORRISON, ILLINOIS

The slow cooker makes easy work of these hearty venison sandwiches. I'm an avid hunter and cook, and the meat always comes out tender and tasty.

PREP: 10 min.
COOK: 8 hours

- 2 cups water
- 1 envelope onion soup mix
- 1 tablespoon dried basil
- 1 tablespoon dried parsley flakes
- 1 teaspoon beef bouillon granules
- 1/2 teaspoon celery salt
- 1/4 teaspoon garlic powder
- 1/4 teaspoon cayenne pepper
- 1/4 teaspoon pepper
- 1 boneless venison roast (3 to 4 pounds), cut into 1-inch cubes
- 10 to 12 sandwich rolls, split

Green pepper rings, optional

- In a 3-qt. slow cooker, combine the first nine ingredients. Add venison and stir. Cover and cook on low for 8 hours or until meat is tender. Using a slotted spoon, spoon into rolls. Top with pepper rings if desired.

Yield: 10-12 servings.

mamesmom
TASTE OF HOME ONLINE COMMUNITY
It takes only seven ingredients to make this mild version of a Southwestern chicken chili. I like to add a dash of hot sauce and some sour cream on top, and serve it with tortilla chips.

Great Northern Bean Chili

PREP: 20 min. ■ **COOK:** 4 hours

- 2 pounds boneless skinless chicken breasts, cut into 1-inch cubes
- 1 tablespoon canola oil
- 1 jar (48 ounces) great northern beans, rinsed and drained
- 1 jar (16 ounces) salsa
- 1 can (14-1/2 ounces) chicken broth
- 1 teaspoon ground cumin, optional
- 2 cups (8 ounces) shredded Monterey Jack cheese

- In a large skillet, brown chicken in oil; drain. In a 4- or 5-qt. slow cooker, combine the beans, salsa, broth, cumin if desired and chicken.

- Cover and cook on low for 4-6 hours or until the chicken is tender. Serve with cheese.

Yield: 8 servings.

Dawn
Fagerstrom
WARREN, MINNESOTA

This recipe turns brisket into tender slices of beef and a delicious au jus. To get very thin slices of beef, chill the brisket first, then slice and reheat in the juices.

Brisket for a Bunch

Brisket for a Bunch

PREP: 20 min. ■ COOK: 7 hours

1 fresh beef brisket (2-1/2 pounds), cut in half	1/4 cup water
1 tablespoon canola oil	1/4 cup sugar
1/2 cup chopped celery	2 tablespoons onion soup mix
1/2 cup chopped onion	1 tablespoon cider vinegar
3/4 cup beef broth	12 hamburger buns, split
1/2 cup tomato sauce	

■ In a large skillet, brown brisket in oil on both sides; transfer to a 3-qt. slow cooker. In the same skillet, saute celery and onion for 1 minute. Gradually add the broth, tomato sauce and water; stir to loosen the browned bits from pan. Add the sugar, soup mix and vinegar; bring to a boil. Pour over brisket.

■ Cover and cook on low for 7-8 hours or until meat is tender. Let stand for 5 minutes before slicing. Skim fat from cooking juices. Serve meat in buns with cooking juices.

Yield: 10 servings.

Editor's Note: This is a fresh beef brisket, not corned beef.

Hearty Black Bean Soup*

Amy Chop
OAK GROVE, LOUISIANA

Cumin and chili powder give spark to this thick, hearty soup. If you have leftover cooked meat, smoked sausage, browned ground beef or roast, toss it in for the last 30 minutes of cooking.

PREP: 10 min.
COOK: 9 hours

    3 medium carrots, halved
       and thinly sliced
    2 celery ribs, thinly sliced
    1 medium onion, chopped
    4 garlic cloves, minced
    1 can (30 ounces) black
       beans, rinsed and drained
    2 cans (14-1/2 ounces *each*)
       chicken *or* vegetable broth
    1 can (15 ounces) crushed
       tomatoes
1-1/2 teaspoons dried basil
  1/2 teaspoon dried oregano
  1/2 teaspoon ground cumin
  1/2 teaspoon chili powder
  1/2 teaspoon hot pepper
       sauce
Hot cooked rice

■ In a 3-qt. slow cooker, combine the first 12 ingredients. Cover and cook on low for 9-10 hours or until vegetables are tender. Serve with rice.

Yield: 8 servings.

*Nutrition Facts: One 1-cup serving (prepared with reduced-sodium broth; calculated without rice) equals 141 calories, 2 g fat (0 saturated fat), 2 mg cholesterol, 477 mg sodium, 24 g carbohydrate, 0 fiber, 9 g protein. Diabetic Exchanges: 1-1/2 starch, 1-1/2 very lean meat.

In a small skillet, saute onions in butter until tender. Transfer to a 3-qt. slow cooker. Stir in remaining ingredients. Cook on high for 5-8 hours or until vegetables are tender.

Yield: 6-8 servings (2-1/2 quarts).

Editor's Note: The stew may also be cooked in a Dutch oven on the stovetop. Cover and simmer for 1-1/2 hours.

When a recipe calls for poultry seasoning, you can make your own at home with this simple recipe. For 1 teaspoon of poultry seasoning, combine 3/4 teaspoon rubbed sage and 1/4 teaspoon dried thyme or marjoram.

Smoked Sausage Soup

Rachel Lyn Grasmick
ROCKY FORD, COLORADO
This rich soup is packed with hearty vegetables, smoked sausage and chunks of chicken. I guarantee it's unlike any other soup you've ever tasted.

Smoked Sausage Soup

PREP: 10 min. ■ COOK: 5 hours

2 cups chopped onions	1/4 cup minced fresh parsley
2 tablespoons butter	2 tablespoons cornstarch
2 cups cubed cooked chicken	2 tablespoons poultry seasoning
1 pound smoked sausage, cut into bite-size pieces	1 teaspoon dried oregano
3 cups sliced celery	1 teaspoon ground cumin
3 cups sliced summer squash	1 teaspoon Liquid Smoke, optional
2 cups chicken broth	1/2 teaspoon pepper
1 can (8 ounces) tomato sauce	

Alice Peacock
GRANDVIEW, MISSOURI

My husband and I created this recipe to replicate the minestrone soup at our favorite Italian restaurant. It's nice to have this ready for our evening meal on days when we have a real busy schedule. To make the soup vegetarian, use vegetable broth instead of beef.

Vegetable Minestrone

PREP: 15 min. ■ COOK: 6-1/2 hours

2 cans (14-1/2 ounces *each*) beef broth

1 can (16 ounces) kidney beans, rinsed and drained

1 can (15 ounces) great northern beans, rinsed and drained

1 can (14-1/2 ounces) Italian-style stewed tomatoes

1 large onion, chopped

1 medium zucchini, thinly sliced

1 medium carrot, shredded

3/4 cup tomato juice

1 teaspoon dried basil

3/4 teaspoon dried oregano

1/4 teaspoon garlic powder

1 cup frozen cut green beans, thawed

1/2 cup frozen chopped spinach, thawed

1/2 cup small shell pasta

1/2 cup shredded Parmesan cheese

■ In a 4- or 5-qt. slow cooker, combine the first 11 ingredients. Cover and cook on low for 6-7 hours or until vegetables are tender.

■ Stir in green beans, spinach and pasta. Cover and cook for 30 minutes or until heated through. Sprinkle with cheese.

Yield: 8 servings (2-1/2 quarts).

Adding garnishes to soup before serving adds color, flavor and texture. Easy ideas include: finely chopped green onions or chives, minced fresh parsley, shredded cheddar cheese, grated or shredded Parmesan cheese, a dollop of sour cream and seasoned croutons.

Barbecued Chicken Sandwiches

Roberta Brown
WAUPACA, WISCONSIN

These sandwiches are great for large gatherings. The chicken can be cooked ahead of time, then added to the homemade barbecue sauce for simmering hours before guests arrive.

PREP: 5 min.
COOK: 6 hours

2 broiler/fryer chickens (3 to 3-1/2 pounds *each*), cooked and shredded

1 large onion, chopped

2 cups water

1-1/4 cups ketchup

1/4 cup packed brown sugar

1/4 cup Worcestershire sauce

1/4 cup red wine vinegar

1 teaspoon *each* salt, celery seed and chili powder

1/4 teaspoon hot pepper sauce

Hamburger buns

■ In a 3-qt. slow cooker or Dutch oven, combine all ingredients except for the buns. Cover and cook on low for 6-8 hours in the slow cooker or simmer for 1-1/2 hours on the stovetop in a Dutch oven. Serve on buns.

Yield: 8-10 servings.

Editor's Note: 6 cups diced cooked chicken may be used instead of the shredded chicken.

Judy
Metzentine
THE DALLES, OREGON

It's easy to fill the slow cooker and let it do the work. I've served this soup often to family and friends on cold nights.

Beef Barley Lentil Soup

Beef Barley Lentil Soup*

PREP: 5 min. ■ COOK: 8 hours

1 pound lean ground beef	8 cups water
1 medium onion, chopped	2 teaspoons beef bouillon granules
2 cups cubed red potatoes (1/4-inch pieces)	1 teaspoon salt
1 cup chopped celery	1/2 teaspoon lemon-pepper seasoning
1 cup chopped carrot	2 cans (14-1/2 ounces *each*) stewed tomatoes
1 cup dried lentils, rinsed	
1/2 cup medium pearl barley	

■ In a nonstick skillet, cook beef and onion over medium heat until meat is no longer pink; drain.

■ Transfer to a 5-qt. slow cooker. Layer with the potatoes, celery, carrots, lentils and barley. Combine the water, bouillon, salt and lemon-pepper; pour over vegetables. Cover and cook on low for 6 hours or until the vegetables and barley are tender.

■ Add the tomatoes; cook 2 hours longer.

Yield: 10 servings.

✱ Nutrition Facts: 1-1/2 cups equals 241 calories, 5 g fat (2 g saturated fat), 17 mg cholesterol, 660 mg sodium, 33 g carbohydrate, 9 g fiber, 18 g protein. **Diabetic Exchanges:** 2 lean meat, 1-1/2 starch, 1 vegetable.

Barbecued Turkey Chili

Melissa Webb
ELLSWORTH, SOUTH DAKOTA

The first time I made this, it won first prize at a chili cook-off. It takes just minutes to mix together, and the slow cooker does the rest. It's often requested by friends and family when we all get together.

PREP: 5 min.
COOK: 4 hours

1 can (16 ounces) kidney beans, rinsed and drained

1 can (15-1/2 ounces) hot chili beans

1 can (15 ounces) turkey chili with beans

1 can (14-1/2 ounces) diced tomatoes, undrained

1/3 cup barbecue sauce

■ In a 3-qt. slow cooker, combine all of the ingredients. Cover and cook on high for 4 hours or until heated through and the flavors are blended.

Yield: 4-6 servings.

A creative way to serve chili is to place mashed potatoes or a split baked potato in serving bowls first, then to spoon the chili over the potatoes. Top each serving with shredded cheddar, sour cream and some chopped green onion for a delicious finish.

Sausage Pepper Sandwiches

Zippy Spanish Rice Soup

Marilyn Schetz
CUYAHOGA FALLS, OHIO

I created this recipe after ruining a dinner of Spanish rice. I tried to salvage the dish by adding more water, cilantro and green chiles. It was a hit with the whole family. It's hearty enough to be a main meal with the addition of a garden salad and some corn bread.

PREP: 25 min.
COOK: 4 hours

- 1 pound lean ground beef
- 1 medium onion, chopped
- 3 cups water
- 1 jar (16 ounces) salsa
- 1 can (14-1/2 ounces) diced tomatoes, undrained
- 1 jar (7 ounces) roasted sweet red peppers, drained and chopped
- 1 can (4 ounces) chopped green chilies
- 1 envelope taco seasoning
- 1 tablespoon dried cilantro flakes
- 1/2 cup uncooked converted rice

- In a small skillet, cook beef and onion over medium heat until meat is no longer pink; drain.

- Transfer the beef mixture to a 4- or 5-qt. slow cooker. Add the water, salsa, tomatoes, red peppers, chilies, taco seasoning and cilantro. Stir in rice. Cover and cook on low for 4-5 hours or until rice is tender.

Yield: 8 servings (about 2 quarts).

Suzette Gessel
ALBUQUERQUE, NEW MEXICO

Peppers and onions add a fresh taste to this zippy sausage filling for sandwiches. My mother gave me this recipe. It's simple to assemble, and it's gobbled up quickly.

Sausage Pepper Sandwiches

PREP: 5 min. ■ **COOK:** 7 hours

- 6 Italian sausage links (4 ounces *each*)
- 1 medium green pepper, cut into 1-inch pieces
- 1 large onion, cut into 1-inch pieces
- 1 can (8 ounces) tomato sauce
- 1/8 teaspoon pepper
- 6 hoagie *or* submarine sandwich buns, split

- In a large skillet, brown the sausage links over medium heat. Cut into 1/2-in. slices; place in a 3-qt. slow cooker. Stir in the green pepper, onion, tomato sauce and pepper.

- Cover and cook on low for 7-8 hours or until sausage is no longer pink and vegetables are tender. Use a slotted spoon to serve on buns.

Yield: 6 servings.

Vermicelli Beef Stew*

PREP: 20 min. ■ **COOK:** 8-1/2 hours

Sharon Delaney-Chronis
SOUTH MILWAUKEE, WISCONSIN

I love to try new recipes for my husband and myself, and also when we entertain friends and relatives. This stew is a little different from most because of the vermicelli.

1-1/2 pounds beef stew meat, cut into 1-inch cubes	1 tablespoon dried basil
1 medium onion, chopped	1 teaspoon salt
2 tablespoons canola oil	1 teaspoon dried oregano
3 cups water	6 ounces uncooked vermicelli, broken into 2-inch pieces
1 can (14-1/2 ounces) diced tomatoes	1/4 cup grated Parmesan cheese
1 package (16 ounces) frozen mixed vegetables, thawed	

■ In a large skillet, brown the meat and onion in oil; drain. Transfer to a 5-qt. slow cooker. Stir in the water, tomatoes, vegetables, basil, salt and oregano. Cover and cook on low for 8-10 hours or until the meat and vegetables are tender.

■ Stir in vermicelli. Cover and cook for 30 minutes or until pasta is tender. Sprinkle with cheese.

Yield: 8 servings (2 quarts).

✱ Nutrition Facts: 1 cup equals 294 calories, 10 g fat (3 g saturated fat), 55 mg cholesterol, 455 mg sodium, 28 g carbohydrate, 5 g fiber, 22 g protein. **Diabetic Exchanges:** 2 lean meat, 2 vegetable, 1 starch, 1 fat.

If your stew needs just a little extra thickening, stir in a few tablespoons of fresh white, whole wheat or rye bread crumbs.

Hearty French Dip Sandwiches

PREP: 30 min.
COOK: 6 hours

- 1 large onion, sliced
- 1 boneless beef rump roast (3 pounds)
- 2 cans (10-1/2 ounces *each*) condensed French onion soup
- 1 loaf (1 pound) French bread, halved lengthwise
- 1/4 cup butter, softened
- 1 tablespoon grated Parmesan cheese
- 1/2 teaspoon garlic salt
- 8 slices part-skim mozzarella cheese

■ Place onion in a 4- or 5-qt. slow cooker. Cut roast in half; place over onion. Pour the soup over beef. Cover and cook on low for 6-8 hours or until meat is tender. Remove meat to a cutting board. Let stand for 10 minutes. Thinly slice meat across the grain and return to the slow cooker. Heat through.

■ Place bread on an ungreased baking sheet. Combine butter, Parmesan cheese and garlic salt; spread over bread. Bake at 400° for 10-12 minutes or until lightly browned. Layer with the cheese, beef and onion. Replace bread top; cut diagonally. Serve with cooking juices.

Yield: 8 servings.

Dorothy Connelley
BELLE FOURCHE, SOUTH DAKOTA

This is a very favorite meal of my husband, who is nicknamed "The Beef Man," because we sell USDA beef in our retail store. Served with a green salad, this makes a wonderful evening meal. It would also work great for sandwiches at a football game party.

Bernice
Muilenburg
MOLALLA, OREGON

The meat for these sandwiches turns out tender and flavorful. I sometimes substitute deer and elk in this recipe, and it never tastes like game.

Teriyaki Sandwiches

Teriyaki Sandwiches

PREP: 30 min. ■ **COOK:** 7 hours

>   2   pounds boneless chuck
>   steak
>   1/4   cup soy sauce
>   1   tablespoon brown sugar
>   1   teaspoon ground ginger
>   1   garlic clove, minced
>   4   teaspoons cornstarch
>   2   tablespoons water
>   8   French rolls, split
>   1/4   cup butter, melted
>   Pineapple rings
>   Chopped green onions

■ Cut steak into thin bite-size slices. In a 3-qt. slow cooker, combine the soy sauce, sugar, ginger and garlic. Add steak. Cover and cook on low for 7-9 hours or until meat is tender.

■ Remove the meat with a slotted spoon; set aside. Carefully pour the liquid into a 2-cup measuring cup; skim fat. Add the water to liquid to measure 1-1/2 cups.

■ Pour into a large saucepan. Combine cornstarch and water until smooth; add to pan. Cook and stir until thick and bubbly, about 2 minutes. Add meat and heat through.

■ Brush rolls with butter; broil 4-5 in. from the heat for 2-3 minutes or until lightly toasted. Fill with meat, pineapple and green onions.

Yield: 8 servings.

Split Pea Soup

Taste of Home
Test Kitchen
GREENDALE, WISCONSIN

Slow cook your split pea soup while you are out for the afternoon, and a delicious dinner will be ready when you arrive back home! This is a real stick-to-your-ribs soup. The ham hock gives a great smoky flavor.

PREP: 15 min.
COOK: 8 hours

>   1   can (49-1/2 ounces)
>   chicken broth
>   1-1/2   pounds smoked ham
>   hocks
>   2   cups *each* chopped
>   onions, celery and carrots
>   1   package (16 ounces) dried
>   green split peas
>   2   bay leaves
>   Salad croutons, optional

■ In a 4- or 5-qt. slow cooker, combine the chicken broth, ham hocks, vegetables, peas and bay leaves. Cover and cook on low for 8-10 hours or until peas are tender.

■ Discard the bay leaves. Remove the meat from bones; cut the ham into small pieces. Cool the soup slightly.

■ In a blender, process soup in batches until smooth. Return all to slow cooker; stir in ham. Heat through. Garnish with croutons if desired.

**Yield: 7 servings
(about 2-1/4 quarts).**

Big Red Soup

- Heat oil in skillet; brown beef stew meat. Place meat in 5-qt. slow cooker; add remaining ingredients except for tortillas and cheese. Cook on low for at least 10 hours.

- When serving, place enough tortilla quarters to cover bottom of each bowl. Pour soup over tortilla pieces; sprinkle with the cheese.

Yield: 10-12 servings.

Shelly Korell
BAYARD, NEBRASKA

We're Nebraska Cornhusker football fans, and on the days when the "Big Red" team is playing, I make up a big pot of this satisfying soup to eat while watching the game!

Big Red Soup

PREP: 20 min. ■ **COOK:** 10 hours

2 tablespoons canola oil	1/4 cup water
2 pounds beef stew meat, cut into 1-inch cubes	1 teaspoon ground cumin
3/4 cup chopped onion	1 teaspoon chili powder
2 cloves garlic, minced	1 teaspoon salt
2 cans (14-1/2 ounces *each*) diced tomatoes in sauce	1/2 teaspoon lemon-pepper seasoning
1 can (10-1/2 ounces) condensed beef broth, undiluted	2 teaspoons Worcestershire sauce
1 can (10-1/2 ounces) condensed chicken broth, undiluted	1/3 cup picante sauce
	8 corn tortillas, cut into quarters
1 can (10-3/4 ounces) condensed tomato soup, undiluted	1 cup (4 ounces) shredded cheddar cheese

Select sharp cheddar cheese when using packaged shredded cheese for recipes that you'd like to have a bolder flavor. If you will be shredding cheese at home from bulk cheddar, you can choose from mild, medium, sharp and extra sharp.

Fresh Pumpkin Soup

- In a 5-qt. slow cooker, combine the first eight ingredients. Cover and cook on low for 8-10 hours or until the pumpkin and apples are tender.

- Meanwhile, toss the pumpkin seeds with oil and salt. Spread the seeds onto an ungreased 15-in. x 10-in. x 1-in. baking pan. Bake at 250° for 45-50 minutes or until golden brown. Set aside.

- Cool the soup slightly; process in batches in a blender. Transfer to a large saucepan and heat through. Garnish with toasted pumpkin seeds.

Yield: 9 servings (about 2 quarts).

* Nutrition Facts: 1 cup equals 102 calories, 2 g fat (0.55 g saturated fat), 0 cholesterol, 567 mg sodium, 22 g carbohydrate, 3 g fiber, 3 g protein. Diabetic Exchanges: 1 starch, 1/2 fruit.

Jane Shapton
IRVINE, CALIFORNIA

This soup features the fall flavors of fresh pumpkin and tart apples, and is sure to warm you up on a crisp autumn day. I top it with a sprinkling of toasted pumpkin seeds.

Fresh Pumpkin Soup*

PREP: 50 min. ■ **COOK:** 8 hours

- 8 cups chopped fresh pumpkin (about 3 pounds)
- 4 cups chicken broth
- 3 small tart apples, peeled and chopped
- 1 medium onion, chopped
- 2 tablespoons lemon juice
- 2 teaspoons minced fresh gingerroot
- 2 garlic cloves, minced
- 1/2 teaspoon salt

TOASTED PUMPKIN SEEDS:
- 1/2 cup fresh pumpkin seeds
- 1 teaspoon canola oil
- 1/8 teaspoon salt

Peeling fresh
pumpkin can be tricky! For easier peeling, cut the pumpkin into large pieces and remove the fibrous strings and seeds. Peel the skin from the pumpkin using a small sharp knife or vegetable peeler.

Marylou LaRue
FREELAND, MICHIGAN

This tangy sandwich filling is a cinch to prepare in the slow cooker, and it's popular at gatherings. I often take it to potlucks, and I'm always asked for my secret ingredient.

Turkey Sloppy Joes

Turkey Sloppy Joes*

PREP: 15 min. ■ **COOK:** 4 hours

1 pound ground turkey breast	1/2 cup ketchup
1 small onion, chopped	1 tablespoon brown sugar
1/2 cup chopped celery	2 tablespoons prepared mustard
1/4 cup chopped green pepper	1/4 teaspoon pepper
1 can (10-3/4 ounces) reduced-sodium condensed tomato soup, undiluted	8 hamburger buns, split

■ In a large saucepan coated with cooking spray, cook the ground turkey, onion, celery and green pepper over medium heat until the meat is no longer pink; drain if necessary. Stir in the soup, ketchup, brown sugar, mustard and pepper.

■ Transfer to a 3-qt. slow cooker. Cover and cook on low for 4 hours. Serve on hamburger buns.

Yield: 8 servings.

✱ Nutrition Facts: 1 sandwich equals 247 calories, 7 g fat (2 g saturated fat), 45 mg cholesterol, 553 mg sodium, 32 g carbohydrate, 2 g fiber, 14 g protein. **Diabetic Exchanges:** 2 starch, 1-1/2 lean meat.

Savory Chicken Sandwiches

Joan Parker
GASTONIA, NORTH CAROLINA

With eight children under the age of 12, I know how to make family-pleasing meals. This tender chicken tastes like you fussed, but requires a handful of ingredients. You can also thicken the juices and serve it over rice.

PREP: 25 min.
COOK: 8 hours

- 4 bone-in chicken breast halves
- 4 bone-in chicken thighs
- 1 envelope onion soup mix
- 1/4 teaspoon garlic salt
- 1/4 cup prepared Italian salad dressing
- 1/4 cup water
- 14 to 16 hamburger buns, split

■ Remove skin from chicken if desired. Place chicken in a 5-qt. slow cooker. Sprinkle with soup mix and garlic salt. Pour dressing and water over chicken.

■ Cover and cook on low for 8-9 hours. Remove chicken; cool slightly. Skim fat from cooking juices. Remove the chicken from bones; cut into bite-size pieces and return to slow cooker. Serve with a slotted spoon on buns.

Yield: 14-16 servings.

Mary Shivers
ADA, OKLAHOMA

I decided to add some extra character to a potato chowder with roasted red peppers. Although the soup is made delicious with bacon, seasonings and Parmesan, the flavor of the red peppers gives a deliciously unique twist to the soup.

Parmesan Potato Soup

PREP: 20 min. ■ **COOK:** 5-1/2 hours

8 medium potatoes, peeled and cut into 1/2-inch cubes	1/8 teaspoon rubbed sage
6 cups chicken broth	1/3 cup all-purpose flour
1 large onion, chopped	2 cups heavy whipping cream, *divided*
1 jar (7 ounces) roasted sweet red peppers, drained and chopped	1 cup grated Parmesan cheese, *divided*
1 small celery rib, chopped	8 bacon strips, cooked and crumbled
1/2 teaspoon garlic powder	2 tablespoons minced fresh cilantro
1/2 teaspoon seasoned salt	
1/2 teaspoon pepper	

■ In a 5- or 6-qt. slow cooker, combine the first nine ingredients. Cover and cook on low for 5-6 hours or until vegetables are tender.

■ In a small bowl, combine flour and 1/2 cup cream; add to slow cooker. Stir in 3/4 cup cheese, bacon, cilantro and remaining cream.

■ Cover and cook for 30 minutes or until slightly thickened. Ladle into bowls; sprinkle with remaining cheese.

Yield: 12 servings (3 quarts).

Always check the date stamp on packages of vacuum-sealed bacon to make sure it's fresh. The date reflects the last date of sale. Once the package is opened, bacon should be used within a week. For long-term storage, freeze bacon for up to 1 month.

Tex-Mex Beef Sandwiches

Brenda Theisen
ADDISON, MICHIGAN

Everyone loves these sandwiches when I serve them. The cocoa is a surprise ingredient that adds a depth of flavor. It's hard to identify, so I'm often asked "what's that yummy flavor?"

PREP: 25 min.
COOK: 8 hours

- 1 boneless beef chuck roast (3 pounds)
- 1 envelope burrito seasoning
- 2 tablespoons baking cocoa
- 1 large green pepper, coarsely chopped
- 1 large sweet red pepper, coarsely chopped
- 1 large onion, chopped
- 1 cup beef broth
- 1/2 cup ketchup
- 8 hoagie buns, split

■ Cut roast in half. Combine burrito seasoning and cocoa; rub over meat. Place the peppers and onion in a 3- or 4-qt. slow cooker. Top with meat; sprinkle with any remaining burrito mixture. Combine the broth and ketchup; pour over meat. Cover and cook on high for 8-10 hours or until meat is tender.

■ Skim fat. When cool enough to handle, shred the meat with two forks and return to the slow cooker; heat through. Using a slotted spoon, spoon 1/2 cup beef mixture onto each bun.

Yield: 8 servings.

Broccoli Potato Soup*

PREP: 25 min. ■ **COOK:** 4-1/2 hours

Crystal Kelso
SANDY, OREGON

For a very comforting soup with a nice, creamy texture, try this one with nutritious broccoli and chunks of potato. The red pepper flakes add a hint of spice, and the fresh herbs make this a truly delicious soup.

- 1 pound small red potatoes, cubed
- 1 large onion, chopped
- 1 large carrot, coarsely chopped
- 7 garlic cloves, minced
- 3 cups water
- 1 can (14-1/2 ounces) condensed cream of broccoli soup, undiluted
- 1 teaspoon *each* minced fresh thyme, basil and parsley
- 1 teaspoon garlic powder
- 1/2 teaspoon salt
- 1/2 teaspoon crushed red pepper flakes
- 1/4 teaspoon pepper
- 2 cups frozen chopped broccoli, thawed and drained
- 1 cup (4 ounces) shredded Havarti cheese

■ Place the potatoes, onion, carrot and garlic in a 4- or 5-qt. slow cooker. Add the water, soup and seasonings. Cover and cook on low for 4-5 hours or until heated through.

■ Stir in broccoli and cheese. Cover and cook for 30 minutes or until the broccoli is tender.

Yield: 8 cups (2 quarts).

❋ Nutrition Facts: 1 cup equals 158 calories, 6 g fat (3 g saturated fat), 15 mg cholesterol, 563 mg sodium, 20 g carbohydrate, 3 g fiber, 7 g protein. **Diabetic Exchanges:** 1-1/2 starch, 1 fat.

Havarti cheese is a Danish, semisoft cheese that gets its name from the farm on which it was originally developed. It's pale yellow with very small holes. Havarti that is young is mild and tangy. When it ages it takes on a sharper, more intense flavor.

Mulligatawny Soup

Mary Ann Marino
WEST PITTSBURG, PENNSYLVANIA

I learned to cook and bake from my mom and grandmother, and often use fresh vegetables, fruits and herbs. This is a hearty soup, which I make with leftover chicken, turkey and sometimes beef, pork or lamb. My family enjoys this on a crisp fall or winter day.

PREP: 20 min.
COOK: 6 hours

- 1 carton (32 ounces) chicken broth
- 1 can (14-1/2 ounces) diced tomatoes
- 2 cups cubed cooked chicken
- 1 large tart apple, peeled and chopped
- 1/4 cup finely chopped onion
- 1/4 cup chopped carrot
- 1/4 cup chopped green pepper
- 1 tablespoon minced fresh parsley
- 2 teaspoons lemon juice
- 1 teaspoon salt
- 1 teaspoon curry powder
- 1/2 teaspoon sugar
- 1/4 teaspoon pepper
- 2 whole cloves

■ In a 3- or 4-qt. slow cooker, combine all ingredients. Cover and cook on low for 6-8 hours or until vegetables are tender. Discard cloves.

Yield: 8 servings (2 quarts).

BBQ Beef Sandwiches

Lime Navy Bean Chili

Connie Thomas
JENSEN, UTAH

A touch of lime flavors this filling family favorite. Fill the cooker in the morning for a great meal later.

PREP: 15 min. + soaking
COOK: 5 hours

- 1-1/4 cups dried navy beans
- 3 cups water
- 2 bone-in chicken breast halves (7 ounces *each*), skin removed
- 1 cup frozen corn
- 1 medium onion, chopped
- 1 can (4 ounces) chopped green chilies
- 4 garlic cloves, minced
- 1 tablespoon chicken bouillon granules
- 1 teaspoon ground cumin
- 1/2 teaspoon chili powder
- 2 tablespoons lime juice

■ Place beans in a large pot; add water to cover by 2 in. Bring to a boil; boil for 2 minutes. Remove from heat; cover and let stand for 1 hour. Drain; rinse beans, discarding liquid.

■ In a 3-qt. slow cooker, combine the beans, water, chicken, corn, onion, chilies, garlic, bouillon, cumin and chili powder. Cover and cook on low for 5-6 hours or until a meat thermometer reads 170° and beans are tender.

■ Remove chicken breasts; remove meat from the bones and cut into bite-size pieces. Discard bones and return chicken to the chili. Stir in lime juice just before serving.

Yield: 6 servings.

Rebecca Rohland
MEDFORD, WISCONSIN

After years of searching, I found a recipe for shredded barbecue beef that's a hit with all my family and friends. It's easy to freeze for future meals, if there's any left over!

BBQ Beef Sandwiches

PREP: 15 min. ■ **COOK:** 8 hours

- 2 cups ketchup
- 1 medium onion, chopped
- 1/4 cup cider vinegar
- 1/4 cup molasses
- 2 tablespoons Worcestershire sauce
- 2 garlic cloves, minced
- 1/2 teaspoon salt
- 1/2 teaspoon ground mustard
- 1/2 teaspoon pepper
- 1/4 teaspoon garlic powder
- 1/4 teaspoon crushed red pepper flakes
- 1 boneless beef chuck roast (3 pounds)
- 14 sesame seed hamburger buns, split

■ In a large bowl, combine the first 11 ingredients. Cut roast in half; place in a 5-qt. slow cooker. Pour ketchup mixture over roast.

■ Cover and cook on low for 8-9 hours or until meat is tender.

■ Remove meat and shred with two forks. Skim fat from cooking juices. Return meat to slow cooker; heat through. Using a slotted spoon, serve beef on buns.

Yield: 14 sandwiches.

Bandito Chili Dogs

Spinach Bean Soup

PREP: 20 min.
COOK: 6-1/4 hours

3 cans (14-1/2 ounces *each*) vegetable broth

1 can (15-1/2 ounces) great northern beans, rinsed and drained

1 can (15 ounces) tomato puree

1/2 cup finely chopped onion

1/2 cup uncooked converted long grain rice

2 garlic cloves, minced

1 teaspoon dried basil

1/2 teaspoon salt

1/4 teaspoon pepper

1 package (6 ounces) fresh baby spinach, coarsely chopped

1/4 cup shredded Parmesan cheese

- In a 4-qt. slow cooker, combine the first nine ingredients. Cover and cook on low for 6-7 hours or until heated through. Stir in spinach. Cover and cook for 15 minutes or until spinach is wilted. Sprinkle with cheese.

Yield: 8 servings (2 quarts).

Marion Lowery
MEDFORD, OREGON

I've brought these beefy chili dogs to family functions for years. Adults and children alike love the cheesy chili sauce that's a snap to make with canned items.

Bandito Chili Dogs

PREP: 15 min. ■ **COOK:** 4 hours

1 package (1 pound) hot dogs

2 cans (15 ounces *each*) chili without beans

1 can (10-3/4 ounces) condensed cheddar cheese soup, undiluted

1 can (4 ounces) chopped green chilies

10 hot dog buns, split

1 medium onion, chopped

1 to 2 cups corn chips, coarsely crushed

1 cup (4 ounces) shredded cheddar cheese

- Place the hot dogs in a 3-qt. slow cooker. In a large bowl, combine the chili, soup and green chilies; pour over hot dogs. Cover and cook on low for 4-5 hours.

- Serve the hot dogs in buns; top with the chili mixture, onion, corn chips and shredded cheese.

Yield: 10 servings.

One bouillon cube or 1 teaspoon of bouillon granules dissolved in 1 cup of boiling water may be substituted for 1 cup of broth in any recipe.

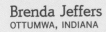

Brenda Jeffers
OTTUMWA, INDIANA

This meatless soup is great for a busy weeknight supper after I get home from my job as a college nursing professor. The soup is full of fresh baby spinach, rice and beans, and provides a hearty meal full of nutrients to keep me healthy.

Beef & Ground Beef

30

40

29

A slow cooker is the perfect way to bring out the full-bodied flavor of beef. These robust and family-friendly recipes will satisfy even the heartiest of appetites, and put dinner on the table in a flash.

So-Easy Spaghetti Sauce

- In a large skillet, cook the beef, onion and celery over medium heat until meat is no longer pink; drain. In a 4- or 5-qt. slow cooker, combine the tomato sauce, tomato juice, tomatoes, tomato paste, sugar, seasonings and beef mixture.

- Cover and cook on low for 5-6 hours until heated through. Discard the bay leaves. Serve with spaghetti; sprinkle with cheese if desired.

Yield: about 2-1/4 quarts.

* Nutrition Facts: 3/4 cup (calculated without spaghetti and cheese) equals 125 calories, 3 g fat (1 g saturated fat), 19 mg cholesterol, 744 mg sodium, 16 g carbohydrate, 4 g fiber, 10 g protein. **Diabetic Exchanges:** 1 lean meat, 1 vegetable, 1/2 starch, 1/2 fat.

Cathy Johnson
SOMERSET, PENNSYLVANIA

This traditional, thick pasta sauce is a cinch to prepare. It has a pleasantly mild flavor and goes with any kind of cooked pasta. If you like, use ground turkey or chicken instead of the beef.

So-Easy Spaghetti Sauce*

PREP: 30 min. ■ **COOK:** 5 hours

1 pound lean ground beef	2 teaspoons chili powder
1 medium onion, finely chopped	1 teaspoon salt
1/4 cup finely chopped celery	1 teaspoon garlic powder
1 can (29 ounces) tomato sauce	1 teaspoon dried basil
2-1/2 cups tomato juice	1 teaspoon dried oregano
1 can (14-1/2 ounces) diced tomatoes	1/2 teaspoon pepper
1 can (12 ounces) tomato paste	4 bay leaves
2 teaspoons sugar	Hot cooked spaghetti
	Grated Parmesan cheese, optional

Garlic bread is an excellent accompaniment to pasta topped with the So-Easy Spaghetti Sauce. Just combine 1/2 cup melted butter with 4 cloves of minced garlic. Brush over the cut side of two halves of a one pound loaf of French bread, then sprinkle with chopped parsley. Broil 4-6 inches from the heat for about 2 minutes.

Flavorful Beef Stew*

PREP: 25 min. ■ **COOK:** 6 hours

jackitt

TASTE OF HOME ONLINE COMMUNITY

This tasty and rich beef stew creates a thick sauce that goes great with bread. I find it much easier to prepare than the stovetop or oven variety.

1/2	pound medium fresh mushrooms, quartered	3/4	teaspoon salt
2	medium red potatoes, cubed	1/4	teaspoon pepper
3	medium carrots, cut into 1/4-inch slices	1	pound beef stew meat, cut into 1-inch cubes
1	medium onion, chopped	1	can (14-1/2 ounces) beef broth
1	celery rib, thinly sliced	4-1/2	teaspoons reduced-sodium teriyaki sauce
1/4	cup all-purpose flour	2	garlic cloves, minced
1	tablespoon paprika	1	bay leaf

■ In a 3- or 4-qt. slow cooker, combine mushrooms, potatoes, carrots, onion and celery. In a large resealable plastic bag, combine the flour, paprika, salt and pepper. Add the cubed beef, a few pieces at a time and shake to coat.

■ Place over vegetable mixture. Combine the broth, teriyaki sauce, garlic and bay leaf. Pour over beef.

■ Cover and cook on low for 6-8 hours or until meat and vegetables are tender. Discard bay leaf.

Yield: 6 servings.

* Nutrition Facts: 1 cup equals 202 calories, 6 g fat (2 g saturated fat), 47 mg cholesterol, 745 mg sodium, 19 g carbohydrate, 3 g fiber, 19 g protein. **Diabetic Exchanges:** 2 lean meat, 1 starch, 1 vegetable.

Fresh mushrooms should be used within a few days of purchase. If that's not possible, you can blanch or saute them in a jiffy, then freeze for up to 1 month for use in soups, sauces and casseroles.

Slow Cooker Sauerbraten

PREP: 20 min.
COOK: 6 hours

1	boneless beef chuck roast *or* rump roast (3 to 4 pounds)
4	cups water
3	bay leaves
1	bottle (14 ounces) ketchup
1	large onion, chopped
3/4	cup packed brown sugar
3/4	cup cider vinegar
1	tablespoon mixed pickling spices
30	gingersnap cookies, crushed

GRAVY:

2	tablespoons cornstarch
1/4	cup cold water

■ Cut roast in half. Place in a 5-qt. slow cooker; add water and bay leaves. In a large bowl, combine ketchup, onion, brown sugar and vinegar; pour over roast.

■ Place pickling spices on a double thickness of cheesecloth; bring up corners of cloth and tie with string to form a bag. Add the spice bag and cookie crumbs to slow cooker.

■ Cover and cook on low for 6-8 hours or until meat is tender.

■ Remove roast and keep warm. Discard bay leaves and spice bag. For gravy, strain cooking juices; transfer 4 cups to a large saucepan. Combine cornstarch and water until smooth; stir into cooking juices. Bring to a boil; cook and stir for 2 minutes or until thickened. Slice roast; serve with gravy.

Yield: 10 servings.

Norma English
BADEN, PENNSYLVANIA

My family is of German Lutheran descent, and although we enjoy the traditional beef roast Sauerbraten, I never liked the amount of time and fuss it takes to make it. This recipe is so good and oh-so-easy. It's great served with dumplings, spaetzle, veggies or a salad.

Valerie Jones
PORTLAND, MAINE

I spice up flank steak with taco seasoning packets, then simmer it all day until the beef is tender. Just fill tortillas and add toppings for a tasty meal.

Steak Burritos

Steak Burritos*

PREP: 15 min. ■ **COOK:** 8 hours

- 2 flank steaks (about 1 pound *each*)
- 2 envelopes taco seasoning
- 1 medium onion, chopped
- 1 can (4 ounces) chopped green chilies
- 1 tablespoon white vinegar
- 10 flour tortillas (8 inches), warmed
- 1-1/2 cups (6 ounces) shredded Monterey Jack cheese
- 1-1/2 cups chopped seeded plum tomatoes
- 3/4 cup sour cream

■ Cut steaks in half; rub with taco seasoning. Place in a 3-qt. slow cooker coated with cooking spray. Top with onion, chilies and vinegar.

■ Cover and cook on low for 8-9 hours or until meat is tender.

■ Remove steaks and cool slightly; shred meat with two forks. Return to slow cooker; heat through.

■ Spoon about 1/2 cup meat mixture down the center of each tortilla. Top with cheese, tomato and sour cream. Fold ends and sides over filling.

Yield: 10 servings.

✱ Nutrition Facts: One serving (prepared with reduced-sodium taco seasoning, fat-free tortillas, reduced-fat cheese and fat-free sour cream) equals 339 calories, 10 g fat (0 saturated fat), 57 mg cholesterol, 580 mg sodium, 31 g carbohydrate, 2 g fiber, 28 g protein. **Diabetic Exchanges:** 3 lean meat, 2 starch, 1 vegetable.

Cajun-Style Pot Roast

Ginger Menzies
OAK CREEK, COLORADO

I often make this zippy roast when expecting dinner guests. It gives me time to visit and everyone always enjoys it, even my friend who's a chef.

PREP: 15 min.
COOK: 6 hours

- 1 boneless beef chuck roast (2 to 3 pounds)
- 2 tablespoons Cajun seasoning
- 1 tablespoon olive oil
- 2 cans (10 ounces *each*) diced tomatoes and green chilies
- 1 medium sweet red pepper, chopped
- 1-1/2 cups chopped celery
- 3/4 cup chopped onion
- 1/4 cup quick-cooking tapioca
- 1-1/2 teaspoons minced garlic
- 1 teaspoon salt

Hot cooked rice

■ Cut roast in half; sprinkle with Cajun seasoning. In a large skillet, brown the roast in oil on all sides; drain. Transfer to a 5-qt. slow cooker.

■ Combine the tomatoes, red pepper, celery, onion, tapioca, garlic and salt; pour over roast. Cover and cook on low for 6-8 hours or until meat is tender. Slice and serve with rice.

Yield: 6 servings.

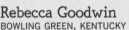
Slow Cooker Lasagna

- In a large skillet, cook the ground beef, green pepper and onion over medium heat until the meat is no longer pink; drain. Stir in the pasta sauce; heat through. In a large bowl, combine mozzarella and ricotta cheeses, Italian seasoning, garlic powder, salt and pepper.

- Spread 1 cup meat sauce in an oval 3-qt. slow cooker. Layer with 1-1/3 noodles, breaking the noodles where necessary, 2/3 cup meat sauce and 1 cup of the cheese mixture. Repeat layers twice. Top with the remaining sauce.

- Cover and cook on low for 4-5 hours or until noodles are tender. Sprinkle with Parmesan cheese. Cover and cook for 15 minutes or until cheese is melted. Let stand for 10 minutes before cutting.

Yield: 6 servings.

Rebecca Goodwin
BOWLING GREEN, KENTUCKY

This favorite is made super easy in a slow cooker. The lasagna cuts well for nice servings. You may need to break the lasagna noodles so they fit into the slow cooker crock.

Slow Cooker Lasagna

PREP: 45 min. ■ **COOK:** 4-1/4 hours + standing

1 pound ground beef	1 tablespoon Italian seasoning
1 medium green pepper, chopped	1/2 teaspoon garlic powder
1 medium onion, chopped	1/2 teaspoon salt
1 jar (26 ounces) herb and garlic pasta sauce	1/4 teaspoon pepper
4 cups (16 ounces) shredded part-skim mozzarella cheese	4 no-cook lasagna noodles
	2 tablespoons shredded Parmesan cheese
1 carton (15 ounces) ricotta cheese	

To sharpen up the Slow Cooker Lasagna recipe, substitute one quarter of the mozzarella cheese with shredded sharp cheddar.

LorskyNY
TASTE OF HOME ONLINE COMMUNITY

Long, gentle cooking turns simple top round steak into delicious, tender cuts of meat. A touch of ground mustard gives it some zip. I like to serve this hearty entree with mashed potatoes, because the vegetable topping makes an excellent sauce.

Veggie-Topped Swiss Steak*

PREP: 35 min. ■ COOK: 6 hours

1-1/2 pounds boneless beef top round steak
1/4 cup all-purpose flour
2 teaspoons ground mustard
3/4 teaspoon salt
1/4 teaspoon pepper
2 tablespoons canola oil
2 tablespoons butter
1 can (14-1/2 ounces) diced tomatoes
2 celery ribs, finely chopped
2 medium carrots, grated
1 medium onion, finely chopped
2 tablespoons Worcestershire sauce
1 tablespoon brown sugar
2 tablespoons minced fresh parsley

■ Cut steak into serving-size pieces. In a large resealable plastic bag, combine the flour, mustard, salt and pepper. Add beef, a few pieces at a time, and shake to coat.

■ In a skillet, brown meat in oil and butter on both sides; drain. Transfer meat to a 3-qt. slow cooker. Combine the tomatoes, celery, carrots, onion, Worcestershire sauce and brown sugar; pour over meat.

■ Cover and cook on low for 6-8 hours or until meat is tender. Sprinkle with parsley.

Yield: 6 servings.

❋ Nutrition Facts: 4 ounces cooked beef with 1/3 cup sauce equals 287 calories, 12 g fat (4 g saturated fat), 74 mg cholesterol, 524 mg sodium, 16 g carbohydrate, 3 g fiber, 28 g protein. **Diabetic Exchanges:** 4 lean meat, 1 vegetable, 1 fat, 1/2 starch.

Dry mustard (referred to as ground mustard in many recipes) is made from mustard seeds that have been finely ground. When a recipe calls for prepared mustard, use yellow or brown mustard commonly served as a condiment.

Sunday Beef Stew

Jeanette Lazary
ROCHESTER, NEW YORK

We had an aunt who served this stew each time there was a special occasion. It brings back wonderful memories. The cinnamon adds a unique flavor.

PREP: 25 min.
COOK: 6 hours

1/3 cup all-purpose flour
3/4 teaspoon salt
3/4 teaspoon ground cinnamon
1/2 teaspoon pepper
2 pounds beef stew meat, cut into 1-inch cubes
2 tablespoons canola oil
1 package (14 ounces) frozen pearl onions
1 cup dry red wine *or* beef broth
3/4 cup water
2 tablespoons red wine vinegar
2 tablespoons tomato paste
1 tablespoon honey
2 bay leaves
1 garlic clove, minced

■ In a large resealable plastic bag, combine the flour, salt, cinnamon and pepper. Add beef, a few pieces at a time, and shake to coat. In a large skillet, brown beef in oil. Transfer to a 3-qt. slow cooker. Stir in the remaining ingredients.

■ Cover and cook on low for 6-8 hours or until beef and onions are tender. Discard bay leaves.

Yield: 6 servings.

All-Day Brisket with Potatoes*

PREP: 30 min. ■ **COOK:** 8 hours

Lana Gryga
GLEN FLORA, WISCONSIN

I think the slow cooker was invented with brisket in mind. This sweet and savory version is perfection itself, because the tender beef melts in your mouth. It's very important to buy "first-cut" or "flat-cut" brisket, which has far less fat than other cuts.

2 medium potatoes, peeled and cut into 1/4-inch slices	1/3 cup tomato paste
2 celery ribs, sliced	1/4 cup red wine vinegar
1 fresh beef brisket (3 pounds)	3 tablespoons brown sugar
1 tablespoon canola oil	3 tablespoons Dijon mustard
1 large onion, sliced	3 tablespoons soy sauce
2 garlic cloves, minced	2 tablespoons molasses
1 can (12 ounces) beer	1/2 teaspoon paprika
1/2 teaspoon beef bouillon granules	1/4 teaspoon salt
3/4 cup stewed tomatoes	1/8 teaspoon pepper
	1 bay leaf

■ Place potatoes and celery in a 5-qt. slow cooker. Cut brisket in half. In a large skillet, brown beef in oil on all sides; transfer to slow cooker. In the same pan, saute onion and garlic until tender; add to slow cooker.

■ Add the beer and bouillon granules to skillet, stirring to loosen browned bits from pan; pour over meat. In a large bowl, combine the remaining ingredients; add to slow cooker.

■ Cover and cook on low for 8-10 hours or until meat and vegetables are tender. Discard bay leaf. To serve, thinly slice across the grain.

Yield: 8 servings.

✱ Nutrition Facts: 1 serving equals 352 calories, 9 g fat (3 g saturated fat), 72 mg cholesterol, 724 mg sodium, 25 g carbohydrate, 2 g fiber, 37 g protein. **Diabetic Exchanges:** 5 lean meat, 1 starch, 1 vegetable, 1/2 fat.

Editor's Note: This is a fresh beef brisket, not corned beef.

Mexican Beef Stew

Pat Dazis
CHARLOTTE, NORTH CAROLINA

Instead of chuck roast, you can also use eye of round for this recipe. You can serve it with noodles, rice or flour tortillas.

PREP: 30 min.
COOK: 6 hours

4 medium potatoes, peeled and cubed

1 can (16 ounces) fat-free refried beans

1 can (14-1/2 ounces) reduced-sodium beef broth

1 can (10 ounces) enchilada sauce

2 cups frozen corn

1 large red onion, chopped

1 can (4 ounces) chopped green chilies

2 tablespoons chopped pickled jalapeno slices

1 tablespoon lime juice

1 teaspoon ground cumin

Dash crushed red pepper flakes

1 boneless beef chuck roast (3 to 4 pounds)

Sour cream

■ In a 5- or 6-qt. slow cooker, combine the first 11 ingredients. Cut roast in half; transfer to slow cooker.

■ Cover and cook on low for 6-8 hours or until the meat and vegetables are tender.

■ Remove meat; cool slightly. Cut into small pieces and return to slow cooker and heat through. Serve with sour cream.

Yield: 8 servings.

Sweet 'n' Tender Cabbage Rolls

Sonja Benz
CARMEL, INDIANA

I've used this recipe for more than 30 years, and the extra time it takes to assemble the rolls is well worth the effort. You can assemble the night before and cook the next day.

Sweet 'n' Tender Cabbage Rolls

PREP: 40 min. ■ COOK: 7 hours

1 large head cabbage	1 teaspoon dried oregano
2 eggs, lightly beaten	1 teaspoon dried basil
1/2 cup milk	1/2 teaspoon pepper
2 cups cooked long grain rice	2 pounds lean ground beef
2 jars (4-1/2 ounces *each*) sliced mushrooms, well drained	SAUCE:
1 small onion, chopped	2 cans (8 ounces *each*) tomato sauce
2 teaspoons salt	1/2 cup packed brown sugar
1 teaspoon dried parsley flakes	2 tablespoons lemon juice
	2 teaspoons Worcestershire sauce

■ Cook cabbage in boiling water just until leaves fall off head. Set aside 14 large leaves for rolls. (Refrigerate remaining cabbage for another use.) Cut out the thick vein from bottom of each reserved leaf, making a V-shaped cut.

■ In a large bowl, combine the eggs, milk, rice, mushrooms, onion and seasonings. Crumble beef over mixture and mix well. Place about 1/2 cup on each cabbage leaf; overlap cut ends and fold in sides, beginning from the cut end. Roll up completely to enclose filling.

■ Place seven rolls, seam side down, in a 5-qt. slow cooker. Combine sauce ingredients; pour half over cabbage rolls. Top with the remaining rolls and sauce.

■ Cover and cook on low for 7-8 hours or until a meat thermometer reads 160°.

Yield: 7 servings.

When buying a head of cabbage, look for crisp-looking leaves that are firmly packed. The head should feel heavy for its size. Store cabbage tightly wrapped in a plastic bag in the refrigerator for up to 2 weeks.

Dennis Kuyper
CRESTON, IOWA

I asked for this recipe after a recent trip to South Africa with my church. The stew includes fresh garden vegetables and meat. I've made it for my friends many times, and they thought it was great and enjoyed the interesting combination of flavors. It's traditionally served with brown rice.

Beef and Lamb Stew*

PREP: 50 min. + marinating ■ COOK: 8-1/2 hours

1/2 cup dry red wine *or* beef broth

1/2 cup olive oil

4 garlic cloves, minced, *divided*

1-1/2 teaspoons dried thyme, *divided*

1-1/4 teaspoons dried marjoram, *divided*

3/4 teaspoon dried rosemary, crushed and *divided*

1-1/2 teaspoons salt, *divided*

3/4 teaspoon pepper, *divided*

1 pound beef stew meat, cut into 1-inch cubes

1 pound lamb stew meat, cut into 1-inch cubes

10 small red potatoes, halved

1/2 pound medium fresh mushrooms, halved

2 medium onions, thinly sliced

2 cups fresh cauliflowerets

1 can (16 ounces) kidney beans, rinsed and drained

1-1/2 cups fresh green beans, trimmed and cut in half

3 medium carrots, cut into 1/2-inch slices

1 celery rib, thinly sliced

1 cup additional beef broth

2 tablespoons minced fresh parsley

2 teaspoons sugar

3 tablespoons cornstarch

1/4 cup water

6 cups cooked brown rice

■ In a large resealable plastic bag, combine the wine, oil, 2 garlic cloves, 1 teaspoon thyme, 3/4 teaspoon marjoram, 1/2 teaspoon rosemary, 1/2 teaspoon salt and 1/4 teaspoon pepper; add beef and lamb. Seal bag and turn to coat; refrigerate for 8 hours.

■ In a 5- or 6-qt. slow cooker, layer potatoes, mushrooms, onions, cauliflower, kidney beans, green beans, carrots, and celery.

■ Drain and discard marinade. Place meats over vegetables. Combine the additional broth, parsley, sugar and remaining garlic, thyme, marjoram, rosemary, salt and pepper; pour over meats.

■ Cover and cook on low for 8-10 hours or until meat and vegetables are tender. Combine cornstarch and water until smooth; stir into stew. Cover and cook for 30 minutes or until gravy is thickened. Serve with rice.

Yield: 12 servings (3 quarts).

* Nutrition Facts: 1 cup meat mixture with 1/2 cup rice equals 377 calories, 12 g fat (3 g saturated fat), 48 mg cholesterol, 499 mg sodium, 44 g carbohydrate, 7 g fiber, 22 g protein. Diabetic Exchanges: 2-1/2 starch, 2 lean meat, 1 vegetable, 1 fat.

Fruited Pot Roast

Linda South
PINEVILLE, NORTH CAROLINA

This is a wonderful variation of a classic pot roast. My family really enjoys it. The fruit is a nice change from the vegetables that normally accompany this dish.

PREP: 15 min.
COOK: 6 hours

1 package (7 ounces) mixed dried fruit

1 large onion, cut into wedges

1 can (5-1/2 ounces) unsweetened apple juice

1 boneless beef chuck roast (2 pounds)

1/2 teaspoon salt

1/4 teaspoon ground allspice

1/4 teaspoon pepper

■ Place fruit and onion in a 3- or 4-qt. slow cooker; add apple juice. Top with roast; sprinkle with seasonings.

■ Cover and cook on low for 6-8 hours or until meat is tender. Serve with fruit mixture.

Yield: 6 servings.

Autumn Pot Roast

PREP: 30 min. ■ COOK: 6 hours

Mary Hankins
KANSAS CITY, MISSOURI

This is one of my all-time favorite slow cooker recipes because it's always comforting to me. When the weather is chilly outside, it's great to come home to this warm, home-cooked meal.

1 boneless beef chuck roast (3 pounds)	1/3 cup sun-dried tomatoes (not packed in oil)
1 teaspoon salt, *divided*	3 garlic cloves, minced
1/2 teaspoon pepper, *divided*	1 teaspoon dried thyme
1 tablespoon olive oil	2 bay leaves
1-1/2 pounds sweet potatoes, cut into 1-inch pieces	1 can (14-1/2 ounces) reduced-sodium beef broth
2 medium parsnips, cut into 1/2 inch pieces	3/4 cup dry red wine *or* additional reduced-sodium beef broth
1 large sweet onion, cut into chunks	

■ Cut the roast in half; sprinkle with 1/2 teaspoon salt and 1/4 teaspoon pepper. In a large skillet, brown meat in oil on all sides; drain.

■ Transfer to a 5-qt. slow cooker. Top with sweet potatoes, parsnips, onion, sun-dried tomatoes, garlic, thyme, bay leaves and remaining salt and pepper. Combine broth and wine; pour over vegetables.

■ Cover and cook on low for 6-8 hours or until meat and vegetables are tender. Skim fat. Discard bay leaves. If desired, thicken pan juices.

Yield: 6 servings.

Sweet onions (such as Vidalias) are mild in flavor, high in sugar and water, and low in tear-inducing compounds. Because of these properties, they shouldn't be stored long-term, and they should be used within a few weeks of purchase. Fortunately, there are many varieties of sweet onions that are available almost all year long.

Sloppy Joe Supper

Karla Wiederholt
CUBA CITY, WISCONSIN

Here's an easy way to serve up the flavor of sloppy joes in a one-dish dinner. The aroma of this flavorful entree simmering in the slow cooker is irresistible.

PREP: 15 min.
COOK: 4 hours

1 package (32 ounces) frozen shredded hash brown potatoes, thawed

1 can (10-3/4 ounces) condensed cheddar cheese soup, undiluted

1/4 cup egg substitute

1 teaspoon salt

1/2 teaspoon pepper

2 pounds ground beef

2 tablespoons finely chopped onion

1 can (15-1/2 ounces) sloppy joe sauce

■ In a large bowl, combine the potatoes, soup, egg substitute, salt and pepper. Spread into a lightly greased 5-qt. slow cooker. In a large skillet, cook the beef and onion over medium heat until meat is no longer pink; drain. Stir in sloppy joe sauce. Spoon over potato mixture.

■ Cover and cook on low for 4 to 4-1/2 hours or until heated through.

Yield: 8 servings.

Hearty Cheese Tortellini

Christine Eilerts
TULSA, OKLAHOMA

This is an easy, wonderful recipe that is simple enough for an everyday meal but good enough for company. It makes a large amount, so it feeds plenty of people.

Hearty Cheese Tortellini

PREP: 30 min. ■ COOK: 6-1/4 hours

1/2 pound bulk Italian sausage

1/2 pound lean ground beef

1 jar (24 ounces) marinara sauce

1 can (14-1/2 ounces) Italian diced tomatoes

1 cup sliced fresh mushrooms

1 package (9 ounces) refrigerated cheese tortellini

1 cup (4 ounces) shredded part-skim mozzarella cheese

■ In a small skillet, cook sausage and beef over medium heat until no longer pink; drain. Transfer meat to a 3-qt. slow cooker. Stir in the marinara sauce, tomatoes and mushrooms.

■ Cover and cook on low for 6-7 hours or until heated through.

■ Prepare tortellini according to package directions. Stir into slow cooker; sprinkle with cheese.

■ Cover and cook for 15 minutes or until cheese is melted.

Yield: 6 servings.

Meat Loaf Burgers

Peggy Burdick
BURLINGTON, MICHIGAN

These hearty sandwiches are great for potluck dinners. Served on hamburger buns, the beef patties get extra flavor when topped with the seasoned tomato sauce.

PREP: 10 min.
COOK: 7 hours

1 large onion, sliced

1 celery rib, chopped

2 pounds lean ground beef

1-1/2 teaspoons salt, *divided*

1/4 teaspoon pepper

2 cups tomato juice

4 garlic cloves, minced

1 tablespoon ketchup

1 teaspoon Italian seasoning

1 bay leaf

6 hamburger buns, split

■ Place onion and celery in a 3-qt. slow cooker. Combine the beef, 1 teaspoon salt and pepper; shape into six patties. Place over onion mixture. Combine the tomato juice, garlic, ketchup, Italian seasoning, bay leaf and remaining salt. Pour over the patties.

■ Cover and cook on low for 7-9 hours or until meat is tender. Discard bay leaf. Separate patties with a spatula if necessary; serve on buns.

Yield: 6 servings.

Italian Stuffed Peppers

Taste of Home Test Kitchen
GREENDALE, WISCONSIN

Cooking the stuffed peppers in a slow cooker is not only convenient, but the longer cooking process also improves the flavor of the filling.

Italian Stuffed Peppers

PREP: 25 min. ■ **COOK:** 4 hours

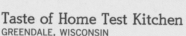

6 large sweet red *or* green peppers

1 pound lean ground beef

2 cups cubed part-skim mozzarella cheese (1/4-inch cubes)

1 cup uncooked converted rice

1 small onion, chopped

2 garlic cloves, minced

1 teaspoon minced fresh parsley

1 teaspoon salt

1/2 teaspoon pepper

1 cup beef broth

1 can (28 ounces) crushed tomatoes

1/2 cup grated Parmesan cheese

■ Cut tops off peppers and remove seeds; set aside. In a large bowl, combine the beef, mozzarella cheese, rice, onion, garlic, parsley, salt and pepper; spoon into peppers. Transfer to an oval 5- or 6-qt. slow cooker. Pour broth over peppers; top with tomatoes.

■ Cover and cook on low for 4-5 hours or until a meat thermometer reaches 160° and peppers are tender. Sprinkle with Parmesan cheese.

Yield: *6 servings.*

Cheesy Pizza Dinner

PREP: 20 min.
COOK: 3 hours

1 package (16 ounces) wide egg noodles

1-1/2 pounds ground beef *or* turkey

1/4 cup chopped onion

1 jar (26 ounces) spaghetti sauce

1 jar (4-1/2 ounces) sliced mushrooms, drained

1-1/2 teaspoons Italian seasoning

1 package (3-1/2 ounces) sliced pepperoni, halved

3 cups (12 ounces) shredded part-skim mozzarella cheese

3 cups (12 ounces) shredded cheddar cheese

■ Cook noodles according to package directions. Meanwhile, in a large skillet, cook beef and onion over medium heat until meat is no longer pink; drain. Stir in the spaghetti sauce, mushrooms and Italian seasoning. Drain noodles.

■ In a 5-qt. slow cooker coated with cooking spray, spread a third of the meat sauce. Cover with a third of the noodles and pepperoni. Sprinkle with a third of the cheddar cheese. Repeat the layers twice.

■ Cover and cook on low for 3-4 hours or until heated through and cheese is melted.

Yield: *6-8 servings.*

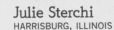

Julie Sterchi
HARRISBURG, ILLINOIS

Always a hit at our church dinners, this hearty casserole keeps folks coming back for more. It's almost better than a regular pizza, because it has all the wonderful flavors, such as pepperoni and ooey-gooey cheese, but the slow cooker does the work for you!

Poultry

52

46

53

You just might find a new favorite recipe after trying one of the chicken or turkey slow cooker dishes shared in this chapter. It's easier than you think to put a delicious dinner on the table.

- Place garlic and celery in a 5-qt. slow cooker. Sprinkle chicken with salt and pepper. In a large nonstick skillet, brown chicken in oil in batches; transfer to slow cooker.

- In a small bowl, combine the remaining ingredients. Pour over chicken. Cover and cook on low for 3-1/2 to 4 hours or until chicken juices run clear.

Yield: 6 servings.

Garlic Clove Chicken

To quickly and easily remove skins from whole garlic cloves, drop them in boiling water for a few seconds, drain and then cool. The skins should slip right off.

Ruth Rigoni
HURLEY, WISCONSIN
Dinner guests and cooks alike will rave about this chicken recipe. Your company will love the tasty poultry, and you'll appreciate the stress-free slow cooker preparation.

Garlic Clove Chicken

PREP: 45 min. ■ **COOK:** 3-1/2 hours

40 garlic cloves, peeled	3 tablespoons lemon juice
4 celery ribs, sliced	2 tablespoons dry vermouth
1 broiler/fryer chicken (3 to 4 pounds), cut up and skin removed	2 tablespoons grated lemon peel
1/2 teaspoon salt	2 tablespoons minced fresh parsley
1/4 teaspoon pepper	2 teaspoons dried basil
1 tablespoon olive oil	1 teaspoon dried oregano
1/4 cup white wine *or* reduced-sodium chicken broth	Dash crushed red pepper flakes

Saucy Mandarin Duck

PREP: 30 min. + marinating ■ **COOK:** 4-3/4 hours

Taste of Home Test Kitchen
GREENDALE, WISCONSIN

For something a little different, try this savory, sweet duck dish that is flavored with Asian seasonings and mandarin oranges. It's a nice change of pace. For some flair, garnish each serving with toasted sesame seeds.

- 1 can (14-1/2 ounces) beef broth
- 1/3 cup tomato paste
- 2 tablespoons brown sugar
- 2 tablespoons orange juice concentrate
- 2 tablespoons soy sauce
- 2 garlic cloves, minced
- 1/2 teaspoon salt
- 1/4 teaspoon pepper
- 1/8 teaspoon ground allspice
- 1 domestic duck (4 to 4-1/2 pounds), skinned, deboned and cut into cubes
- 1/4 pound sliced fresh mushrooms
- 1/2 cup green pepper strips (1/4 in. thick)
- 1 tablespoon butter
- 3 tablespoons cornstarch
- 1/4 teaspoon ground ginger
- 1/4 cup milk
- 1 can (11 ounces) mandarin oranges, drained

Hot cooked rice, optional

■ For the marinade, combine the first nine ingredients. Pour 3/4 cup into a large resealable plastic bag; add the duck. Seal bag and turn to coat; refrigerate for 8 hours. Cover and refrigerate remaining marinade.

■ Drain and discard marinade. Transfer duck to a 1-1/2-qt. slow cooker; add reserved marinade. Cover and cook on low for 4-5 hours or until tender. Skim fat.

■ In a small saucepan, saute mushrooms and green pepper in butter. Combine the cornstarch, ginger and milk until smooth. Stir into the mushroom mixture; add to slow cooker.

■ Cover and cook on high for 45 minutes or until sauce is thickened. Just before serving, stir in oranges. Serve with rice if desired.

Yield: 3 servings.

Ducks are all inspected at the state or federal level. A USDA Grade A shield on a duck is an indication of quality. To receive a Grade A rating, a duck must be plump, meaty and have skin free from cuts, bruises and tears. There can be no broken bones, missing parts and few pin feathers.

Lemon Chicken Breasts with Veggies

PREP: 25 min.
COOK: 8 hours

- 1 pound fresh baby carrots
- 3 cups cubed red potatoes
- 1 package (14 ounces) frozen pearl onions, thawed
- 2 celery ribs, thinly sliced
- 6 bone-in chicken breast halves (10 ounces *each*), skin removed
- 1 can (14-1/2 ounces) condensed cream of chicken soup, undiluted
- 1/2 cup water
- 1/2 cup lemon juice
- 1 teaspoon dried parsley flakes
- 1 teaspoon dried thyme
- 1/2 teaspoon pepper
- 1/4 teaspoon salt

■ In a 5- or 6-qt. slow cooker, combine the carrots, potatoes, onions and celery. Top with chicken. Combine the soup, water, lemon juice, parsley, thyme, pepper and salt.

■ Cover and cook on low for 8-9 hours or until the chicken and vegetables are tender.

Yield: 6 servings.

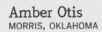

Amber Otis
MORRIS, OKLAHOMA

For a hearty, comforting dish with a nice, subtle lemon flavor, try this delicious chicken dish. The tasty carrots, potatoes and pearl onions make this a satisfying meal. It also adds a touch of class to fancier get-togethers when company is over.

Chicken Saltimbocca

- Flatten chicken to 1/4-in. thickness. Top each piece with a slice of ham and cheese. Roll up tightly; secure with toothpicks. In a shallow bowl, combine flour, Parmesan cheese, salt and pepper. Roll chicken in flour mixture; refrigerate for 1 hour.

- In a large skillet, brown roll-ups in oil on all sides; transfer to a 3-qt. slow cooker. Combine the soup and wine or broth; pour over chicken.

- Cover and cook on low for 4-5 hours or until meat is no longer pink. Remove roll-ups and stir sauce. Discard the toothpicks. Serve with rice.

Yield: 6 servings.

Carol McCollough
MISSOULA, MONTANA

White wine dresses up cream of chicken soup to make a lovely sauce for chicken, ham and Swiss cheese roll-ups. The tried-and-true recipe comes from my mother.

Chicken Saltimbocca

PREP: 25 min. + chilling ■ **COOK:** 4 hours

- 6 boneless skinless chicken breast halves (4 ounces *each*)
- 6 thin slices deli ham
- 6 slices Swiss cheese
- 1/4 cup all-purpose flour
- 1/4 cup grated Parmesan cheese
- 1/2 teaspoon salt
- 1/4 teaspoon pepper
- 2 tablespoons canola oil
- 1 can (10-3/4 ounces) condensed cream of chicken soup, undiluted
- 1/2 cup dry white wine *or* chicken broth
- Hot cooked rice

To flatten chicken for saltimbocca, place boneless chicken breasts between two pieces of waxed paper or plastic wrap or in a resealable plastic bag. Starting in the center and working out to edges, pound lightly with the flat side of a meat mallet until the chicken is even in thickness.

Shelli
McWilliam
SALEM, OREGON

*Slow cooked and
savory, this easy-to-
fix Italian classic is
perfect for any night
of the week, but ele-
gant enough for
company. It is sure
to become a treas-
ured dinner staple
in your home.*

Chicken Merlot with Mushrooms

Chicken Merlot with Mushrooms

PREP: 10 min. ■ **COOK:** 5 hours

3/4 pound sliced fresh mushrooms	2 tablespoons quick-cooking tapioca
1 cup chopped onion	2 teaspoons sugar
2 teaspoons minced garlic	1-1/2 teaspoons dried basil
3 pounds boneless skinless chicken thighs	1/2 teaspoon salt
1 can (6 ounces) tomato paste	1/4 teaspoon pepper
	2 tablespoons grated Parmesan cheese
3/4 cup chicken broth	Hot cooked pasta, optional
1/4 cup merlot *or* additional chicken broth	

■ Place the mushrooms, onion and garlic in a 5-qt. slow cooker. Top with the chicken thighs.

■ In a small bowl, combine the tomato paste, broth, wine, tapioca, sugar, basil, salt and pepper. Pour over chicken. Cover and cook on low for 5-6 hours or until chicken is tender.

■ Sprinkle with Parmesan cheese. Serve with pasta if desired.

Yield: *5 servings.*

Sweet and Saucy Chicken

Patricia Weir
CHILLIWACK, BRITISH COLUMBIA

*I can't remember where this
recipe came from, but I've been
making it for several years. Everyone who tries it enjoys it.*

PREP: 30 min.
COOK: 6 hours

1 broiler/fryer chicken (4 pounds), cut up and skin removed
3/4 cup packed brown sugar
1/4 cup all-purpose flour
2/3 cup water
1/3 cup white vinegar
1/3 cup reduced-sodium soy sauce
2 tablespoons ketchup
1 tablespoon dried minced onion
1 teaspoon prepared mustard
1/4 teaspoon garlic powder
1/4 teaspoon salt
1/4 teaspoon pepper
Hot cooked rice *or* egg noodles, optional

■ Place chicken in a 3-qt. slow cooker. In a small saucepan combine brown sugar and flour. Stir in the water, vinegar and soy sauce. Add the ketchup, onion, mustard, garlic powder, salt and pepper. Bring to a boil; cook and stir for 1-2 minutes or until thickened. Pour over chicken.

■ Cover and cook on low for 6-8 hours or until chicken juices run clear. Serve with rice or noodles if desired.

Yield: *6 servings.*

Diane
Twait Nelsen
RINGSTED, IOWA

These sandwiches have been such a hit at office potlucks that I keep copies of the recipe in my desk to hand out. They're easy to make and always a bit hit.

Slow-Cooked Turkey Sandwiches

Slow-Cooked Turkey Sandwiches

PREP: 15 min. ■ **COOK:** 3 hours

6 cups cubed cooked turkey
2 cups cubed process cheese (Velveeta)
1 can (10-3/4 ounces) condensed cream of chicken soup, undiluted
1 can (10-3/4 ounces) condensed cream of mushroom soup, undiluted
1/2 cup finely chopped onion
1/2 cup chopped celery
22 wheat sandwich buns, split

■ In a 3-qt. slow cooker, combine the first six ingredients. Cover and cook on low for 3-4 hours or until onion and celery are tender and cheese is melted. Stir before spooning onto buns.

Yield: 22 servings.

An easy slaw goes great with the turkey sandwiches. In a large bowl, combine 1 package broccoli coleslaw mix, 1 package dried cranberries, 6 green onions cut into 1/2-inch pieces and 1/4 cup bottled coleslaw dressing. Toss to coat and refrigerate until serving.

Tangy Chicken Thighs

dutchmom4MI
TASTE OF HOME ONLINE COMMUNITY

I love this dish because it turns affordable chicken thighs into a delicious meal. The creamy, tangy sauce is what makes this dish.

PREP: 25 min.
COOK: 4-3/4 hours

1 envelope Italian salad dressing mix
1/2 teaspoon pepper
6 boneless skinless chicken thighs (3-1/2 pounds)
2 tablespoons butter, melted
1 large onion, chopped
2 garlic cloves, minced
1 can (10-3/4 ounces) condensed cream of chicken soup, undiluted
1 package (8 ounces) cream cheese, softened and cubed
1/4 cup chicken broth
Hot cooked rice *or* noodles, optional

■ Combine the salad dressing mix and pepper. In a 3-qt. slow cooker, layer half of the chicken, butter, salad dressing mixture, onion and garlic. Repeat layers. Cover and cook on low for 4-5 hours or until chicken is tender. Skim fat.

■ In a small bowl, combine soup, cream cheese and broth until blended; add to slow cooker. Cover and cook for 45 minutes or until heated through.

■ Remove chicken to a serving platter; stir sauce until smooth. Serve chicken with sauce and rice or noodles if desired.

Yield: 6 servings.

Corsican Chicken

Mary Bergfeld
EUGENE, OREGON

Moist, tender chicken thighs make a delicious entree for winter months. I set the table with sunny Mediterranean hues that look gorgeous with this colorful meal.

Corsican Chicken

PREP: 20 min. ■ **COOK:** 4-1/2 hours

3 tablespoons butter, softened

2 tablespoons herbes de Provence

1 teaspoon salt

2 garlic cloves, minced

1/2 teaspoon coarsely ground pepper

2 pounds boneless skinless chicken thighs

1 large onion, chopped

1/2 cup oil-packed sun-dried tomatoes, julienned

1 can (10-1/2 ounces) condensed beef consomme, undiluted

1/2 cup dry vermouth *or* orange juice

1/2 cup pitted Greek olives, quartered

1 teaspoon grated orange peel

2 teaspoons cornstarch

1 tablespoon cold water

2 tablespoons minced fresh basil

2 tablespoons diced pimientos

2 tablespoons minced fresh parsley

■ In a small bowl, combine the butter, herbes de Provence, salt, garlic and pepper; rub over chicken. Place in a 5-qt. slow cooker. Add the onion, tomatoes, consomme and vermouth or orange juice. Cover and cook on low for 4-5 hours or until chicken is no longer pink. Add olives and orange peel. Cover and cook on high for 30 minutes.

■ Remove chicken and keep warm. Pour cooking juices into a small saucepan; skim fat. Combine cornstarch and water until smooth; gradually stir into cooking juices. Bring to a boil; cook and stir for 2 minutes or until smooth. Pour over chicken. Sprinkle with basil, pimientos and parsley.

Yield: 6-8 servings.

Editor's Note: Look for herbes de Provence in the spice aisle. It is also available from Penzeys Spices. Call 1-800-741-7787 or visit www.penzeys.com.

Kalamata olives,

also called Greek olives, are purple-black, almond-shaped olives native to Greece. They're usually packed in either olive oil or vinegar, giving them a stronger flavor than most other olives. Kalamata olives can be found in larger supermarkets as well as smaller ethnic grocery stores.

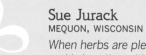

Sue Jurack
MEQUON, WISCONSIN

When herbs are plentiful in my garden, I prepare this recipe. The turkey stays moist in the slow cooker and is bursting with flavor. When I served this to our Bible study potluck group, everyone enjoyed the dish so much that they wanted the recipe!

Slow-Cooked Herbed Turkey

PREP: 15 min. + marinating ■ COOK: 3-1/2 hours + standing

1 can (14-1/2 ounces) chicken broth	2 tablespoons Dijon mustard
1/2 cup lemon juice	1 tablespoon minced fresh marjoram
1/4 cup packed brown sugar	1-1/2 teaspoons paprika
1/4 cup minced fresh sage	1 teaspoon garlic powder
1/4 cup minced fresh thyme	1 teaspoon pepper
1/4 cup lime juice	1/2 teaspoon salt
1/4 cup cider vinegar	2 frozen boneless turkey breast roasts, thawed (3 pounds *each*)
1/4 cup olive oil	
1 envelope onion soup mix	

■ In a blender, combine the first 15 ingredients; cover and process until blended. Place turkey breasts in a gallon-size resealable plastic bag; add half of marinade. Seal bag and turn to coat; seal and refrigerate overnight. Pour remaining marinade into a bowl; cover and refrigerate.

■ Transfer turkey breasts to a 5-qt. slow cooker; discard marinade. Add reserved marinade; cover and cook on high for 4-1/2 to 5 hours or until juices run clear and a meat thermometer reads 170°. Let stand for 10 minutes before slicing.

Yield: 14-16 servings.

Leftover turkey is a great opportunity to make even more delicious entrees for your family. To make your dollar stretch, try the Next Day Turkey Primavera on page 124, the Mushroom Turkey Tetrazzini on page 201 or the Slow-Cooked Turkey Sandwiches on page 48.

Southwest Chicken*

Maddymoo
TASTE OF HOME ONLINE COMMUNITY

Chicken is cooked with corn, beans and salsa until tender for a delicious meal with Southwestern flair. The garnishes really complete the meal.

PREP: 15 min.
COOK: 4 hours

- 1 can (15-1/4 ounces) whole kernel corn, drained
- 1 can (15 ounces) black beans, rinsed and drained
- 1 jar (16 ounces) mild salsa
- 4 boneless skinless chicken breast halves (5 ounces *each*)

Sweet red and yellow pepper strips, sour cream, shredded cheddar cheese and sliced green onions, optional

■ In a 4-qt. slow cooker, layer three-fourths each of the corn and beans and half of the salsa. Arrange the chicken over salsa; top with remaining corn, beans and salsa. Cover and cook on low for 4-6 hours or until the chicken is tender.

■ Shred chicken with two forks and return to the slow cooker; heat through. Top with the peppers, sour cream, cheese and onions if desired.

Yield: 6 servings.

✱ Nutrition Facts: 1 cup (calculated without optional ingredients) equals 234 calories, 3 g fat (1 g saturated fat), 52 mg cholesterol, 678 mg sodium, 23 g carbohydrate, 4 g fiber, 24 g protein. **Diabetic Exchanges:** 3 very lean meat, 1 starch, 1 vegetable.

Sharon Johannes
ASHLEY, ILLINOIS

With a full-time job and active child, I'm known as the "Slow Cooker Queen" in my family. I've made this recipe for years. After making a few tweaks, it's become a treasured favorite.

Rosemary Chicken with White Beans

Rosemary Chicken with White Beans

PREP: 15 min. ■ **COOK:** 3 hours

- 6 boneless skinless chicken breast halves (6 ounces *each*)
- 1 tablespoon canola oil
- 2 cans (15-1/2 ounces *each*) great northern beans, rinsed and drained
- 1 cup sliced fresh carrots
- 1/2 cup sliced celery
- 2/3 cup Italian salad dressing
- 2 teaspoons dried rosemary, crushed
- 1/2 teaspoon salt
- 1 teaspoon pepper

■ In a large skillet, brown chicken in oil in batches on both sides. Place the beans, carrots and celery in a 5-qt. slow cooker; top with chicken.

■ Combine the salad dressing, rosemary, salt and pepper; pour over chicken. Cover and cook on low for 3-4 hours or until a meat thermometer reads 170°.

Yield: 6 servings.

Herbed Chicken and Tomatoes

Rebecca Popke
LARGO, FLORIDA

I put a tangy spin on chicken by adding just a few ingredients. Recipes such as this are really a plus when you work a full-time job but still want to put a healthy, satisfying meal on the table.

PREP: 5 min.
COOK: 5 hours

- 1 pound boneless skinless chicken breasts, cut into 1-1/2-inch pieces
- 2 cans (14-1/2 ounces *each*) Italian diced tomatoes
- 1 envelope savory herb with garlic soup mix
- 1/4 teaspoon sugar
Hot cooked pasta
Shredded Parmesan cheese

■ In a 3-qt. slow cooker, combine the chicken, tomatoes, soup mix and sugar. Cover and cook on low for 5-6 hours or until chicken is no longer pink. Serve with pasta; sprinkle with Parmesan cheese.

Yield: 4 servings.

Lime Chicken Tacos

- Place the chicken in a 3-qt. slow cooker. Combine lime juice and chili powder; pour over chicken. Cover and cook on low for 5-6 hours or until chicken is tender.

- Remove chicken; cool slightly. Shred and return to the slow cooker. Stir in the corn and salsa. Cover and cook on low for 30 minutes or until heated through. Serve in tortillas with sour cream, cheese and lettuce if desired.

Yield: 12 tacos.

* Nutrition Facts: 1 taco (prepared with fat-free tortillas; calculated without sour cream and cheese) equals 148 calories, 2 g fat (trace saturated fat), 31 mg cholesterol, 338 mg sodium, 18 g carbohydrate, 1 g fiber, 14 g protein. **Diabetic Exchanges:** 2 very lean meat, 1 starch.

Here are some sweet and savory ways to use up leftover tortillas:

- Brush with butter and sprinkle with herbs or cinnamon-sugar. Bake until crisp.
- Spread with peanut butter or cream cheese, then roll.
- Dry until brittle, then crumble over soups or salads.

Tracy Gunter
BOISE, IDAHO

Lime adds zest to this easy tortilla filling, and leftovers make a refreshing topping to taco salad. This fun recipe is great and simple for a casual dinner with friends or family.

Lime Chicken Tacos*

PREP: 10 min. ■ **COOK:** 5-1/2 hours

1-1/2 pounds boneless skinless chicken breasts

3 tablespoons lime juice

1 tablespoon chili powder

1 cup frozen corn

1 cup chunky salsa

12 flour tortillas (6 inches), warmed

Sour cream, shredded cheddar cheese and shredded lettuce, optional

- Place the turkey, skin side up, in a 5-qt. slow cooker. Brush with butter. Sprinkle with parsley, salt, tarragon and pepper. Top with mushrooms. Pour wine over all. Cover and cook on low for 7-8 hours or until a meat thermometer reads 170°.

- Remove turkey and keep warm. Skim fat from cooking juices. In a small saucepan, combine the cornstarch and water until smooth. Gradually add cooking juices. Bring to a boil; cook and stir for 2 minutes or until thickened. Serve with turkey.

Yield: 8 servings.

Turkey with Mushroom Sauce

Myra Innes
AUBURN, KANSAS

When we were first married, I didn't have an oven, so I made this tender turkey in the slow cooker. Now I rely on this recipe to free up the oven to make other dishes for get-togethers.

When cooking

with white wine, use dry varieties, such as Chardonnay, Sauvignon Blanc or Pinot Grigio.

Turkey with Mushroom Sauce

PREP: 10 min. ■ COOK: 7-8 hours

- 1 boneless turkey breast (3 pounds), cut in half
- 2 tablespoons butter, melted
- 2 tablespoons dried parsley flakes
- 1/2 teaspoon salt
- 1/2 teaspoon dried tarragon
- 1/8 teaspoon pepper

- 1 jar (4-1/2 ounces) sliced mushrooms, drained *or* 1 cup sliced fresh mushrooms
- 1/2 cup white wine *or* chicken broth
- 2 tablespoons cornstarch
- 1/4 cup cold water

Mushroom Meat Loaf

PREP: 30 min. ■ COOK: 3-1/4 hours

Tyler Sherman
WILLIAMSBURG, VIRGINIA

Although I don't consider myself much of a cook, this recipe is delicious. It's moist, tender and the sauce has a nice zip to it. The mushrooms and ground turkey are a nice combination.

2 eggs, lightly beaten	1/2 teaspoon dried thyme
1-1/3 cups soft bread crumbs	1/4 teaspoon pepper
8 ounces large portobello mushrooms, stems removed and finely chopped	1 pound lean ground turkey
	1/4 cup chili sauce
1 small onion, finely chopped	2 teaspoons stone-ground mustard
2 garlic cloves, minced	1/8 teaspoon cayenne pepper
3/4 teaspoon salt	

■ In a large bowl, combine the eggs, bread crumbs, mushrooms, onion, garlic, salt, thyme and pepper. Crumble turkey over mixture and mix well. Shape into a 7-1/2-in. x 4-in. loaf.

■ Cut three 20-in. x 3-in. strips of heavy-duty aluminum foil; crisscross so they resemble spokes of a wheel. Place strips on the bottom and up the sides of a 3-qt. slow cooker coated with cooking spray. Coat strips with cooking spray. Place meat loaf in the center.

■ Cover and cook on low for 3-4 hours or until no pink remains and a meat thermometer reads 165°.

■ In a small bowl, combine the chili sauce, mustard and cayenne; pour over meat. Cover and cook for 15 minutes or until heated through. Using foil strips as handles, remove meat loaf to a platter.

Yield: 6 servings.

To make soft bread crumbs, tear a few slices of bread into 1-1/2-in. pieces and place in a food processor or blender jar. Cover and pulse until the bread turns to crumbs. The more "pulses," the finer the crumbs. You can process a sprig of fresh parsley or another herb along with the bread for added flavor.

Ham 'n' Swiss Chicken

Dorothy Witmer
EPHRATA, PENNSYLVANIA

This saucy casserole allows you to enjoy all the rich flavor of chicken cordon bleu with less effort. It's a snap to layer the ingredients and let them cook all afternoon.

PREP: 10 min.
COOK: 4 hours

2 eggs
2 cups milk, *divided*
1/2 cup butter, melted
1/2 cup chopped celery
1 teaspoon finely chopped onion
8 slices bread, cubed
12 thin slices deli ham, rolled up
2 cups (8 ounces) shredded Swiss cheese
2-1/2 cups cubed cooked chicken
1 can (10-3/4 ounces) condensed cream of chicken soup, undiluted

■ In a large bowl, whisk eggs and 1-1/2 cups milk. Stir in the butter, celery and onion. Stir in bread crumbs.

■ Place half of the mixture in a greased 3-qt. slow cooker; top with half of the rolled-up ham, cheese and chicken. Combine soup and remaining milk; pour half over the chicken. Repeat layers once.

■ Cover and cook on low for 4-5 hours or until a thermometer inserted into bread mixture reads 160°.

Yield: 6 servings.

Sesame Orange Chicken

PREP: 20 min.
COOK: 4 hours

 1/2 cup all-purpose flour
  16 boneless skinless chicken thighs (4 ounces *each*)
 2/3 cup teriyaki sesame ginger barbecue sauce
 2/3 cup orange marmalade
 1/2 cup orange juice
 1/4 cup soy sauce
   1 tablespoon minced fresh gingerroot
 1/2 teaspoon crushed red pepper flakes
   2 tablespoons sesame seeds, toasted

Hot cooked rice

- Place flour in a large resealable plastic bag. Add the chicken, a few pieces at a time, and shake to coat. Transfer to a 4- or 5-qt. slow cooker.

- In a large bowl, combine the barbecue sauce, marmalade, orange juice, soy sauce, ginger and pepper flakes. Pour over chicken. Cover and cook on low for 4-6 hours or until meat is tender. Sprinkle with sesame seeds. Serve with rice.

Yield: 8 servings.

Taste of Home Test Kitchen
GREENDALE, WISCONSIN

Break out the slow cooker and start the week off on an easy note with this all-in-one recipe. A cup of chicken broth may be substituted for the water and chicken bouillon granules.

Creamy Tarragon Chicken

Creamy Tarragon Chicken

PREP: 10 min. ■ **COOK:** 6-1/4 hours

   7 boneless skinless chicken breast halves (6 ounces *each*)
   1 cup chopped onion
   1 cup water
   2 ounces prosciutto *or* deli ham, chopped
   3 tablespoons quick-cooking tapioca
   2 teaspoons chicken bouillon granules
   2 teaspoons dried tarragon
   1 teaspoon minced garlic
 1/4 teaspoon salt
 1/4 teaspoon pepper
   3 cups frozen broccoli-cauliflower blend, thawed
 1/2 cup half-and-half cream
 1-1/2 cups uncooked orzo pasta

- In a 5-qt. slow cooker, combine the first 10 ingredients. Cover and cook on low for 6-7 hours or until chicken juices run clear.

- Remove three chicken breast halves; cool. Cover and refrigerate to save for another use.

- Stir vegetables and cream into the slow cooker. Cover and cook 15 minutes longer or until vegetables are heated through. Meanwhile, cook orzo according to package directions. Serve with chicken and vegetables.

Yield: 4 servings.

Darlene Brenden
SALEM, OREGON

The enticing aroma of oranges and barbecue awaits you after removing the lid from this tasty dish. Summertime doesn't mean you can't enjoy a hot, hearty meal! If you have a rice cooker, you can make a side dish of rice to serve with the chicken.

Other Entrees

69

70

60

Slow cookers aren't just for meat and poultry any more! You'll want to check out all of the new and delicious meals you can create in this chapter, such as pork ribs, hearty stew, salmon loaf, ham dishes and even breakfast staples. You won't be disappointed!

- Place pork chops in a 3-qt. slow cooker. Combine the teriyaki sauce, vinegar, pepper flakes and garlic; pour over meat. Cover and cook on low for 6 hours or until meat is tender.

- Remove the pork and cut into bite-size pieces; keep warm. Strain cooking juices into a large saucepan. Combine cornstarch and water until smooth; stir into juices. Bring to a boil; cook and stir for 2 minutes or until thickened. Stir in peanut butter; add meat.

- Serve with rice. Sprinkle with onions and peanuts. Drizzle with lime juice if desired.

Yield: 6 servings.

Thai-Style Pork

Amy Van Orman
ROCKFORD, MICHIGAN

A creamy peanut butter sauce coats moist slices of pork in this delectable dish. This recipe is from a friend in my cooking club, and it's always a favorite.

Thai-Style Pork

PREP: 15 min. ■ **COOK:** 6-1/4 hours

2	pounds boneless pork loin chops
1/4	cup teriyaki sauce
2	tablespoons rice vinegar
1	teaspoon crushed red pepper flakes
1	teaspoon minced garlic
1	tablespoon cornstarch

- 1/4 cup cold water
- 1/4 cup creamy peanut butter

Hot cooked rice
- 1/2 cup chopped green onions
- 1/2 cup dry roasted peanuts

Lime juice, optional

To add a selection of toppings for Thai-Style Pork, place plain yogurt, toasted flaked coconut and minced fresh cilantro each in separate bowls. Guests can top their dish with whatever garnishes they prefer.

Susan Blair
STERLING, MICHIGAN

I modified a recipe to reduce the fat without sacrificing flavor. I've served this at numerous places, and folks are always surprised to find out they're eating healthy.

Ham Tetrazzini

Ham Tetrazzini*

PREP: 15 min. ■ COOK: 4 hours

1 can (10-3/4 ounces) reduced-sodium condensed cream of mushroom soup, undiluted

1 cup sliced fresh mushrooms

1 cup cubed fully cooked lean ham

1/2 cup fat-free evaporated milk

2 tablespoons white wine *or* water

1 teaspoon prepared horseradish

1 package (7 ounces) spaghetti

1/2 cup shredded Parmesan cheese

■ In a 3-qt. slow cooker, combine the soup, mushrooms, ham, milk, wine or water and horseradish. Cover and cook on low for 4 hours. Cook spaghetti according to package directions; drain. Add the spaghetti and cheese to slow cooker; toss to coat.

Yield: 6 servings.

✱ Nutrition Facts: One serving (3/4 cup) equals 231 calories, 5 g fat (2 g saturated fat), 18 mg cholesterol, 607 mg sodium, 32 g carbohydrate, 1 g fiber, 14 g protein. **Diabetic Exchanges:** 2 starch, 1 lean meat, 1/2 fat.

For 8 ounces of pasta, bring 3 quarts of water to a boil. Add 1 tablespoon salt if desired. Follow the package cooking directions. To test for doneness, remove a single piece of pasta, rinse in cold water and taste. Pasta should be cooked until "al dente," or firm yet tender. Avoid overcooking, which can result in a mushy texture.

Herbed Pork Roast*

PREP: 25 min.
COOK: 8 hours

1 boneless whole pork loin roast (4 pounds)

1 cup water

1/4 cup butter, softened

2 tablespoons rubbed sage

2 tablespoons dried parsley flakes

2 teaspoons pepper

1 teaspoon minced garlic

1 teaspoon dried oregano

1/2 teaspoon salt

1 small onion, thinly sliced

1 teaspoon browning sauce, optional

■ Cut roast in half. Place pork and water in a 4-qt. slow cooker. Spread butter over meat. Combine the sage, parsley, pepper, garlic, oregano and salt; rub over meat. Top with onion. Cover and cook on low for 8-10 hours or until a meat thermometer reads 160°.

■ Remove and discard onion. If desired, thicken cooking juices. Stir in browning sauce if desired.

Yield: 12 servings.

✱ Nutrition Facts: 4 ounces cooked meat with about 2 tablespoons gravy (calculated without browning sauce) equals 227 calories, 11 g fat (5 g saturated fat), 85 mg cholesterol, 171 mg sodium, 1 g carbohydrate, trace fiber, 29 g protein. **Diabetic Exchanges:** 4 lean meat, 1 fat.

Shelia Letchworth
VERSAILLES, MISSOURI

The herb rub and sliced onion add loads of flavor to this pork roast. I like to serve the pork with a side of parslied potatoes and a green salad for a well-rounded dinner. The wonderful thing about this recipe is that it cooks all day so you can use your time to run errands or spend with your family.

Brat Sauerkraut Supper

Ann Christensen
MESA, ARIZONA

This stick-to-your-ribs German dish is sure to satisfy even the biggest appetite at your house. Sliced apple and apple juice lend mellowing sweetness to the tangy sauerkraut.

Brat Sauerkraut Supper

PREP: 15 min. ■ COOK: 4 hours

- 1 jar (32 ounces) sauerkraut, rinsed and well drained
- 2 medium red potatoes, peeled, halved and cut into thin slices
- 1 medium tart apple, peeled and cut into thick slices
- 1 small onion, chopped
- 1/2 cup apple juice
- 1/4 cup water
- 2 tablespoons brown sugar
- 1 teaspoon chicken bouillon granules
- 1 teaspoon caraway seeds
- 1 garlic clove, minced
- 1 bay leaf
- 1 pound fully cooked bratwurst links
- 6 bacon strips, cooked and crumbled

■ In a 5-qt. slow cooker, combine the first 11 ingredients. Top with bratwurst. Cover and cook on high for 4-5 hours or until potatoes are tender. Discard bay leaf. Sprinkle with bacon.

Yield: 6 servings.

Easy and Elegant Ham

Denise DiPace
MEDFORD, NEW JERSEY

I fix this moist, tender ham to serve my large family. It can be readied quickly in the morning, frees up my oven, tastes outstanding and can feed a crowd. Covered with colorful pineapple slices, cherries and orange glaze, the showstopping appearance appeals to both children and adults.

PREP: 5 min.
COOK: 6 hours + standing

- 2 cans (20 ounces *each*) sliced pineapple
- 1 fully cooked boneless ham (about 6 pounds), halved
- 1 jar (6 ounces) maraschino cherries, well drained
- 1 jar (12 ounces) orange marmalade

■ Drain the pineapple, reserving juice; set juice aside. Place half of the pineapple in an ungreased 5-qt. slow cooker. Top with the ham. Add the cherries, remaining sliced pineapple and the reserved pineapple juice. Spoon marmalade over ham.

■ Cover and cook on low for 6-7 hours or until heated through. Remove to a warm serving platter. Let stand for 10-15 minutes before slicing. Serve the pineapple and cherries with sliced ham.

Yield: 18-20 servings.

Terry Paull
EAGLE RIVER,
WISCONSIN

We live in the "north woods," so we usually have an ample supply of venison. This is a recipe our mom made often, and it's one of our favorites.

Hunter's Delight

Hunter's Delight

PREP: 15 min. ■ **COOK:** 6 hours

1/2	pound sliced bacon, diced
2-1/2	pounds red potatoes, thinly sliced
2	medium onions, sliced
1-1/2	pounds boneless venison steak, cubed

2	cans (14-3/4 ounces *each*) cream-style corn
3	tablespoons Worcestershire sauce
1	teaspoon sugar
1/2	to 1 teaspoon seasoned salt

■ In a large skillet, cook bacon over medium heat until crisp; drain. Place potatoes and onions in a 5-qt. slow cooker. Top with venison and bacon.

■ In a large bowl, combine the corn, Worcestershire sauce, sugar and seasoned salt; pour over the top.

■ Cover; cook on low for 6-8 hours or until meat and potatoes are tender.

Yield: 8 servings.

To cut the wild flavor of venison, try sprinkling on a little apple pie spice and ground black pepper. When venison is cooked this way in a slow cooker, it tastes similar to beef.

Egg and Broccoli Casserole

Janet Sliter
KENNEWICK, WASHINGTON

For years, I've prepared this egg casserole, which is delicious for brunch, in my slow cooker. It's an unusual recipe for this appliance but is welcomed when I serve it. Folks always go back for seconds.

PREP: 10 min.
COOK: 3-1/2 hours

3	cups (24 ounces) 4% cottage cheese
3	cups frozen chopped broccoli, thawed and drained
2	cups (8 ounces) shredded cheddar cheese
6	eggs, lightly beaten
1/3	cup all-purpose flour
1/4	cup butter, melted
3	tablespoons finely chopped onion
1/2	teaspoon salt

Additional shredded cheddar cheese, optional

■ In a large bowl, combine the first eight ingredients. Pour into a greased 3-qt. slow cooker. Cover and cook on high for 1 hour. Stir.

■ Reduce heat to low; cover and cook 2-1/2 to 3 hours longer or until a thermometer placed in the center reads 160° and the eggs are set. Sprinkle with cheese if desired.

Yield: 6 servings.

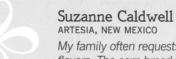

Suzanne Caldwell
ARTESIA, NEW MEXICO

My family often requests this economical, slow cooker favorite. It's loaded with fresh Southwestern flavors. The corn bread topping is a wonderful complement to the flavorful beans. One batch makes several servings, but it never lasts long at our house!

Corn Bread-Topped Frijoles

PREP: 20 min. ■ **COOK:** 3 hours

- 1 medium onion, chopped
- 1 medium green pepper, chopped
- 2 garlic cloves, minced
- 1 tablespoon canola oil
- 1 can (16 ounces) kidney beans, rinsed and drained
- 1 can (15 ounces) pinto beans, rinsed and drained
- 1 can (14-1/2 ounces) diced tomatoes, undrained
- 1 can (8 ounces) tomato sauce
- 1 teaspoon chili powder
- 1/2 teaspoon pepper
- 1/8 teaspoon hot pepper sauce

CORN BREAD TOPPING:

- 1 cup all-purpose flour
- 1 cup yellow cornmeal
- 1 tablespoon sugar
- 1-1/2 teaspoons baking powder
- 1/2 teaspoon salt
- 2 eggs, lightly beaten
- 1-1/4 cups fat-free milk
- 1 can (8-3/4 ounces) cream-style corn
- 3 tablespoons canola oil

■ In a large skillet, saute the onion, green pepper and garlic in oil until tender. Transfer to a greased 5-qt. slow cooker.

■ Stir in the beans, tomatoes, tomato sauce, chili powder, pepper and hot pepper sauce. Cover and cook on high for 1 hour.

■ In a large bowl, combine the flour, cornmeal, sugar, baking powder and salt. Combine the eggs, milk, corn and oil; add to dry ingredients and mix well. Spoon evenly over bean mixture.

■ Cover and cook on high 2 hours longer or until a toothpick inserted near the center of corn bread comes out clean.

Yield: 8 servings.

Frijoles [free-HOH-lehs] is simply the Mexican word for "beans." But when used in the context of a recipe, it usually means beans or refried beans that are flavored with spices and aromatic ingredients such as garlic, onion and green pepper.

Sweet & Sour Pork Ribs

Merle Dyck
ELKFORD, BRITISH COLUMBIA

For years I wondered why people raved about ribs. I didn't have the patience or energy to bother with them, until I made this recipe. Now I'm a believer, too.

PREP: 30 min.
COOK: 8 hours

- 2 cups packed brown sugar
- 1/4 cup all-purpose flour
- 1/2 cup cider vinegar
- 1/3 cup water
- 2 tablespoons soy sauce
- 2 tablespoons ketchup
- 3 garlic cloves, minced
- 8 bone-in country-style pork ribs (3 inches thick and 8 ounces *each*)

■ In a small saucepan, combine brown sugar and flour. Stir in the vinegar, water, soy sauce, ketchup and garlic. Bring to a boil; cook and stir for 2 minutes or until thickened.

■ Place ribs in a 5-qt. slow cooker. Top with sauce. Cover and cook on low for 8-10 hours or until meat is tender. Skim fat. Serve ribs with sauce.

Yield: 8 servings.

Chinese Pork Ribs

June Ross
BELMONT, NORTH CAROLINA

This is one of the only dishes that both of my young boys love. They even come back for seconds.

PREP: 10 min.
COOK: 6 hours

- 1/4 cup soy sauce
- 1/3 cup orange marmalade
- 3 tablespoons ketchup
- 2 garlic cloves, minced
- 3 to 4 pounds bone-in country-style pork ribs

■ In a bowl, combine the soy sauce, marmalade, ketchup and garlic. Pour half into a 5-qt. slow cooker. Top with ribs; drizzle with the remaining sauce. Cover and cook on low for 6 hours or until tender. Thicken cooking juices if desired.

Yield: 6-8 servings.

Kimberly Burke
CHICO, CALIFORNIA
Pork slowly stews with jalapenos, onion, green enchilada sauce and spices in this flavor-packed Mexican dish. It's great with sour cream, cheese or olives on the side.

Pork Chili Verde

Pork Chili Verde

PREP: 25 min. ■ **COOK:** 6-1/2 hours

- 1 boneless pork sirloin roast (3 pounds), cut into 1-inch cubes
- 4 medium carrots, sliced
- 1 medium onion, thinly sliced
- 1 cup minced fresh cilantro
- 4 garlic cloves, minced
- 3 tablespoons canola oil
- 1 can (28 ounces) green enchilada sauce
- 2 jalapeno peppers, seeded and chopped
- 1 tablespoon cornstarch
- 1/4 cup cold water
- Hot cooked rice
- Flour tortillas, warmed

■ In a large skillet, saute the pork, carrots, onion, cilantro and garlic in oil in batches until pork is browned. Transfer to a 5-qt. slow cooker. Add the enchilada sauce and jalapenos. Cover and cook on low for 6 hours or until meat is tender.

■ In a small bowl, combine cornstarch and water until smooth; stir into pork mixture. Cover and cook on high for 30 minutes or until thickened. Serve with rice and tortillas.

Yield: 8 servings.

Editor's Note: When cutting hot peppers, disposable gloves are recommended. Avoid touching your face.

Country-style ribs are meaty ribs from the rib end of the pork loin. They are sold with and without bones, both in slabs and individually.

Sweet Potato Lentil Stew

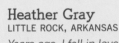

Heather Gray
LITTLE ROCK, ARKANSAS
Years ago, I fell in love with the spicy flavor and wonderful aroma of this hearty slow cooker recipe. You can serve the stew alone or as a topper for meat or poultry.

Sweet Potato Lentil Stew

PREP: 5 min. ■ **COOK:** 5 hours

    4   cups vegetable broth
    3   cups sweet potatoes,
        peeled and cubed (about
        1-1/4 pounds)
1-1/2   cups dried lentils, rinsed
    3   medium carrots, cut into
        chunks
    1   medium onion, chopped

    4   garlic cloves, minced
  1/2   teaspoon ground cumin
  1/4   teaspoon ground ginger
  1/4   teaspoon cayenne pepper
  1/4   cup minced fresh cilantro
  1/4   teaspoon salt

■ In a 3-qt. slow cooker, combine the first nine ingredients. Cover and cook on low for 5-6 hours or until the vegetables are tender. Stir in the minced cilantro and salt.

Yield: 6 servings.

Slow Cooker Salmon Loaf

Kelly Ritter
DOUGLASVILLE, GEORGIA

As a stay-at-home mom with two small children, I'm always looking for quick, easy recipes that can be prepared ahead of time. I also don't like to heat up my oven during our hot Georgia summers. I adapted this recipe from one I found in an old slow cooker book of my grandma's.

PREP: 10 min.
COOK: 4 hours

    2   eggs, lightly beaten
    2   cups seasoned stuffing
        croutons
    1   cup chicken broth
    1   cup grated Parmesan
        cheese
  1/4   teaspoon ground mustard
    1   can (14-3/4 ounces)
        salmon, drained, bones
        and skin removed

■ In a bowl, combine the first five ingredients. Add salmon and mix well. Transfer to a 3-qt. slow cooker coated with cooking spray. Gently shape mixture into a loaf. Cover and cook on low for 4-6 hours or until a meat thermometer reads 160°.

Yield: 6 servings.

John Vale
HARDIN, MONTANA

We love this hearty, nutritious cooked cereal that is flavored with cinnamon, chopped fruit and nuts. We enjoy it with plain yogurt and sliced bananas or blueberries.

Warm 'n' Fruity Breakfast Cereal

Warm 'n' Fruity Breakfast Cereal*

PREP: 10 min. ■ **COOK:** 6 hours

5 cups water	1/4 cup dried cranberries
2 cups seven-grain cereal	1/4 cup raisins
1 medium apple, peeled and chopped	1/4 cup chopped dates
1 cup unsweetened apple juice	1/4 cup maple syrup
	1 teaspoon ground cinnamon
1/4 cup dried apricots, chopped	1/2 teaspoon salt
	Chopped walnuts, optional

■ In a 5-qt. slow cooker, combine the first 11 ingredients. Cover and cook on low for 6-7 hours or until fruits are softened. Sprinkle individual servings with walnuts if desired.

Yield: 10 cups.

✱ Nutrition Facts: 1 cup (calculated without walnuts) equals 185 calories, 3 g fat (trace saturated fat), 0 cholesterol, 120 mg sodium, 37 g carbohydrate, 5 g fiber, 5 g protein. **Diabetic Exchanges:** 1 starch, 1 fruit, 1/2 fat.

When chopping dried fruit, to prevent it from sticking to the knife blade, sprinkle the fruit first with a little flour (for savory recipes) or powdered sugar (for sweet recipes).

Pork Roast Dinner*

PREP: 30 min. + marinating
COOK: 8 hours

- 1 boneless whole pork loin roast (3 to 4 pounds)
- 2 teaspoons minced garlic
- 2 teaspoons fennel seeds, crushed
- 1-1/2 teaspoons dried rosemary, crushed
- 1 teaspoon dried oregano
- 1 teaspoon paprika
- 3/4 teaspoon salt
- 1/4 teaspoon pepper
- 1-1/2 pounds medium potatoes, peeled and cut into chunks
- 1-1/2 pounds large sweet potato, peeled and cut into chunks
- 2 large sweet onions, cut into eighths
- 1/2 cup chicken broth

■ Cut the roast in half. Combine the garlic, fennel, rosemary, oregano, paprika, salt and pepper; rub over pork. Cover and refrigerate for 8 hours.

■ Place potatoes and onions in a 5-qt. slow cooker. Top with pork. Pour broth over meat.

■ Cover and cook on low for 8-10 hours or until a meat thermometer reads 160° and the vegetables are tender.

Yield: 8 servings.

✱ Nutrition Facts: 1 serving equals 369 calories, 9 g fat (3 g saturated fat), 99 mg cholesterol, 349 mg sodium, 29 g carbohydrate, 3 g fiber, 41 g protein. **Diabetic Exchanges:** 5 lean meat, 2 starch.

Lisa Chamberlain
ST. CHARLES, ILLINOIS

I am single and love to cook, so I often cook for friends that either don't cook or who work nights. They love new recipes, and this was one of their favorites. The leftover meat makes great barbecue pork sandwiches the next day.

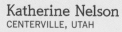

Katherine Nelson
CENTERVILLE, UTAH

Pork roast is slow-cooked with savory and sweet ingredients, including a can of cola, to create tender, shredded pork burritos. A fresh tomatillo dressing, made easy (and extra delicious) with the addition of dressing mix, tops the pork for an out-of-this-world entree.

Shredded Pork Burritos

PREP: 25 min. ■ COOK: 9 hours

1 bone-in pork shoulder roast (5 pounds)
2 tablespoons plus 1/2 cup packed brown sugar
4 teaspoons paprika, *divided*
2 teaspoons crushed red pepper flakes
2 teaspoons ground cumin
1 teaspoon kosher salt
1 can (12 ounces) cola
1 cup chicken broth
1 large sweet onion, thinly sliced
2 garlic cloves, minced

TOMATILLO DRESSING:
1 cup mayonnaise
1/2 cup milk
2 tomatillos, husks removed and rinsed
3/4 cup fresh cilantro
1 jalapeno pepper, seeded and cut into coarse chunks
1 envelope ranch salad dressing mix
1 tablespoon lime juice
1 garlic clove, minced
1/8 teaspoon cayenne pepper
16 flour tortillas (8 inches)

■ Cut the roast in half. Combine 2 tablespoons brown sugar, 2 teaspoons paprika, red pepper flakes, cumin and salt; rub over meat. Place in a 4-qt. slow cooker. Add the cola, broth, onion and garlic. Cover and cook on low for 8-10 hours or until meat is tender. When cool enough to handle, remove meat from bones; discard bones. Shred meat with two forks. Skim fat from cooking juices and return meat to slow cooker. Stir in the remaining brown sugar and paprika. Cover and cook on low for 1 hour or until heated through.

■ Meanwhile, in a blender, combine the mayonnaise, milk, tomatillos, cilantro, jalapeno, salad dressing, lime juice, garlic and cayenne. Cover and process until blended. Pour into a small bowl. Chill until serving.

■ Using a slotted spoon, spoon 1/2 cup filling off center on each tortilla. Drizzle with the tomatillo dressing. Fold the sides and ends over filling and roll up.

Yield: 16 servings.

Editor's Note: When cutting hot peppers, disposable gloves are recommended. Avoid touching your face.

A tomatillo [tohm-ah-TEE-oh], looks like a small, green tomato that is encased in a thin, papery skin. It's related to the tomato, and is available in specialty grocery stores and Latin American markets.

Barbecued Pork Chop Supper

Jacqueline Jones
ROUND LAKE BEACH, ILLINOIS

I start this mouthwatering barbecued pork chop recipe in the morning in the slow cooker. Later in the day, I enjoy a tasty supper without any last-minute work.

PREP: 10 min.
COOK: 8 hours

6 small red potatoes, cut into quarters
6 medium carrots, cut into 1-inch pieces
8 bone-in pork loin *or* rib chops (1/2 inch thick and 8 ounces *each*)
1 teaspoon salt
1/4 teaspoon pepper
1 bottle (28 ounces) barbecue sauce
1 cup ketchup
1 cup cola
2 tablespoons Worcestershire sauce

■ Place potatoes and carrots in a 5-qt. slow cooker. Top with the pork chops. Sprinkle with salt and pepper. Combine the barbecue sauce, ketchup, cola and the Worcestershire sauce; pour over the pork chops.

■ Cover and cook on low for 8-9 hours or until meat and vegetables are tender.

Yield: 8 servings.

Jennifer Fulk
MORENO VALLEY,
CALIFORNIA

I love anything Cajun, so I came up with this slow cooker jambalaya that's restaurant-good. If you can't find andouille sausage, hot links, smoked sausage or chorizo will also work.

Hearty Jambalaya

Hearty Jambalaya

PREP: 15 min. ■ **COOK:** 6-1/4 hours

1 can (28 ounces) diced tomatoes, undrained

1 pound fully cooked andouille sausage links, cubed

1/2 pound boneless skinless chicken breasts, cut into 1-inch cubes

1 can (8 ounces) tomato sauce

1 cup diced onion

1 small sweet red pepper, diced

1 small green pepper, diced

1 cup chicken broth

1 celery rib with leaves, chopped

2 tablespoons tomato paste

2 teaspoons dried oregano

2 teaspoons Cajun seasoning

1-1/2 teaspoons minced garlic

2 bay leaves

1 teaspoon Louisiana-style hot sauce

1/2 teaspoon dried thyme

1 pound cooked medium shrimp, peeled and deveined

Hot cooked rice

■ In a 5-qt. slow cooker, combine the first 16 ingredients. Cover and cook on low for 6-7 hours or until chicken juices run clear. Stir in shrimp. Cover and cook 15 minutes longer or until heated through. Discard bay leaves. Serve with rice.

Yield: 8 servings.

Bavarian Pork Loin

PREP: 25 min.
COOK: 6 hours

1 boneless whole pork loin roast (3 to 4 pounds)

1 can (14 ounces) Bavarian sauerkraut, rinsed and drained

1-3/4 cups chopped carrots

1 large onion, finely chopped

1/2 cup unsweetened apple juice

2 teaspoons dried parsley flakes

3 large tart apples, peeled and quartered

■ Cut the roast in half; place in a 5-qt. slow cooker. Combine the sauerkraut, chopped carrots, onion, apple juice and parsley; spoon over roast. Cover and cook on low for 4 hours.

■ Add the apples to slow cooker. Cover and cook 2 to 2-1/2 hours longer or until a meat thermometer reads 160°.

■ Remove roast; let stand for 5 minutes before slicing. Serve with sauerkraut mixture.

Yield: 10 servings.

If you like your saurkraut to have a sweeter flavor, for the Bavarian Pork Loin, use a sweet onion, such as a Vidalia, in the recipe.

Edie DeSpain

LOGAN, UTAH

I got the recipe for this tender pork roast from an aunt, who made it all the time. What a delicious taste sensation with sauerkraut, carrots, onions and apples. It's truly a versatile recipe, because you can serve it both as a weeknight dinner or as a special meal.

Side Dishes

77

86

81

For easy side dish recipes for your potluck, family gathering or any social function, let a slow cooker do the work for you! It will conveniently cook macaroni and cheese, rice, mashed potatoes or stuffing to perfection, and will keep the food warm, too.

Sweet Potato Stuffing

Kelly Pollock
LONDON, ONTARIO
Mom likes to make sure there will be enough stuffing to satisfy our large family for the holidays. She slow-cooks this dressing in addition to the stuffing cooked inside the turkey.

Sweet Potato Stuffing

PREP: 15 min. ■ **COOK:** 4 hours

1/2 cup chopped celery	1/4 cup chopped pecans
1/2 cup chopped onion	1/2 teaspoon poultry seasoning
1/4 cup butter, cubed	1/2 teaspoon rubbed sage
6 cups dry bread cubes	1/2 teaspoon salt, optional
1 large sweet potato, cooked, peeled and finely chopped	1/2 teaspoon pepper
1/2 cup chicken broth	

■ In a large skillet, saute celery and onion in butter until tender. Stir in the remaining ingredients. Transfer to a greased 3-qt. slow cooker. Cover and cook on low for 4 hours or until vegetables are tender.

Yield: 10 servings.

In recipes calling for "rubbed" sage, take the whole dried leaf and crush or rub it to make a finely textured powder. Most dried sage sold in the spice section of the grocery store is made this way.

Hash Browns With Ham

lightningbug
TASTE OF HOME ONLINE COMMUNITY
Convenient grocery store items like frozen hash browns and a can of chicken soup create this easy-to-make dish. Both kids and adults love it because it's super tasty and chock-full of cheese.

PREP: 15 min.
COOK: 3-1/4 hours

1 package (32 ounces) frozen Southern-style hash brown potatoes, thawed

1 cup cubed fully cooked ham

1 small onion, chopped

2 cups (8 ounces) shredded cheddar cheese, *divided*

1 can (14-3/4 ounces) condensed cream of chicken soup, undiluted

1/2 cup butter, melted

1 cup (8 ounces) sour cream

■ In a 3-qt. slow cooker, combine the potatoes, ham, onion and 1 cup cheese. Combine the soup and butter; pour over the potato mixture. Cover and cook on low for 3-4 hours or until the potatoes are tender.

■ Stir in the sour cream. Sprinkle with remaining cheese. Cover and cook for 15 minutes or until cheese is melted.

Yield: 8 servings.

Trudy Vincent
VALLES MINES,
MISSOURI

Sour cream, butter and cream cheese add richness to these make-ahead potatoes. They're wonderful because they don't require any last-minute mashing.

Slow Cooker Mashed Potatoes

Slow Cooker Mashed Potatoes

PREP: 5 min. ■ COOK: 2 hours

- 1 package (3 ounces) cream cheese, softened
- 1/2 cup sour cream
- 1/4 cup butter, softened
- 1 envelope ranch salad dressing mix
- 1 teaspoon dried parsley flakes
- 6 cups warm mashed potatoes (without added milk and butter)

■ In a large bowl, combine the cream cheese, sour cream, butter, salad dressing mix and parsley; stir in potatoes. Transfer to a 3-qt. slow cooker. Cover and cook on low for 2-4 hours.

Yield: 8-10 servings.

Editor's Note: This recipe was tested with fresh potatoes (not instant) in a slow cooker with heating elements surrounding the unit, not only in the base.

Saucy Scalloped Potatoes

PREP: 15 min.
COOK: 7 hours

- 4 cups thinly sliced peeled potatoes (about 2 pounds)
- 1 can (10-3/4 ounces) condensed cream of celery soup *or* mushroom soup, undiluted
- 1 can (12 ounces) evaporated milk
- 1 large onion, sliced
- 2 tablespoons butter
- 1/2 teaspoon salt
- 1/4 teaspoon pepper
- 1-1/2 cups chopped fully cooked ham

■ In a 3-qt. slow cooker, combine the first seven ingredients. Cover and cook on high for 1 hour. Stir in ham. Reduce heat to low; cook 6-8 hours longer or until potatoes are tender.

Yield: 8 servings.

To soften butter quickly, microwave the sticks at 70 percent power in 10-second intervals from two to four times. The butter should be ready to use.

Elaine Kane
KEIZER, OREGON

For old-fashioned flavor, try these scalloped potatoes. They cook up tender, creamy and comforting, and are made with easy-to-find ingredients. I like them because they taste like au gratin, but unlike a potato side dish cooked in the oven, the slow cooker does the work while I stay busy with other tasks.

Slow-Cooked Creamy Rice

Laura Crane
LEETONIA, OHIO

This wonderful side dish goes well with any meat stew. I use fresh herbs on hand along with the chopped parsley to add even more flavor.

PREP: 25 min.
COOK: 2-1/2 hours

    3 cups cooked rice
    2 eggs, lightly beaten
    1 can (12 ounces) evaporated milk
    1 cup (4 ounces) shredded Swiss cheese
    1 cup (4 ounces) shredded cheddar cheese
    1 medium onion, chopped
  1/2 cup minced fresh parsley
    6 tablespoons water
    2 tablespoons canola oil
    1 garlic clove, minced
  1-1/2 teaspoons salt
  1/4 teaspoon pepper

■ In a 3-qt. slow cooker, combine all ingredients. Cover and cook on low for 2-1/2 to 3 hours or until a thermometer reads 160°.

Yield: 8 servings.

Melissa Marzolf
MARYSVILLE, MICHIGAN

For a comforting recipe that feeds a crowd, try these saucy slow-cooked potatoes. A simple topping of buttered croutons tops the rich and creamy combination.

Cheesy Potatoes

Cheesy Potatoes

PREP: 10 min. ■ **COOK:** 8 hours

    6 medium potatoes, peeled and cut into 1/4-inch strips
    2 cups (8 ounces) shredded cheddar cheese
    1 can (10-3/4 ounces) condensed cream of chicken soup, undiluted
    1 small onion, chopped *or* 1 tablespoon dried minced onion
    7 tablespoons butter, melted, *divided*
    1 teaspoon salt
    1 teaspoon pepper
    1 cup (8 ounces) sour cream
    2 cups seasoned stuffing cubes

■ Toss the potatoes and cheese; place in a 5-qt. slow cooker. Combine the soup, onion, 4 tablespoons butter, salt and pepper; pour over the potato mixture.

■ Cover and cook on low for 8-10 hours or until the potatoes are tender. Stir in sour cream. Toss stuffing cubes and remaining butter; sprinkle over the potatoes.

Yield: 10-12 servings.

Plain yogurt can be substituted in equal amounts for sour cream in baking recipes as well as in casseroles, dips and sauces. You may notice dips and sauces might be thinner in consistency when using yogurt, and nonfat yogurt does not work well in recipes that are baked.

Partytime Beans

- In a 5-qt. slow cooker, combine the first 10 ingredients. Stir in the beans and peas. Cover and cook on low for 5-7 hours or until onion and peppers are tender. Discard bay leaves.

Yield: 16 servings.

* Nutrition Facts: 1/2 cup (prepared with no-salt-added ketchup) equals 162 calories, trace fat (trace saturated fat), 0 cholesterol, 305 mg sodium, 34 g carbohydrate, 6 g fiber, 7 g protein. **Diabetic Exchanges:** 2 starch, 1 meat.

Jean Cantner
BOSTON, VIRGINIA

A friend brought this colorful bean dish to my house for a potluck dinner. As soon as I tasted the slightly sweet baked beans, I had to have the recipe.

Partytime Beans*

PREP: 10 min. ■ **COOK:** 5 hours

1-1/2 cups ketchup
1 medium onion, chopped
1 medium green pepper, chopped
1 medium sweet red pepper, chopped
1/2 cup water
1/2 cup packed brown sugar
2 bay leaves
2 to 3 teaspoons cider vinegar
1 teaspoon ground mustard

1/8 teaspoon pepper
1 can (16 ounces) kidney beans, rinsed and drained
1 can (15-1/2 ounces) great northern beans, rinsed and drained
1 can (15-1/4 ounces) lima beans
1 can (15 ounces) black beans, rinsed and drained
1 can (15-1/2 ounces) black-eyed peas, rinsed and drained

Diced bell peppers can be frozen without boiling in water first. Simply wash and dry the peppers, remove the stems and seeds and chop as desired. Pack into freezer bags or containers. The peppers will keep in your freezer for 3 to 6 months. When a cooked dish calls for diced peppers, you can use them directly from the freezer.

Apple Sausage Beans

PREP: 30 min. ■ **COOK:** 5 hours

Becky Gourley
SEQUIM, WASHINGTON

This is a nice way to jazz up ordinary canned beans. To make things fun, when it comes time to serve the beans, whoever was the best helper in my kitchen gets to eat the apple.

- 1 package (12 ounces) uncooked maple breakfast sausage links
- 1/2 cup finely chopped onion
- 1 garlic clove, minced
- 1/2 cup unsweetened apple juice
- 2 tablespoons brown sugar
- 2 tablespoons maple syrup
- 2 tablespoons molasses
- 1/2 teaspoon apple pie spice
- 1/4 teaspoon ground nutmeg
- 2 cans (28 ounces *each*) baked beans
- 1 large red apple, cubed

■ Cut the sausage links into 1/2-in. pieces. In a large skillet, cook the sausage, onion and garlic over medium heat until the meat is no longer pink and the vegetables are tender; drain if necessary. Transfer to a 3- or 4-qt. slow cooker.

■ In a small bowl, combine the apple juice, brown sugar, maple syrup, molasses, pie spice and nutmeg. Stir into same skillet, stirring to loosen browned bits from pan. Cook and stir until sugar is dissolved.

■ Add the beans, apple and apple juice mixture to the slow cooker. Cover and cook on low for 5-6 hours or until apple is tender.

Yield: 12 servings.

It's easy to make your own apple pie spice. For 1 teaspoon, simply combine 1/2 teaspoon ground cinnamon, 1/4 teaspoon ground nutmeg and 1/8 teaspoon each of ground cardamom and ground allspice.

Green Beans And New Potatoes*

PREP: 15 min.
COOK: 6 hours

- 1 pound fresh green beans, trimmed
- 1 pound small potatoes, quartered
- 1/2 pound medium fresh mushrooms, halved
- 1/2 cup thinly sliced sweet onion
- 2 cans (14-1/2 ounces *each*) beef broth
- 2 tablespoons beefy onion soup mix
- 2 teaspoons Worcestershire sauce
- 1 teaspoon grated lemon peel
- 1/2 teaspoon salt
- 1/2 teaspoon pepper
- 1/4 teaspoon garlic powder

■ In a 5-qt. slow cooker, layer the green beans, potatoes, mushrooms and onion. Combine the remaining ingredients and pour over vegetables.

■ Cover and cook on low for 6-7 hours or until the vegetables are tender. Serve with a slotted spoon.

Yield: 10 servings.

✱ Nutrition Facts: 3/4 cup equals 58 calories, trace fat (trace saturated fat), 0 cholesterol, 192 mg sodium, 12 g carbohydrate, 3 g fiber, 3 g protein. **Diabetic Exchanges:** 1 vegetable, 1/2 starch.

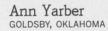

Ann Yarber
GOLDSBY, OKLAHOMA

This tasty vegetable side dish made in a slow cooker frees up your stove or oven. The vegetables come out tender, and the onion soup mix and onion add lots of flavor to the broth. It really is a colorful accompaniment to any entree.

Creamy Macaroni and Cheese

Jennifer Babrock
CHICOPEE, MASSACHUSETTS

This is a great way to make America's most popular comfort food. The dish turns out cheesy, rich and creamy. Preparation is so easy and convenient.

Creamy Macaroni and Cheese

PREP: 25 min. ■ **COOK:** 2 hours

- 3 cups uncooked elbow macaroni
- 1 pound process cheese (Velveeta), cubed
- 2 cups (8 ounces) shredded Mexican cheese blend
- 2 cups (8 ounces) shredded white cheddar cheese
- 1-3/4 cups milk
- 1 can (12 ounces) evaporated milk
- 3/4 cup egg substitute
- 3/4 cup butter, melted

■ Cook macaroni according to package directions; drain. Place in a greased 5-qt. slow cooker. Stir in remaining ingredients.

■ Cover and cook on low for 2-3 hours or until a thermometer reads 160°, stirring once.

Yield: 16 servings (3/4 cup each).

Italian Spaghetti Squash

Melissa Brooks
SPARTA, WISCONSIN

This is a unique and easy way to cook spaghetti squash. Be sure the squash is small or medium in size so that it fits into the slow cooker after being cut in half.

PREP: 15 min.
COOK: 6-1/4 hours

- 1 medium spaghetti squash
- 1 cup sliced fresh mushrooms
- 1 can (14-1/2 ounces) diced tomatoes, undrained
- 1 teaspoon dried oregano
- 1 teaspoon salt
- 1/4 teaspoon pepper
- 3/4 cup shredded part-skim mozzarella cheese

■ Cut squash in half lengthwise; discard seeds. Place squash, cut side up, in a 6- or 7-qt. slow cooker. Layer with the mushrooms, tomatoes, oregano, salt and pepper. Cover and cook on low for 6-8 hours or until the squash is tender.

■ Sprinkle with cheese. Cover and cook for 15 minutes or until cheese is melted. When squash is cool enough to handle, use a fork to separate the spaghetti squash strands.

Yield: 4 servings.

Kathy
Westendorf
WESTGATE, IOWA

*My sister-in-law
shared this recipe
with me. I simmer
garden-fresh vegeta-
bles into a tasty side
dish. It's a favorite
at holiday gather-
ings and potlucks.*

Slow-Cooked Vegetables

Slow-Cooked Vegetables*

PREP: 10 min. ■ **COOK:** 7 hours

- 4 celery ribs, cut into 1-inch pieces
- 4 small carrots, cut into 1-inch pieces
- 2 medium tomatoes, cut into chunks
- 2 medium onions, thinly sliced
- 2 cups cut fresh green beans (1-inch pieces)
- 1 medium green pepper, cut into 1-inch pieces
- 1/4 cup butter, melted
- 3 tablespoons quick-cooking tapioca
- 1 tablespoon sugar
- 2 teaspoons salt, optional
- 1/8 teaspoon pepper

■ Place the vegetables in a 3-qt. slow cooker. In a small bowl, combine the butter, tapioca, sugar, salt if desired and pepper; pour over vegetables and stir well.

■ Cover and cook on low for 7-8 hours or until vegetables are tender. Serve with a slotted spoon.

Yield: 8 servings.

✳ Nutrition Facts: One 1-cup serving (prepared with margarine and without salt) equals 118 calories, 99 mg sodium, 0 cholesterol, 16 gm carbohydrate, 2 gm protein, 6 gm fat. **Diabetic Exchanges:** 2 vegetable, 1 fat.

Give limp celery a second chance to season entrees, soups and stews. Cut the end from a limp stalk. Place in a jar or glass of cold water. Place in the refrigerator for several hours or overnight.

Peachy Sweet Potatoes

Taste of Home Test Kitchen
GREENDALE, WISCONSIN

It only takes five ingredients to create this sweet potato side dish. I find it's a great way to free up my oven for other dishes. The recipe is on the sweet side, and the granola adds extra crunch.

PREP: 20 min.
COOK: 5 hours

- 2-1/4 pounds cubed peeled sweet potatoes
- 3/4 teaspoon salt
- 1/8 teaspoon pepper
- 1 cup peach pie filling
- 2 tablespoons butter, melted
- 1/4 teaspoon ground cinnamon
- 1/2 cup granola without raisins, optional

■ Place potatoes in a 3-qt. slow cooker coated with cooking spray. Toss with salt and pepper. Top with pie filling and drizzle with butter. Sprinkle with cinnamon.

■ Cover and cook on low for 5-7 hours or until the potatoes are tender. Sprinkle with granola if desired.

Yield: 6 servings.

Chunky Applesauce

Lisa Roessner
FORT RECOVERY, OHIO

My mother gave me the recipe for this warm and cinnamony apple dish. Simmering it in a slow cooker fills the house with a wonderful aroma. You can also serve it with cream for dessert.

Chunky Applesauce*

PREP: 5 min. ■ **COOK:** 6 hours

    8 to 10 large tart apples, peeled and cut into chunks

Sugar substitute equivalent to 1/2 to 1 cup sugar

1/2 cup water

1 teaspoon ground cinnamon

■ Combine apples, sugar, water and cinnamon in a 3-qt. slow cooker; stir gently. Cover and cook on low for 6-8 hours or until apples are tender.

Yield: 5 cups.

*Nutrition Facts: One 3/4-cup serving (prepared with sugar substitute equivalent to 1/2 cup sugar) equals 93 calories, 0 fat (0 saturated fat), 0 cholesterol, 77 mg sodium, 25 g carbohydrate, 4 g fiber, 1 g protein. **Diabetic Exchanges:** 2-1/2 fruit, 1 meat.

Slow-Cooked Sausage Dressing

PREP: 20 min.
COOK: 3 hours

    1/2 pound reduced-fat bulk pork sausage

    2 celery ribs, chopped

    1 large onion, chopped

    7 cups seasoned stuffing cubes

    1 can (14-1/2 ounces) reduced-sodium chicken broth

    1 medium tart apple, chopped

    1/3 cup chopped pecans

    2 tablespoons reduced-fat butter, melted

1-1/2 teaspoons rubbed sage

    1/2 teaspoon pepper

■ In a large nonstick skillet, cook the sausage, celery and onion over medium heat until meat is no longer pink; drain. Transfer to a large bowl; stir in the remaining ingredients.

■ Transfer to a 5-qt. slow cooker coated with cooking spray. Cover; cook on low for 3-4 hours or until heated through and apple is tender, stirring once.

Yield: 8 cups.

Editor's Note: This recipe was tested with Land O'Lakes light stick butter.

Raquel Haggard
EDMOND, OKLAHOMA

This dressing is so delicious no one will know it uses reduced-fat butter. The pork sausage add loads of flavor, and the pecans and apples add a delicious touch. And best of all, it cooks effortlessly in the slow cooker, so the stove and oven are freed up for other dishes!

Carol Greco
CENTEREACH,
NEW YORK

Working full-time, I wasn't always able to cook the meals my family loved. So I re-created many of our favorites in the slow cooker. This cinnamony treatment for squash is one of them.

Spiced Acorn Squash

Spiced Acorn Squash

PREP: 10 min. ■ **COOK:** 4 hours

3/4 cup packed brown sugar
1 teaspoon ground cinnamon
1 teaspoon ground nutmeg
2 small acorn squash, halved and seeded
3/4 cup raisins
4 tablespoons butter
1/2 cup water

■ In a small bowl, combine the brown sugar, cinnamon and nutmeg; spoon into squash halves. Sprinkle with raisins. Top each with 1 tablespoon of butter. Wrap each squash half individually in heavy-duty foil; seal tightly.

■ Pour water into a 5-qt. slow cooker. Place the squash, cut side up, in slow cooker (packets may be stacked). Cover and cook on high for 4 hours or until the squash is tender. Open foil packets carefully to allow steam to escape.

Yield: 4 servings.

Marmalade-Glazed Carrots

Barb Rudyk
VERMILION, ALBERTA

This side dish is ideal when you'd like to serve your vegetables in a different way for a special dinner. Cinnamon and nutmeg season baby carrots that are simmered with orange marmalade and brown sugar.

PREP: 10 min.
COOK: 5-1/2 hours

2 pounds fresh baby carrots
1/2 cup orange marmalade
3 tablespoons cold water, *divided*
2 tablespoons brown sugar
1 tablespoon butter, melted
1/2 teaspoon ground cinnamon
1/4 teaspoon salt
1/4 teaspoon ground nutmeg
1/8 teaspoon pepper
1 tablespoon cornstarch

■ In a 3-qt. slow cooker, combine the carrots, orange marmalade, 1 tablespoon water, brown sugar, butter and seasonings. Cover and cook on low for 5-6 hours or until carrots are tender.

■ Combine cornstarch and the remaining water until smooth; stir into carrot mixture. Cover and cook on high for 30 minutes or until thickened. Serve with a slotted spoon.

Yield: 6 servings.

Slow-Cooked Bean Medley

Peggy Gwillim
STRASBOURG, SASKATCHEWAN

I often change the variety of beans in this recipe, using whatever I have on hand to total five 15- to 16-ounce cans. The sauce makes any combination delicious!

Slow-Cooked Bean Medley

PREP: 25 min. ■ COOK: 5 hours

1-1/2 cups ketchup

2 celery ribs, chopped

1 medium onion, chopped

1 medium green pepper, chopped

1 medium sweet red pepper, chopped

1/2 cup packed brown sugar

1/2 cup water

1/2 cup Italian salad dressing

2 bay leaves

1 tablespoon cider vinegar

1 teaspoon ground mustard

1/8 teaspoon pepper

1 can (16 ounces) kidney beans, rinsed and drained

1 can (15-1/2 ounces) black-eyed peas, rinsed and drained

1 can (15-1/2 ounces) great northern beans, rinsed and drained

1 can (15-1/4 ounces) whole kernel corn, drained

1 can (15-1/4 ounces) lima beans, rinsed and drained

1 can (15 ounces) black beans, rinsed and drained

■ In a 5-qt. slow cooker, combine the first 12 ingredients. Stir in remaining ingredients. Cover and cook on low for 5-7 hours or until onion and peppers are tender. Discard bay leaves.

Yield: 12 servings.

Vegetable Medley*

Terry Maly
OLATHE, KANSAS

This is a wonderful side dish to make when garden vegetables are plentiful. The colorful combination complements the entree.

PREP: 5 min.
COOK: 5 hours

4 cups diced peeled potatoes

1-1/2 cups frozen whole kernel corn *or* 1 can (15-1/4 ounces) whole kernel corn, drained

4 medium tomatoes, seeded and diced

1 cup sliced carrots

1/2 cup chopped onion

3/4 teaspoon salt

1/2 teaspoon sugar

1/2 teaspoon dill weed

1/8 teaspoon pepper

■ In a 3-qt. slow cooker, combine all ingredients. Cover and cook on low for 5-6 hours or until vegetables are tender.

Yield: 8 servings.

*Nutrition Facts: One 1-cup serving (prepared with frozen corn) equals 116 calories, 1 g fat (trace saturated fat), 0 cholesterol, 243 mg sodium, 27 g carbohydrate, 4 g fiber, 3 g protein. **Diabetic Exchange:** 1-1/2 starch.

Snacks & Sweets

91

98

101

When it's time to celebrate, use your slow cooker! There are plenty of fun and delicious recipes to help you plan your next party. Your guests will rave after tasting delicious dips, chicken wings, spiced cider, crunchy snacks, savory appetizers and irresistible sweets.

Spinach Artichoke Dip

Barbecue Sausage Bites

Rebekah Randolph
GREER, SOUTH CAROLINA

This popular, sweet-and-tangy appetizer pairs pineapple chunks with barbecue sauce and three kinds of sausage.

PREP: 10 min.
COOK: 2-1/2 hours

- 1 package (1 pound) miniature smoked sausages
- 3/4 pound fully cooked bratwurst links, cut into 1/2-inch slices
- 3/4 pound smoked kielbasa *or* Polish sausage, cut into 1/2-inch slices
- 1 bottle (18 ounces) barbecue sauce
- 2/3 cup orange marmalade
- 1/2 teaspoon ground mustard
- 1/8 teaspoon ground allspice
- 1 can (20 ounces) pineapple chunks, drained

■ In a 3-qt. slow cooker, combine the sausages. In a small bowl, whisk the barbecue sauce, marmalade, mustard and all-spice. Pour over the sausage mixture; stir to coat.

■ Cover and cook on high for 2-1/2 to 3 hours or until heated through. Stir in the pineapple. Serve with toothpicks.

Yield: 12-14 servings.

Jan Haberstich
WATERLOO, IOWA

This rich and creamy dip is perfect for special occasions. It tastes especially good when served warm with crackers. The red onion adds flavor and color.

Spinach Artichoke Dip

PREP: 15 min. ■ **COOK:** 2 hours

- 1 can (14 ounces) water-packed artichoke hearts, rinsed, drained and chopped
- 1 cup fresh baby spinach, chopped
- 1/2 cup sour cream
- 1/2 cup mayonnaise
- 1/2 cup shredded part-skim mozzarella cheese
- 1/2 cup shredded Parmesan cheese
- 1/3 cup chopped red onion
- 1/4 teaspoon garlic powder

Assorted crackers *or* breads

■ In a 1-1/2-qt. slow cooker, combine the first eight ingredients. Cover and cook on low for 2-3 hours or until heated through. Serve with crackers or breads.

Yield: 3 cups.

Easy Chocolate Clusters

Doris Reynolds
MUNDS PARK, ARIZONA
You can use this simple recipe to make a big batch of choco-late candy without a lot of fuss. I've sent these clusters, along with the recipe, to my husband's office many times.

Easy Chocolate Clusters

PREP: 10 min. + standing ■ **COOK:** 2 hours

- 2 pounds white candy coating, broken into small pieces
- 2 cups (12 ounces) semisweet chocolate chips
- 1 package (4 ounces) German sweet chocolate
- 1 jar (24 ounces) dry roasted peanuts

■ In a 3-qt. slow cooker, combine the candy coating, chocolate chips and German chocolate. Cover and cook on high for 1 hour. Reduce heat to low; cover and cook 1 hour longer or until melted, stirring every 15 minutes.

■ Stir in peanuts. Drop by teaspoonfuls onto waxed paper. Let stand until set. Store at room temperature.

Yield: 3-1/2 dozen.

Caramel Pear Pudding

PREP: 20 min.
COOK: 3 hours

- 1 cup all-purpose flour
- 1/2 cup sugar
- 1-1/2 teaspoons baking powder
- 1/2 teaspoon ground cinnamon
- 1/4 teaspoon salt
- 1/8 teaspoon ground cloves
- 1/2 cup milk
- 4 medium pears, peeled and cubed
- 1/2 cup chopped pecans
- 3/4 cup packed brown sugar
- 1/4 cup butter, softened
- 1/2 cup boiling water
- Vanilla ice cream, optional

■ In a large bowl, combine the flour, sugar, baking powder, cinnamon, salt and cloves. Stir in milk until smooth. Add pears and pecans. Spread evenly into a 3-qt. slow cooker coated with cooking spray.

■ In a small bowl, combine the brown sugar and butter; stir in boiling water. Pour over batter (do not stir). Cover and cook on low for 3-4 hours or until pears are tender. Serve warm with ice cream if desired.

Yield: 10 servings.

Diane Halferty
CORPUS CHRISTI, TEXAS

This is a lovely dessert that uses pears that are seasonally available. It's easy to fix and a comforting treat after any meal. The sugars, spices and milk create a decadent caramel sauce. I enjoy snacking on it in front of the fireplace.

- Sprinkle chicken wings with a dash of salt and pepper. Broil 4-6 in. from the heat for 5-10 minutes on each side or until golden brown. Transfer to a greased 5-qt. slow cooker.

- Combine the ketchup, brown sugar, vinegar, Worcestershire sauce, mustard, garlic, Liquid Smoke if desired and remaining salt; pour over wings. Toss to coat. Cover and cook on low for 3-1/4 to 3-3/4 hours or until the chicken juices run clear. Sprinkle with the sesame seeds if desired.

Yield: about 2-1/2 dozen.

Liquid Smoke

comes packaged in a bottle and is actually derived from the condensation that forms while wood is smoked. It can usually be found with other condiments at the grocery store. Be sure to check the label of ingredients to help you decide which brand to purchase.

Sweet 'n' Tangy Chicken Wings

Ida Tuey
KOKOMO, INDIANA

This slow cooker recipe is perfect for parties. Put the wings in before you prepare for the party, and in a few hours, you'll have wonderful appetizers!

Sweet 'n' Tangy Chicken Wings

PREP: 20 min. ■ **COOK:** 3-1/4 hours

    3   pounds chicken wingettes
        (about 30)
  1/2   teaspoon salt, divided
Dash pepper
1-1/2   cups ketchup
  1/4   cup packed brown sugar
  1/4   cup red wine vinegar

    2   tablespoons Worcestershire
        sauce
    1   tablespoon Dijon mustard
    1   teaspoon minced garlic
    1   teaspoon Liquid Smoke,
        optional
Sesame seeds, optional

Pat Sparks
ST. CHARLES, MISSOURI

This old-fashioned favorite goes to-gether quickly, and it's such a treat to come home to the heavenly aroma of cinnamony baked apples. It's just like Mom used to make!

Hot Caramel Apples

Hot Caramel Apples

PREP: 15 min. ■ **COOK:** 4 hours

4 large tart apples, cored	1/4 cup butter
1/2 cup apple juice	8 caramels
1/2 cup packed brown sugar	1/4 teaspoon ground cinnamon
12 red-hot candies	Whipped cream, optional

■ Peel about 3/4 in. off the top of each apple; place in a 3-qt. slow cooker. Pour juice over apples. Fill the center of each apple with 2 tablespoons of sugar, three red-hots, 1 tablespoon butter and two caramels. Sprinkle with cinnamon.

■ Cover and cook on low for 4-6 hours or until the apples are tender. Serve immediately with whipped cream if desired.

Yield: 4 servings.

Spiced Apricot Cider

Connie Cummings
GLOUCESTER, NEW JERSEY

You'll need just six ingredients to simmer together this hot, spiced beverage. Each delicious mugful is rich with apricot flavor.

PREP: 5 min.
COOK: 2 hours

> 2 cans (12 ounces *each*) apricot nectar
> 2 cups water
> 1/4 cup lemon juice
> 1/4 cup sugar
> 2 whole cloves
> 2 cinnamon sticks (3 inches)

■ In a 3-qt. slow cooker, combine all ingredients. Cover and cook on low for 2 hours or until the cider reaches desired temperature. Discard the cloves and cinnamon sticks.

Yield: 6 servings.

When choosing apples for the Hot Caramel Apples, firm-fleshed apples are best for baking whole. Varieties include Empire, Fuji, Golden Delicious, Jonagold, Rome Beauty and Royal Gala.

Jennifer Bennett
SALEM, INDIANA

For an old-fashioned sweet treat just like Grandma made, try this creamy pudding. It has a rich cinnamon flavor and is made wonderfully light after whipped cream is stirred into it at the end. Vanilla and lemon extract add wonderful aroma and flavor to the dessert.

Rice Pudding

PREP: 15 min. ■ COOK: 3 hours + chilling

1-1/4	cups milk	1	teaspoon butter, melted
1/2	cup sugar	1	teaspoon vanilla extract
1/2	cup uncooked converted rice	3/4	teaspoon lemon extract
1/2	cup raisins	1	cup heavy whipping cream, whipped
2	eggs, lightly beaten	1/8	teaspoon ground nutmeg
1	teaspoon ground cinnamon		

■ In a 1-1/2-qt. slow cooker, combine the first nine ingredients. Cover and cook on low for 2 hours; stir. Cover and cook for 1-2 hours or until rice is tender. Transfer to a small bowl.

■ Cover and refrigerate for at least 1 hour. Just before serving, fold in whipped cream; sprinkle with nutmeg.

Yield: 4 servings.

Also known as parboiled rice, converted rice has gone through a steam-pressure process before milling. This gives it a firmer grain so that it cooks up fluffier, and the grains of rice are more separated than regular white rice.

Marmalade Meatballs*

Jeanne Kiss
GREENSBURG, PENNSYLVANIA

We had a pre-Superbowl potluck at work, so I started cooking these meatballs in the morning. By lunch time they were ready. They were a big hit!

PREP: 10 min.
COOK: 4 hours

- 1 bottle (16 ounces) Catalina salad dressing
- 1 cup orange marmalade
- 3 tablespoons Worcestershire sauce
- 1/2 teaspoon crushed red pepper flakes
- 1 package (32 ounces) frozen fully cooked meatballs, thawed

■ In a 3-qt. slow cooker, combine the salad dressing, marmalade, Worcestershire sauce and red pepper flakes. Stir in meatballs. Cover and cook on low for 4-5 hours or until heated through.

Yield: about 5 dozen.

* Nutrition Facts: 1 meatball equals 73 calories, 4 g fat (1 g saturated fat), 12 mg cholesterol, 126 mg sodium, 6 g carbohydrate, trace fiber, 2 g protein. **Diabetic Exchanges:** 1 fat, 1/2 starch.

Kelly Byler
GOSHEN, INDIANA

Guests will go crazy when you serve this cheesy nacho casserole. You won't need to worry about filling the chip bowl, because the tortilla chips are baked right in!

Southwestern Nachos

Southwestern Nachos

PREP: 40 min. ■ COOK: 7-1/4 hours

  2 boneless whole pork loin roasts (3-1/2 pounds *each*)
  1 cup unsweetened apple juice
  6 garlic cloves, minced
  1 teaspoon salt
  1 teaspoon Liquid Smoke, optional
2-1/2 cups barbecue sauce, *divided*
  1/3 cup packed brown sugar
  2 tablespoons honey
  1 package (10 ounces) tortilla chip scoops
1-1/2 cups frozen corn

  1 can (15 ounces) black beans, rinsed and drained
  1 medium tomato, seeded and chopped
  1 medium red onion, chopped
  1/3 cup minced fresh cilantro
  1 jalapeno pepper, seeded and chopped
  2 teaspoons lime juice
  1 package (16 ounces) process cheese (Velveeta), cubed
  2 tablespoons milk

■ Cut each roast in half; place in two 5-qt. slow cookers. Combine the apple juice, garlic, salt and Liquid Smoke if desired; pour over meat. Cover and cook on low for 7-8 hours or until tender.

■ Shred pork with forks; place in a large bowl. Stir in 2 cups barbecue sauce, brown sugar and honey. Divide chips between two greased 13-in. x 9-in. baking dishes; top with pork mixture. Combine corn, beans, tomato, onion, cilantro, jalapeno and lime juice; spoon over pork mixture.

■ Bake, uncovered, at 375° for 15-20 minutes or until heated through. Meanwhile, in a small saucepan, melt cheese with milk. Drizzle cheese sauce and remaining barbecue sauce over nachos.

Yield: 30 servings.

Editor's Note: When cutting hot peppers, disposable gloves are recommended. Avoid touching your face.

Slow Cooker Party Mix

Dana Hughes
GRESHAM, OREGON

This mildly seasoned snack mix is always a party favorite. Served warm right from a slow cooker, the munchable mixture is very satisfying.

PREP: 5 min.
COOK: 3 hours

  4 cups Wheat Chex
  4 cups Cheerios
  3 cups pretzel sticks
  1 can (12 ounces) salted peanuts
  1/4 cup butter, melted
  2 to 3 tablespoons grated Parmesan cheese
  1 teaspoon celery salt
  1/2 to 3/4 teaspoon seasoned salt

■ In a 5-qt. slow cooker, combine cereals, pretzels and peanuts. Combine the butter, Parmesan cheese, celery salt and seasoned salt; drizzle over cereal mixture and mix well. Cover and cook on low for 1 to 1-1/2 hours, stirring every 20 minutes. Serve warm or at room temperature.

Yield: about 3 quarts.

Cranberry Sauerkraut Meatballs

Lisa Castelli
PLEASANT PRAIRIE, WISCONSIN

I tried these meatballs at a birthday party for a friend, and now I make them all the time. They are super easy to make and perfect for a potluck or a Sunday afternoon football game.

Cranberry Sauerkraut Meatballs*

PREP: 15 min. ■ COOK: 4 hours

1 can (14 ounces) whole-berry cranberry sauce

1 can (14 ounces) sauerkraut, rinsed and well drained

1 bottle (12 ounces) chili sauce

3/4 cup packed brown sugar

1 package (30 ounces) frozen fully cooked meatballs, thawed

■ In a 4-qt. slow cooker, combine the cranberry sauce, sauerkraut, chili sauce and brown sugar. Stir in meatballs. Cover and cook on low for 4-5 hours or until heated through.

Yield: 5-1/2 dozen.

* Nutrition Facts: 1 meatball with about 1 tablespoon sauce equals 53 calories, 2 g fat (1 g saturated fat), 11 mg cholesterol, 142 mg sodium, 8 g carbohydrate, trace fiber, 2 g protein. **Diabetic Exchange:** 1/2 starch.

Spiced Coffee

Joanne Holt
BOWLING GREEN, OHIO

Even those who usually don't drink coffee will find this special blend with a hint of chocolate appealing. I keep a big batch simmering at parties.

PREP: 10 min.

COOK: 2 hours

8 cups brewed coffee

1/3 cup sugar

1/4 cup chocolate syrup

1/2 teaspoon anise extract

4 cinnamon sticks (3 inches)

1-1/2 teaspoons whole cloves

Additional cinnamon sticks, optional

■ In a 3-qt. slow cooker, combine the coffee, sugar, chocolate syrup and anise extract. Place cinnamon sticks and cloves in a double thickness of cheese-cloth; bring up corners of cloth and tie with string to form a bag. Add to slow cooker. Cover and cook on low for 2-3 hours.

■ Discard spice bag. Ladle coffee into mugs; garnish each with a cinnamon stick if desired.

Yield: 8 cups.

To preserve flavor, store fresh ground or whole bean coffee in an airtight container in the refrigerator for up to 2 weeks. Long-term storage is best done in the freezer for up to 1 year.

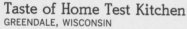
Warm Pomegranate Punch

Pepperoni Pizza Dip

PREP: 20 min.
COOK: 2-1/2 hours

- 4 cups (16 ounces) shredded cheddar cheese
- 4 cups (16 ounces) shredded part-skim mozzarella cheese
- 1 cup mayonnaise
- 1 jar (6 ounces) sliced mushrooms, drained
- 2 cans (2-1/4 ounces *each*) sliced ripe olives, drained
- 1 package (3-1/4 ounces) sliced pepperoni, quartered
- 1 tablespoon dried minced onion

Assorted crackers

- In a 3-qt. slow cooker, combine cheeses, mayonnaise, mushrooms, olives, pepperoni and onion. Cover and cook on low for 1-1/2 hours; stir.

- Cover and cook for 1 hour or until heated through. Serve with crackers.

Yield: 5 cups.

Taste of Home Test Kitchen
GREENDALE, WISCONSIN

If you're looking for something special to serve on a chilly evening, try this warming punch. It has a subtle tea flavor, and the juices create just the right balance of sweet and tart.

Warm Pomegranate Punch

PREP: 10 min. ■ **COOK:** 2 hours

- 1 quart pomegranate juice
- 1 quart unsweetened apple juice
- 2 cups brewed tea
- 1/2 cup sugar
- 1/3 cup lemon juice
- 3 cinnamon sticks (3 inches)
- 12 whole cloves

- In a 4- or 5-qt. slow cooker, combine the first five ingredients. Place cinnamon sticks and cloves on a double thickness of cheesecloth; bring up corners of cloth and tie with string to form a bag. Add to slow cooker.

- Cover and cook on low for 2-4 hours or until punch is heated through. Discard spice bag. Serve warm.

Yield: 2-1/2 quarts.

A bread bowl is the perfect container for the Pepperoni Pizza Dip. To warm the filled bowl, put it in an oven cooking bag, seal and place in the oven. It can be transported easily and still be warm when it's served.

Lisa Francis
ELBA, ALABAMA

This is so easy to make and transport, and you won't have to keep it warm long, because it'll be gone in a flash. The easy ingredient list creates a popular pizza flavor, making this simple dish a great appetizer for any party.

Chili Cheese Dip*

PREP: 20 min. ■ COOK: 4-1/2 hours

Sandra Fick
LINCOLN, NEBRASKA

After trying to create a Mexican soup, I ended up with this outstanding dip that eats like a meal. My husband and two young children love it! Now it's popular for football game days or family gatherings.

1 pound lean ground beef	3 teaspoons chili powder
1 cup chopped onion	1/2 teaspoon dried oregano
1 can (16 ounces) kidney beans, rinsed and drained	1/2 teaspoon chipotle hot pepper sauce
1 can (15 ounces) black beans, rinsed and drained	1/4 teaspoon garlic powder
1 can (14-1/2 ounces) diced tomatoes in sauce	1/4 teaspoon ground cumin
1 cup frozen corn	1 package (16 ounces) reduced-fat process cheese (Velveeta), cubed
3/4 cup water	
1 can (2-1/4 ounces) sliced ripe olives, drained	Corn chips

■ In a large skillet, cook beef and onion over medium heat until no longer pink; drain. Transfer to a 5-qt. slow cooker. Stir in the beans, tomatoes, corn, water, olives, chili powder, oregano, pepper sauce, garlic powder and cumin.

■ Cover and cook on low for 4-5 hours or until heated through; stir in cheese. Cover and cook for 30 minutes or until cheese is melted. Serve with corn chips.

Yield: 8 cups.

✳ Nutrition Facts: 1/4 cup (calculated without chips) equals 87 calories, 3 g fat (1 g saturated fat), 12 mg cholesterol, 330 mg sodium, 9 g carbohydrate, 2 g fiber, 7 g protein. **Diabetic Exchanges:** 1 lean meat, 1/2 starch.

Glazed Kielbasa

Jody Sands Taylor
RICHMOND, VIRGINIA

You'll need only three ingredients to prepare this pleasantly sweet treatment for sausage. Serve it as a main dish or with toothpicks for a hearty appetizer. Fat-free or turkey kielbasa can be used instead of the sausage.

PREP: 5 min.
COOK: 4 hours

3 pounds fully cooked kielbasa or Polish sausage, cut into 1-inch chunks
1/2 cup packed brown sugar
1-1/2 cups ginger ale

■ Place the sausage in a 3-qt. slow cooker; sprinkle with brown sugar. Pour ginger ale over the top. Cover and cook on low for 4-5 hours or until heated through. Serve with a slotted spoon.

Yield: 12-16 servings.

Chipotles are smoked-dried chili peppers that can add loads of flavor to your favorite Mexican, Tex-Mex or Southwestern meal. If you are unable to find chipotle hot pepper sauce, you can also use chipotles in adobo sauce, which comes in a can, or dried chipotle chili powder, which can often be found along with other dried spices.

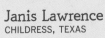
Apple Granola Dessert

Minister's Delight

Mary Ann Potter
BLUE SPRINGS, MISSOURI

You'll need a can of cherry pie filling, a yellow cake mix and just two other ingredients to simmer up this warm dessert. A friend gave me the recipe several years ago, saying that a minister's wife fixed it every Sunday, so she named it accordingly.

PREP: 5 min.
COOK: 2 hours

- 1 can (21 ounces) cherry *or* apple pie filling
- 1 package (18-1/4 ounces) yellow cake mix
- 1/2 cup butter, melted
- 1/3 cup chopped walnuts, optional

■ Place pie filling in a 1-1/2-qt. slow cooker. Combine cake mix and butter (mixture will be crumbly); sprinkle over filling. Sprinkle with walnuts if desired. Cover and cook on low for 2-3 hours. Serve in bowls.

Yield: 10-12 servings.

Janis Lawrence
CHILDRESS, TEXAS

I would be lost without my slow cooker. Besides using it to prepare our evening meal, I often make desserts in it, including these apples that get a tasty addition from granola.

Apple Granola Dessert

PREP: 10 min. ■ **COOK:** 6 hours

- 4 medium tart apples, peeled and sliced
- 2 cups granola cereal with fruit and nuts
- 1/4 cup honey
- 2 tablespoons butter, melted
- 1 teaspoon ground cinnamon
- 1/2 teaspoon ground nutmeg
- Whipped topping, optional

■ In a 1-1/2-qt. slow cooker, combine apples and cereal. In a bowl, combine the honey, butter, cinnamon and nutmeg; pour over apple mixture and mix well. Cover and cook on low for 6-8 hours. Serve with whipped topping if desired.

Yield: 4-6 servings.

If you love the crunch of nuts, but cannot use them, substitute with granola (check the package to be sure it doesn't contain nuts), crisp rice cereal or Grape-Nuts.

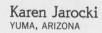

Karen Jarocki
YUMA, ARIZONA

I adapted my mom's yummy cobbler recipe for slow cooking. With the hot summers here in Arizona, we can still enjoy this comforting dessert, and I don't have to turn on the oven. Although the recipe calls for frozen yogurt, you can also serve this simply with a dollop of whipped topping.

Slow Cooker Berry Cobbler

PREP: 15 min. ■ **COOK:** 2 hours

1-1/4 cups all-purpose flour, *divided*

2 tablespoons plus 1 cup sugar, *divided*

1 teaspoon baking powder

1/4 teaspoon ground cinnamon

1 egg, lightly beaten

1/4 cup fat-free milk

2 tablespoons canola oil

1/8 teaspoon salt

2 cups unsweetened raspberries

2 cups unsweetened blueberries

2 cups reduced-fat frozen vanilla yogurt, optional

■ In a large bowl, combine 1 cup flour, 2 tablespoons sugar, baking powder and cinnamon. Combine the egg, milk and oil; stir into dry ingredients just until moistened (batter will be thick). Spread the batter evenly onto the bottom of a 5-qt. slow cooker coated with cooking spray.

■ In a large bowl, combine the salt and remaining flour and sugar; add berries and toss to coat. Spread over batter.

■ Cover and cook on high for 2 to 2-1/2 hours or until a toothpick inserted into cobbler comes out without crumbs. Top each serving with 1/4 cup frozen yogurt if desired.

Yield: 8 servings.

Fresh berries should be stored covered in your refrigerator and washed just before using. Use them within 10 days of purchase. To wash berries, place berries a few at a time in a colander in the sink. Gently spray with sink sprayer. Then spread out on paper towels to pat dry.

Fruit Compote Dessert

Laura Bryant German
WEST WARREN, MASSACHUSETTS

This is one of the first desserts I learned to make in the slow cooker, and it's the one guests still enjoy most. It tastes like it came from a fancy restaurant.

PREP: 15 min.
COOK: 3 hours

2 medium tart apples, peeled

2 medium peaches, peeled and cubed

2 cups unsweetened pineapple chunks

1-1/4 cups unsweetened pineapple juice

1/4 cup honey

2 lemon slices (1/4 inch)

1 cinnamon stick (3-1/2 inches)

1 medium firm banana, thinly sliced

Whipped cream, sliced almonds and maraschino cherries, optional

■ Cut the apples into 1/4-in. slices and then in half; place in a 3-qt. slow cooker. Add the peaches, pineapple, pineapple juice, honey, lemon and cinnamon. Cover and cook on low for 3-4 hours.

■ Just before serving, stir in banana slices. Serve with a slotted spoon if desired. Garnish with whipped cream, almonds and cherries if desired.

Yield: 8 servings.

STOVETOP
SUPPERS

Beef & Ground Beef

111

120

119

A one-pot or single-skillet supper means less time in the kitchen, and more time with your family. There are plenty of quick and hearty beef and ground beef dishes to choose from. You may even find a new family favorite!

Beef Fettuccine Dinner

Barbara Spohn
BROKEN ARROW, OKLAHOMA

Because I get home late, I need something fast and easy, so this recipe is perfect. It's a big hit with my husband and two children. I fix it twice a month and never have any leftovers!

Beef Fettuccine Dinner

PREP/TOTAL TIME: 20 min.

1 pound ground beef

1-1/2 cups water

1 package (4.3 ounces) fettuccine and beef-flavored sauce mix

1 can (8 ounces) tomato sauce

2 teaspoons chili powder

1 can (11 ounces) whole kernel corn, drained

1 cup (4 ounces) shredded cheddar cheese, *divided*

■ In a large skillet, cook beef over medium heat until no longer pink; drain. Add water; bring to a boil. Stir in the fettuccine mix, tomato sauce and chili powder. Return to a boil. Reduce heat; simmer, uncovered, for 7 minutes or until thickened.

■ Stir in corn and 2/3 cup cheese; heat through. Sprinkle with remaining cheese.

Yield: 4 servings.

Freezing ground

beef, after it's been cooked and browned, is a good way to have it on hand. On a day when you have the time, crumble and brown several pounds of ground beef. Spread on a cookie sheet, cover and freeze until solid. Transfer in 1/2- or 1-pound amounts to freezer bags. Use them for any recipe that uses browned ground beef.

African Beef Curry

Heather Ewald
BOTHELL, WASHINGTON

This dish is from my Aunt Linda, who was a missionary in Nigeria for 45 years. The stew, which is served over rice and sprinkled with toppings, is popular with family and friends.

African Beef Curry*

PREP: 15 min. ■ COOK: 1-1/2 hours

1 pound lean beef stew meat, cut into 1/2-inch cubes

1 can (14-1/2 ounces) diced tomatoes, undrained

1 small onion, chopped

1 small sweet red pepper, chopped

1 small green pepper, chopped

1 to 2 tablespoons curry powder

1/2 teaspoon salt

Hot cooked rice

Raisins, chopped salted peanuts and flaked coconut, optional

■ In a large saucepan, combine the first seven ingredients. Bring to a boil. Reduce heat; cover and simmer for 1-1/2 to 2 hours or until meat is tender.

■ Serve with rice. Garnish with raisins, chopped peanuts and coconut if desired.

Yield: 4 servings.

*Nutrition Facts: 1 cup (calculated without rice or garnishes) equals 205 calories, 8 g fat (3 g saturated fat), 70 mg cholesterol, 474 mg sodium, 10 g carbohydrate, 3 g fiber, 23 g protein. Diabetic Exchanges: 3 lean meat, 2 vegetable.

Hungarian Goulash

Robert Fallon
SAYVILLE, NEW YORK

This stew uses paprika for flavor. The beef turns out super tender.

PREP: 5 min.
COOK: 2-3/4 hours

1 pound boneless beef chuck roast *or* boneless beef rump roast, cut into 1-inch pieces

2 tablespoons canola oil

1/2 cup sliced onion

1 garlic clove, minced

1/3 cup ketchup

2 to 4 tablespoons Worcestershire sauce

1/2 teaspoon white vinegar

1/2 teaspoon brown sugar

1-1/4 teaspoons paprika

1 teaspoon salt

1/2 teaspoon ground mustard

Dash crushed red pepper flakes

1-2/3 cups water, *divided*

1 tablespoon all-purpose flour

Hot cooked egg noodles

■ In a Dutch oven, brown the beef in oil over medium-high heat. Add the onion and garlic; cook until tender.

■ In a small bowl, combine the ketchup, Worcestershire sauce, vinegar, brown sugar, seasonings and 1-1/2 cups water. Stir into beef. Reduce heat; cover and simmer for 2 to 2-1/2 hours or until meat is tender.

■ Combine flour and remaining water; gradually stir into beef mixture. Cook and stir for 2-3 minutes or until thickened. Serve with noodles.

Yield: 4 servings.

Pineapple Beef Stir-Fry

PREP/TOTAL TIME: 30 min.

Connie Braisted
OCEANSIDE, CALIFORNIA

This tasty sweet-and-sour stir-fry features sirloin instead of chicken for a fun change of pace. Pineapple, red pepper, celery and green onion create a colorful feast for the eyes that's perfect for company or everyday dining.

1/2 cup soy sauce	1 cup sliced green onions
2 garlic cloves, minced	1 cup sliced fresh mushrooms
1 teaspoon ground ginger	1 can (20 ounces) pineapple chunks
1 pound boneless beef sirloin steak, cut into 1/4-inch thin strips	1 can (8 ounces) sliced water chestnuts, drained
1 tablespoon canola oil	2 to 3 tablespoons cornstarch
2 celery ribs, thinly sliced	1/2 cup water
1 cup cubed sweet red pepper	Hot cooked rice

■ In a large resealable plastic bag, combine the soy sauce, garlic and ginger. Add beef; turn to coat. Let stand for 15 minutes.

■ In a large skillet, stir-fry beef mixture in oil for 2 minutes. Add celery and red pepper; stir-fry for 2 minutes. Add onions and mushrooms; cook 2 minutes longer.

■ Drain pineapple, reserving juice. Stir pineapple and water chestnuts into skillet. Combine cornstarch, water and reserved pineapple juice until smooth. Gradually stir into the beef and vegetables. Bring to a boil; cook and stir for 1-2 minutes or until thickened. Serve with rice.

Yield: 4 servings.

Here's an excellent idea for a soy sauce substitute. Dissolve 3 tablespoons beef bouillon granules in 1-1/2 cups boiling water. Stir in 1/4 cup plus 1 teaspoon cider vinegar, 2 tablespoons sesame oil, 1 tablespoon dark molasses and a dash of pepper. Store in the refrigerator and shake well before using. Makes about 2 cups.

Skillet Bow Tie Lasagna

Arleta Schurle
CLAY CENTER, KANSAS

This Italian-style meal tastes just like lasagna, but offers the ease and convenience of quick stovetop preparation. My family loves it when this dish is on the menu.

PREP: 5 min.
COOK: 35 min.

- 1 pound ground beef
- 1 small onion, chopped
- 1 garlic clove, minced
- 1 can (14-1/2 ounces) diced tomatoes, undrained
- 1-1/2 cups water
- 1 can (6 ounces) tomato paste
- 1 tablespoon dried parsley flakes
- 2 teaspoons dried oregano
- 1 teaspoon salt
- 2-1/2 cups uncooked bow tie pasta
- 3/4 cup 4% cottage cheese
- 1/4 cup grated Parmesan cheese

■ In a large skillet, cook beef, onion and garlic until meat is no longer pink; drain. Add the tomatoes, water, tomato paste, parsley, oregano and salt. Stir in pasta; bring to a boil. Reduce the heat; cover and simmer for 20-25 minutes or until pasta is tender, stirring once.

■ Combine cheeses; drop by rounded tablespoonfuls onto pasta mixture. Cover and cook for 5 minutes.

Yield: 4 servings.

Pat Habiger
SPEARVILLE, KANSAS

My family tells me these hearty stuffed beef rolls with a creamy sauce "taste like home." The dish is impressive, yet economical and easy to prepare.

Steak Roll-Ups

Steak Roll-Ups

PREP: 20 min. ■ **COOK:** 2 hours

1-1/2 pounds boneless beef round steak

1/4 cup chopped onion

1/4 cup butter, melted

2 cups fresh bread cubes

1/2 cup chopped celery

1 tablespoon dried parsley flakes

1/2 teaspoon salt

1/2 teaspoon poultry seasoning

1/4 teaspoon pepper

1 cup all-purpose flour

2 tablespoons canola oil

1 can (10-3/4 ounces) condensed cream of mushroom soup, undiluted

1-1/3 cups water

3/4 teaspoon browning sauce, optional

■ Flatten steak to 1/3-in. thickness. Cut into six pieces. In a small bowl, combine the next eight ingredients. Place 1/3 cup on each piece of steak; roll up and fasten with a toothpick. Roll in flour.

■ In a large skillet, brown roll-ups in oil. Combine the soup, water and browning sauce if desired; pour over roll-ups. Cover and simmer for 2 hours or until meat is tender, turning occasionally.

Yield: 6 servings.

Store toothpicks in an empty, clean spice bottle with a shaker top and screw-on lid. It's easy to remove the lid and gently shake out a toothpick through the holes. The bottle keeps the toothpicks handy.

Greek-Style Supper*

PREP/TOTAL TIME: 30 min.

1/2 pound ground beef

1/2 cup chopped onion

1 can (14-1/2 ounces) beef broth

1 can (14-1/2 ounces) diced tomatoes, undrained

1-1/2 cups uncooked penne pasta

1-1/2 cups frozen cut green beans, thawed

2 tablespoons tomato paste

2 teaspoons dried oregano

1/2 teaspoon garlic powder

1/4 teaspoon ground cinnamon

3/4 cup crumbled feta cheese

■ In a large skillet, cook beef and onion over medium heat until meat is no longer pink. Meanwhile, in a large saucepan, bring broth and tomatoes to a boil; add pasta. Reduce heat; simmer, uncovered, for 15-20 minutes or until pasta is tender, stirring occasionally.

■ Drain beef mixture; add to pasta. Stir in the beans, tomato paste, oregano, garlic powder and cinnamon; heat through. Sprinkle with feta cheese.

Yield: 4 servings.

*Nutrition Facts: 1-1/2 cups equals 300 calories, 10 g fat (5 g saturated fat), 39 mg cholesterol, 792 mg sodium, 33 g carbohydrate, 6 g fiber, 20 g protein. **Diabetic Exchanges:** 2 lean meat, 2 vegetable, 1-1/2 starch, 1/2 fat.

Alice Bower
ROANOKE, ILLINOIS

This robust Greek-inspired dinner is an all-in-one meal that's sure to become a favorite. I add a pinch of cinnamon to make the dish shine, and feta cheese offers just the right flavor. Better still, there's minimal prep work, and cleanup is just as easy!

Favorite Pot Roast

- In a Dutch oven, brown the roast on all sides in oil. Combine the salt, pepper and thyme; sprinkle over the meat. Add the bay leaf and 2 cups water; bring to a boil. Reduce heat; cover and simmer for 2-1/2 hours.

- Add the potatoes, carrots and onions. Cover and simmer 45 minutes longer or until meat and vegetables are tender. Remove roast and vegetables to a serving platter; keep warm. Discard bay leaf.

- Skim fat from pan juices; add enough water to pan juices to measure 2 cups. In a bowl, combine flour and remaining water until smooth; gradually stir into juices. Bring to a boil; cook and stir for 2 minutes or until thickened and bubbly. Stir in browning sauce if desired. Season with salt and pepper. Slice roast; serve with vegetables and gravy.

Yield: 8 servings.

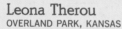

Leona Therou
OVERLAND PARK, KANSAS

I love cooking a pot roast on the weekend because it can simmer while I'm doing other things. This meal makes enough for a family of four with plenty left over.

Favorite Pot Roast

PREP: 15 min. ■ **COOK:** 3-1/2 hours

1 boneless beef rump roast (4 pounds)	8 large carrots, cut into 2-inch chunks
2 tablespoons canola oil	1 pound small onions, peeled
2 teaspoons salt	1/2 cup all-purpose flour
1/2 teaspoon pepper	1/2 teaspoon browning sauce, optional
1/2 teaspoon dried thyme	Additional salt and pepper to taste
1 bay leaf	
3 cups water, *divided*	
8 medium potatoes, peeled and quartered	

Pot roasts are done when a long-handled fork can be inserted into the thickest part of the roast easily. If the pot roast is cooked until it falls apart, the meat is actually overcooked and will be stringy, tough and dry.

Stovetop Hamburger Casserole

Edith Landinger
LONGVIEW, TEXAS

Here is comfort food at its best! It's not only loaded with ground beef, pasta, veggies and cheddar, but it goes together in a jiffy.

PREP: 10 min.
BAKE: 25 min.

1	package (7 ounces) small pasta shells
1-1/2	pounds ground beef
1	large onion, chopped
3	medium carrots, chopped
1	celery rib, chopped
3	garlic cloves, minced
3	cups cubed cooked red potatoes
1	can (15-1/4 ounces) whole kernel corn, drained
2	cans (8 ounces *each*) tomato sauce
1-1/2	teaspoons salt
1/2	teaspoon pepper
1	cup (4 ounces) shredded cheddar cheese

- Cook pasta according to package directions. Meanwhile, in a large skillet, cook beef and onion over medium heat until meat is no longer pink; drain. Add the carrots, celery and garlic; cook and stir for 5 minutes or until vegetables are crisp-tender.

- Stir in the potatoes, corn, tomato sauce, salt and pepper; heat through. Drain pasta and add to skillet; toss to coat. Sprinkle with cheese. Cover and cook until cheese is melted.

Yield: 6 servings.

Cathie Beard
PHILOMATH, OREGON

When our two grown children and grandchildren visit, I like to serve this Mexican-style dinner. Saucy and cheesy, it always disappears fast and never disappoints.

Skillet Enchiladas

Skillet Enchiladas

PREP: 10 min. ■ **COOK:** 35 min.

1	pound ground beef
1	medium onion, chopped
1	can (10-3/4 ounces) condensed cream of mushroom soup, undiluted
1	can (10 ounces) enchilada sauce
1/3	cup milk
1	to 2 tablespoons canned chopped green chilies
	Canola oil
8	corn tortillas
2-1/2	cups (10 ounces) finely shredded cheddar cheese, *divided*
1/2	cup chopped ripe olives

- In a large skillet, cook beef and onion over medium heat until meat is no longer pink; drain. Stir in the soup, enchilada sauce, milk and chilies. Bring to a boil. Reduce heat; cover and simmer for 20 minutes, stirring occasionally.

- Meanwhile, in another skillet, heat 1/4 in. of oil. Dip each tortilla in hot oil for 3 seconds on each side or just until limp; drain on paper towels. Top each tortilla with 1/4 cup cheese and 1 tablespoon olives. Roll up and place over beef mixture, spooning some of mixture over the enchiladas.

- Cover and cook until heated through, about 5 minutes. Sprinkle with the remaining cheese; cover and cook until cheese is melted.

Yield: 8 enchiladas.

Denise Barteet
SHREVEPORT, LOUISIANA

This recipe is so good that I truly enjoy sharing it with others. I've always liked Salisbury steak, but I had to search a long time to find a recipe this tasty. It's handy, too because it can be prepared ahead, kept in the refrigerator and warmed up later.

Salisbury Steak Deluxe

PREP/TOTAL TIME: 30 min.

1 can (10-3/4 ounces) condensed cream of mushroom soup, undiluted
1 tablespoon prepared mustard
2 teaspoons Worcestershire sauce
1 teaspoon prepared horseradish
1 egg
1/4 cup dry bread crumbs
1/4 cup finely chopped onion
1/2 teaspoon salt
Dash pepper
1-1/2 pounds ground beef
1 to 2 tablespoons canola oil
1/2 cup water
2 tablespoons chopped fresh parsley

■ Combine the soup, mustard, Worcestershire sauce and horseradish; blend well. Set aside. In another bowl, lightly beat the egg. Add the bread crumbs, onion, salt, pepper and 1/4 cup of the soup mixture. Crumble beef over mixture and mix well. Shape into six patties.

■ In a large skillet, brown the patties in oil; drain. Combine remaining soup mixture with water; pour over patties. Cover and cook over low heat for 10-15 minutes or until meat is no longer pink and a meat thermometer reads 160°. Remove patties to a serving platter; spoon sauce over meat. Sprinkle with parsley.

Yield: 6 servings.

Chopping parsley is simple with a pair of kitchen shears. No need to clean up a cutting board! After the parsley leaves have been washed and patted dry with paper towels, place in a small glass container and snip with kitchen shears until minced.

Wagon Wheel Supper

Taste of Home
Test Kitchen
GREENDALE, WISCONSIN

Kids will really enjoy this cheesy pasta dish souped up with corn and beef; it's perfect for a cool spring night.

PREP/TOTAL TIME: 25 min.

1/2 pound uncooked wagon wheel pasta
1 pound ground beef
1/2 cup chopped onion
1-3/4 cups water
1 can (10-3/4 ounces) condensed tomato soup, undiluted
1 can (8-3/4 ounces) whole kernel corn, drained
1 envelope spaghetti sauce mix
1/8 teaspoon pepper
4 ounces sliced Colby cheese, cut into strips

■ Cook pasta according to package directions. Meanwhile, in a large skillet, cook beef and onion over medium heat until meat is no longer pink; drain.

■ Stir in the water, soup, corn, spaghetti sauce mix and pepper. Bring to a boil. Reduce the heat and simmer, uncovered, for 2-3 minutes or until heated through.

■ Drain the pasta; stir into beef mixture. Top with cheese; cook and stir for 2 minutes or until cheese is melted.

Yield: 4 servings.

Marcy Cella
L'ANSE, MICHIGAN

This dish is a family favorite that I created, and named, myself! The spinach packs it with a real Popeye punch. The other vegetables combined with the ground beef make it a hearty meal.

Popeye Special

Popeye Special

PREP/TOTAL TIME: 15 min.

1 pound ground beef	1/4 cup chopped sweet red pepper
1/2 pound fresh mushrooms, sliced	1 teaspoon garlic salt
1/2 pound fresh spinach, torn	1/2 teaspoon pepper
6 green onions, sliced	6 eggs, lightly beaten
1/4 cup chopped celery	

■ In a large skillet, cook beef and mushrooms over medium heat until meat is no longer pink; drain. Add the spinach, onions, celery, red pepper, garlic salt and pepper. Cook and stir for 1 minute. Add eggs; cook and stir just until the eggs are set. Serve immediately.

Yield: 4-6 servings.

Hash in A Flash

Wendy Masters
GRAND VALLEY, ONTARIO

I cook more roast beef than we need for one meal so that we'll have leftovers for this homey hash. We always look forward to this satisfying supper.

PREP/TOTAL TIME: 20 min.

- 1 medium onion, chopped
- 2 tablespoons canola oil
- 3 cups frozen shredded hash brown potatoes
- 3 cups finely chopped cooked roast beef
- 1/2 cup beef gravy
- 2 tablespoons ketchup
- 1 teaspoon salt
- 1/2 teaspoon ground mustard
- 1/8 teaspoon pepper

■ In a large skillet, saute onion in oil until tender. Stir in remaining ingredients. Cook over medium heat (do not stir) until browned, about 10 minutes. Turn; brown the remaining side.

Yield: 4 servings.

When a recipe calls for fresh spinach, 1 pound of fresh spinach will yield 10-12 cups of torn leaves, which will cook down to about 1 cup. For the Popeye Special, you will need about 6 cups of fresh spinach leaves.

Beef Rouladen

- Spread steak pieces with mustard. Sprinkle with thyme, salt and pepper. Layer the steak pieces with a quarter each of pickle slices, carrot sticks and a wedge of onion. Roll up and secure with a toothpick. Coat each roll with flour.

- In a large skillet, heat oil over medium-high. Brown beef in oil on all sides. Add the water, bouillon, ketchup and remaining carrots. Cover and simmer 1 hour or until meat is tender. Thicken gravy if desired. Serve with noodles.

Yield: 4 servings.

*Nutrition Facts: 1 serving equals 250 calories, 10 g fat (0 saturated fat), 70 mg cholesterol, 1,012 mg sodium, 12 g carbohydrate, 0 fiber, 26 g protein. **Diabetic Exchanges:** 3 lean meat, 1 vegetable, 1/2 starch, 1/2 fat.

Diana Schurrer
MCHENRY, ILLINOIS

My family came to America from Germany in the late 1950s and brought with them many wonderful recipes like this one. This dish reminds me of my grandmother's kitchen.

Beef Rouladen*

PREP: 20 min. ■ **COOK:** 1 hour 5 min.

1 pound thin cut beef round steak, cut into 4 pieces	2 tablespoons all-purpose flour
Coarse-ground prepared mustard	1 tablespoon canola oil
1/4 teaspoon dried thyme	2 cups water
Salt and pepper to taste	2 teaspoons beef bouillon granules
1 medium dill pickle, quartered lengthwise	3 tablespoons ketchup
3 carrots, cut into sticks, *divided*	Cooked noodles
1 small onion, cut into wedges	

To remove the odor from your hands after slicing or chopping onions, sprinkle your hands with table salt, rub them together a few times, then wash them.

Irish Beef Stew

PREP: 40 min. ■ **COOK:** 3-1/4 hours

Carrie Karleen
ST-NICOLAS, QUEBEC

Rich and hearty, this stew is my husband's favorite. The beef is incredibly tender. Served with crusty bread, it's an ideal cool-weather meal and perfect for any Irish holiday.

    8 bacon strips, diced
  1/3 cup all-purpose flour
    1 teaspoon salt
  1/2 teaspoon pepper
    3 pounds beef stew meat, cut into 1-inch cubes
    1 pound whole fresh mushrooms, quartered
    3 medium leeks (white portion only), chopped
    2 medium carrots, chopped
  1/4 cup chopped celery
    1 tablespoon canola oil
    4 garlic cloves, minced
    1 tablespoon tomato paste
    4 cups reduced-sodium beef broth
    1 cup dark stout beer *or* additional reduced-sodium beef broth
    2 bay leaves
    1 teaspoon dried thyme
    1 teaspoon dried parsley flakes
    1 teaspoon dried rosemary, crushed
    2 pounds Yukon Gold potatoes, cut into 1-inch cubes
    2 tablespoons cornstarch
    2 tablespoons cold water
    1 cup frozen peas

■ In a soup kettle, cook bacon over medium heat until crisp. Using a slotted spoon, remove to paper towels. In a large resealable plastic bag, combine flour, salt and pepper. Add beef, a few pieces at a time, and shake to coat. Brown beef in the bacon drippings. Remove and set aside.

■ In the same pan, saute the mushrooms, leeks, carrots and celery in oil until tender. Add garlic; saute 2 minutes longer. Stir in tomato paste until blended. Add the broth, beer, bay leaves, thyme, parsley and rosemary. Return beef and bacon to pan. Bring to a boil. Reduce heat; cover and simmer for 2 hours.

■ Add potatoes. Return to a boil. Reduce heat; cover and simmer 1 hour longer or until potatoes are tender. Combine cornstarch and water until smooth; stir into stew. Bring to a boil; cook and stir for 2 minutes or until thickened. Add peas; heat through. Discard bay leaves.

Yield: 15 servings (3-3/4 quarts).

Beef Fried Rice

PREP/TOTAL TIME: 30 min.

      1 tablespoon plus 1 teaspoon olive oil, *divided*
      3 eggs, lightly beaten
      3 boneless beef petite sirloin steaks (5 ounces *each*), cut into thin strips
  2-1/2 cups coleslaw mix
    1/2 pound fresh asparagus, trimmed and cut into 1-1/2-inch pieces
    1/2 cup chopped onion
      4 cups cold cooked instant rice
      3 tablespoons butter, cubed
      3 tablespoons soy sauce
    1/8 teaspoon pepper

■ In a large skillet or wok, heat 1 tablespoon oil until hot. Add eggs; cook and stir over medium heat until completely set. Remove and keep warm.

■ In the same pan, stir-fry the beef, coleslaw, asparagus and onion in remaining oil for 4-6 minutes or until vegetables are crisp-tender.

■ Add rice and butter; cook and stir over medium heat for 1-2 minutes or until heated through. Add eggs; stir in soy sauce and pepper.

Yield: 6 servings.

Taste of Home Test Kitchen
GREENDALE, WISCONSIN

Moist beef strips partner with crisp asparagus and shredded cabbage in this standout medley that is made with Asian-style seasonings. It's almost easier to do than ordering take-out, because the dish is made with coleslaw mix and cooked instant rice.

Chili Skillet

- In a large skillet over medium heat, cook beef, onion, pepper and garlic until meat is no longer pink; drain. Add tomato juice, kidney beans, chili powder, oregano, salt and rice; cover and simmer about 25 minutes or until rice is tender.

- Stir in corn and olives; cover and cook 5 minutes more. Sprinkle with cheese; cover and cook about 5 minutes or until cheese is melted.

Yield: 4 servings.

Katherine Brown
FREDERICKTOWN, OHIO

Like most farmers, my husband loves chili. And with all of the vegetables, cheese and meat in it, this quick dish makes a real meal-in-one. I serve it frequently in fall and winter.

Chili Skillet

PREP: 10 min. ■ **COOK:** 35 min.

- 1 pound ground beef
- 1 cup chopped onion
- 1/2 cup chopped green pepper
- 1 garlic clove, minced
- 1 cup tomato juice
- 1 can (16 ounces) kidney beans, rinsed and drained
- 4 teaspoons chili powder
- 1 teaspoon dried oregano
- 1 teaspoon salt
- 1/2 cup uncooked long grain rice
- 1 cup canned *or* frozen corn
- 1/2 cup sliced ripe olives
- 1 cup (4 ounces) shredded cheddar *or* Monterey Jack cheese

It's important to use long grain rice for the Chili Skillet recipe. Instant rice, which is precooked before it is packaged, requires a different amount of liquid during cooking than long grain rice. They cannot be substituted measure for measure.

Jean Wright
CLARKSTON,
WASHINGTON

This recipe was in a cookbook my mother gave me in 1944. Inside, she wrote, "When and if Jean ever gets married." Since then, I've cooked this dish, plus others from the book, for over 55 years!

Veal Shank Fricassee

Veal Shank Fricassee

PREP: 30 min. ■ **COOK:** 1-1/2 hours

2 tablespoons all-purpose flour	1-1/2 cups water, *divided*
2 teaspoons salt	1 medium onion, chopped
1/2 teaspoon dried thyme	1 celery rib, chopped
1/2 teaspoon dried parsley flakes	1 bay leaf
1/8 teaspoon pepper	4 medium carrots, cut into 1-inch slices
1/8 teaspoon cayenne pepper	2 medium potatoes, peeled and cut into 1-inch cubes
2 veal shanks (about 1 pound)	2 tablespoons cornstarch
1 tablespoon canola oil	

■ In a large resealable plastic bag, combine flour and seasonings. Add veal shanks; seal and turn to coat.

■ In a Dutch oven or large skillet, brown veal in oil over medium heat. Pour 1-1/4 cups water into pan; add the onion, celery and bay leaf. Bring to a boil over medium heat. Reduce heat; cover and simmer for 1 hour.

■ Add carrots and potatoes; cover and cook 30 minutes longer or until meat and vegetables are tender. Remove meat and vegetables to a serving platter and keep warm. Pour drippings and loosened browned bits into a measuring cup. Skim fat and discard bay leaf.

■ In a small saucepan, combine cornstarch and the remaining water until smooth. Gradually stir in the drippings. Bring to a boil; cook and stir for 2 minutes or until thickened. Serve with meat and vegetables.

Yield: 2 servings.

Spanish Noodles 'n' Ground Beef

Kelli Jones
PERIS, CALIFORNIA

Smoky bacon adds flavor to this comforting stovetop supper my mom frequently made when we were growing up. Now I prepare it for my family.

PREP/TOTAL TIME: 30 min.

    1 pound ground beef
    1 small green pepper, chopped
1/3 cup chopped onion
3-1/4 cups uncooked medium egg noodles
    1 can (14-1/2 ounces) diced tomatoes, undrained
    1 cup water
1/4 cup chili sauce
    1 teaspoon salt
1/8 teaspoon pepper
    4 bacon strips, cooked and crumbled

■ In a large skillet, cook the beef, green pepper and onion over medium heat until the meat is no longer pink; drain. Stir in the noodles, tomatoes, water, chili sauce, salt and pepper. Cover and cook over low heat for 15-20 minutes or until the noodles are tender, stirring frequently. Top with bacon.

Yield: 5 servings.

Poultry

127

137

135

With the right ingredients and a good recipe, there's always time for a home-cooked dinner! In this chapter, all the delicious dishes use versatile chicken or turkey. And every one-dish wonder cooks up in a flash on the stovetop.

Curry Chicken

Tracy Simiele
CHARDON, OHIO

This is a big hit in our home. My young son and daughter gobble it up. With its irresistible blend of curry and rich coconut milk, your family will love it, too.

Curry Chicken

PREP/TOTAL TIME: 30 min.

1-1/2 cups uncooked instant rice	1 tablespoon canola oil
1 pound boneless skinless chicken breasts, cut into 1-inch pieces	1 can (14 ounces) coconut milk
2 teaspoons curry powder	2 tablespoons tomato paste
3/4 teaspoon salt	3 cups fresh baby spinach
1/4 teaspoon pepper	1 cup chopped tomato
1/2 cup chopped onion	

■ Cook rice according to package directions. Meanwhile, sprinkle the chicken with curry, salt and pepper. In a large skillet, saute chicken and onion in oil until chicken is no longer pink.

■ Stir in coconut milk and tomato paste. Bring to a boil. Reduce heat; simmer, uncovered, for 5 minutes or until thickened. Add spinach and tomato; cook 2-3 minutes longer or until spinach is wilted. Serve with rice.

Yield: 4 servings.

Editor's Note: You may substitute 1/4 teaspoon coconut extract and 1 cup milk, cream or other dairy product for each cup of coconut milk.

Parmesan Chicken Pasta

Taste of Home Test Kitchen
GREENDALE, WISCONSIN

Pasta sauce mix simplifies the assembly of this skillet supper that's loaded with tender chicken. Be sure you have water, milk and butter on hand to prepare the mix as directed on the package.

PREP/TOTAL TIME: 25 min.

- 2 packages (4.3 ounces *each*) Parmesan cheese pasta sauce mix
- 1 pound boneless skinless chicken breasts, cut into strips
- 1 cup sliced fresh mushrooms
- 1 cup fresh green beans, cut into 1-inch pieces
- 2 tablespoons canola oil
- 1 medium tomato, chopped

■ Prepare pasta mix according to package directions. Meanwhile, in a large skillet, cook the chicken, mushrooms and green beans in oil over medium heat for 10-15 minutes or until meat is no longer pink and vegetables are tender; drain. Add to pasta and sauce. Stir in tomato.

Yield: 4 servings.

Editor's Note: This recipe was tested with Lipton Pasta Sides fettuccine and spinach pasta in a Parmesan cheese sauce mix.

Garlic Chicken Penne

Anne Nock
AVON LAKE, OHIO

All it takes is four ingredients and 20 minutes to have this hearty dish ready for the table. Chicken, snap peas and pasta star in this supper, and the garlicky sauce ties it all together nicely.

PREP/TOTAL TIME: 20 min.

- 8 ounces uncooked penne pasta
- 1-1/2 cups frozen sugar snap peas
- 1 package (1.6 ounces) garlic-herb pasta sauce mix
- 1 package (6 ounces) sliced cooked chicken

■ In a large saucepan, cook pasta in boiling water for 6 minutes. Add the peas; return to a boil. Cook for 4-5 minutes or until pasta is tender. Meanwhile, prepare the sauce mix according to the package directions.

■ Drain the pasta mixture; add the chicken. Drizzle with sauce and toss to coat.

Yield: 4 servings.

Robyn Hardisty
LAKEWOOD, CALIFORNIA

I make this recipe around the holidays. It's a wonderful way to use leftover turkey without feeling like it's a "repeat" meal. I love pasta, and the creamy sauce is so easy to make.

Next Day Turkey Primavera

Next Day Turkey Primavera

PREP/TOTAL TIME: 30 min.

- 1 cup uncooked penne pasta
- 8 fresh asparagus spears, trimmed and cut into 1-inch pieces
- 2/3 cup julienned carrot
- 3 tablespoons butter
- 4 large fresh mushrooms, sliced
- 1/2 cup chopped yellow summer squash
- 1/2 cup chopped zucchini
- 1-1/2 cups shredded cooked turkey
- 1 medium tomato, chopped
- 1 envelope Italian salad dressing mix
- 1 cup heavy whipping cream
- 1/4 cup grated Parmesan cheese

■ Cook pasta according to package directions. Meanwhile, in a large skillet, saute asparagus and carrot in butter for 3 minutes. Add the mushrooms, yellow squash and zucchini; saute until crisp-tender.

■ Stir in the turkey, tomato, dressing mix and cream. Bring to a boil; cook and stir for 2 minutes.

■ Drain pasta; add to vegetable mixture and toss to combine. Sprinkle with cheese and toss again.

Yield: 4 servings.

Lynn Skilsky
TUCSON, ARIZONA
This dish was a favorite of mine at a local restaurant. When I saw the recipe, I made some changes to suit my family's taste, and now it's one of our favorites.

Favorite Chicken Pasta

PREP/TOTAL TIME: 30 min.

1-1/4 cups uncooked bow tie pasta

1/2 cup boiling water

1/4 cup chopped sun-dried tomatoes (not packed in oil)

1 teaspoon chopped shallot

1 garlic clove, minced

2 teaspoons olive oil

1/4 cup white wine *or* reduced-sodium chicken broth

2 tablespoons sliced ripe olives

1 tablespoon prepared pesto

1/8 teaspoon pepper

1-1/2 teaspoons all-purpose flour

1/2 cup fat-free half-and-half

1 package (6 ounces) ready-to-use grilled chicken breast strips

1 tablespoon shredded Parmesan cheese

2 teaspoons pine nuts, toasted

- Cook pasta according to package directions. Meanwhile, in a small bowl, combine water and sun-dried tomatoes; cover and let stand for 5 minutes.

- In a large skillet over medium heat, cook and stir shallot and garlic in oil for 2 minutes. Stir in the wine or broth, olives, pesto and pepper; cook 1 minute longer.

- Combine flour and half-and-half until smooth; stir into the pan. Bring to a boil; cook and stir for 1-2 minutes or until thickened.

- Drain pasta and tomatoes; add to shallot mixture. Stir in the chicken; heat through. Sprinkle with Parmesan cheese and pine nuts.

Yield: 2 servings.

To cook pasta more evenly, prevent it from sticking together and avoid boil-overs, always cook pasta in a large kettle or Dutch oven. Pasta should be cooked until "al dente," or firm yet tender. Test often while cooking to avoid overcooking, which can result in a soft or mushy texture.

Skillet Chicken Supper

PREP: 30 min. ■ **COOK:** 30 min.

Marlene Muckenhirn
DELANO, MINNESOTA

This tasty chicken is a hearty main dish. It's gently spiced with a vegetable medley. Try frozen mixed vegetables instead of the peas if that's what you have on hand.

1 cup all-purpose flour
1 teaspoon garlic powder
1 teaspoon pepper
1 broiler/fryer chicken (3 to 4 pounds), cut up
2 tablespoons canola oil
1-3/4 cups water, *divided*
1/2 cup soy sauce
1/2 teaspoon dried oregano
3 medium red potatoes, cut into 1-inch chunks
3 large carrots, cut into 1-inch pieces
3 celery ribs, cut into 1-inch pieces
1 package (10 ounces) frozen peas

■ In a small bowl, combine the flour, garlic powder and pepper. Pour half the flour mixture into a large resealable plastic bag. Add chicken, one piece at a time, and shake to coat; set the remaining flour mixture aside.

■ In a large skillet, cook chicken in oil until browned on all sides; drain. Combine 1-1/4 cups water, soy sauce and oregano; pour over chicken. Add the vegetables. Bring to a boil; reduce heat. Cover and simmer for 30-40 minutes or until chicken juices run clear. Remove chicken and vegetables; keep warm.

■ Combine reserved flour mixture and remaining water until smooth; add to the cooking juices. Bring to a boil; cook and stir for 2 minutes or until thickened. Serve with the chicken and vegetables.

Yield: 6 servings.

A broiler/fryer chicken is about 7 weeks old and weighs 2-1/2 to 4-1/2 pounds. A cut up broiler/fryer should have two breast halves, two thighs, two drumsticks and two wings. It may or may not have the back.

Thai Chicken Fettuccine

PREP: 25 min.
COOK: 15 min. + cooling

1 cup salsa
1/4 cup creamy peanut butter
2 tablespoons orange juice
2 tablespoons honey
1 teaspoon soy sauce
8 ounces uncooked fettuccine
3/4 pound boneless skinless chicken breasts, cut into strips
1 tablespoon canola oil
1 medium sweet red pepper, julienned
1/4 cup minced fresh cilantro

■ For sauce, in a microwave-safe bowl, combine the first five ingredients. Cover and microwave on high for 1 minute; stir. Set aside.

■ Cook fettuccine according to package directions. Meanwhile, in a large skillet, cook chicken in oil over medium heat for 3-5 minutes or until chicken juices run clear. Add red pepper; cook and stir until crisp-tender.

■ Drain the fettuccine; top with chicken mixture and sauce. Sprinkle with cilantro.

Yield: 4 servings.

Michelle Van Loon
ROUND LAKE, ILLINOIS

Salsa, peanut butter, orange juice, honey and soy sauce create a taste-tempting sauce in this unique chicken recipe. Its innovative flavor combination, fresh taste and ease of preparation will bowl you over. It's a great way to satisfy a craving for Southeast Asian cooking.

Skillet Arroz con Pollo

- In a large nonstick skillet coated with cooking spray, saute the onion, red pepper and garlic in olive oil for 1 minute. Add the rice; cook and stir for 4-5 minutes or until lightly browned.

- Stir in the broth, sherry or water, lemon peel, salt and cayenne. Bring to a boil. Reduce heat; cover and simmer for 15 minutes.

- Stir in the chicken, peas and olives. Cover and simmer 3-6 minutes longer or until rice is tender and chicken is heated through. Sprinkle with cilantro.

Yield: 4 servings.

*Nutrition Facts: 1-1/2 cups equals 373 calories, 6 g fat (1 g saturated fat), 54 mg cholesterol, 582 mg sodium, 49 g carbohydrate, 4 g fiber, 28 g protein. Diabetic Exchanges: 3 starch, 3 very lean meat, 1 vegetable, 1/2 fat.

Cheryl Battaglia
DALTON, PENNSYLVANIA

This chicken-and-rice dish is great for both family and special occasion dinners. It's a tasty main course made all in one skillet, and it smells so good while it cooks!

Skillet Arroz con Pollo*

PREP: 15 min. ■ COOK: 25 min.

- 1 medium onion, chopped
- 1 medium sweet red pepper, cut into 1/2-inch pieces
- 1 garlic clove, minced
- 2 teaspoons olive oil
- 1 cup uncooked long grain rice
- 1 can (14-1/2 ounces) reduced-sodium chicken broth
- 1/4 cup sherry *or* water
- 1/2 teaspoon grated lemon peel
- 1/4 teaspoon salt
- 1/4 teaspoon cayenne pepper
- 2 cups cubed cooked chicken breast
- 1 cup frozen peas, thawed
- 1/4 cup sliced ripe olives, drained
- 2 tablespoons minced fresh cilantro

Cilantro adds a distinctive and aromatic flavor to Mexican, Latin American and Asian dishes. Like all other fresh herbs, cilantro should be used as soon as possible. Store the freshly cut stems in about 2 inches of water.

Taste of Home
Test Kitchen
GREENDALE,
WISCONSIN

This amazing recipe gives you authentic fajita flavor in 30 minutes! Pineapple and tomato combine for a real treat that will have everybody coming back for seconds.

Fajita Skillet

Fajita Skillet

PREP/TOTAL TIME: 30 min.

- 2 flour tortillas (10 inches), cut into 1/2-inch strips
- 3 tablespoons olive oil, *divided*
- 1/2 pound boneless skinless chicken breasts, cut into strips
- 1/2 pound boneless beef sirloin steak, cut into thin strips
- 1 medium green pepper, sliced
- 1 small onion, sliced
- 2 tablespoons soy sauce
- 2 teaspoons brown sugar
- 1/2 teaspoon chili powder
- 1/2 teaspoon ground cumin
- 1/4 teaspoon pepper
- 1 teaspoon cornstarch
- 2 tablespoons lime juice
- 1 cup cubed fresh pineapple
- 1 medium tomato, coarsely chopped

■ In a large skillet, fry tortilla strips in 2 tablespoons oil on both sides for 1 minute or until golden brown. Drain on paper towels.

■ In the same skillet, cook the chicken, beef, green pepper, onion, soy sauce, brown sugar, chili powder, cumin and pepper in remaining oil for 3-4 minutes or until chicken is no longer pink.

■ In a small bowl, combine cornstarch and lime juice until smooth. Stir into skillet. Bring to a boil; cook and stir for 1 minute or until thickened. Stir in pineapple and tomato; heat through. Serve with tortilla strips.

Yield: 4 servings.

Lemon Chicken And Rice*

Kat Thompson
PRINEVILLE, OREGON

On our busy ranch, we often need meals we can put on the table in a hurry. This all-in-one chicken dish, with its delicate lemon flavor, fits the bill. And it's inexpensive to boot.

PREP/TOTAL TIME: 30 min.

- 1 pound boneless skinless chicken breasts, cut into strips
- 1 medium onion, chopped
- 1 large carrot, thinly sliced
- 2 garlic cloves, minced
- 2 tablespoons butter
- 1 tablespoon cornstarch
- 1 can (14-1/2 ounces) chicken broth
- 2 tablespoons lemon juice
- 1/2 teaspoon salt, optional
- 1-1/2 cups uncooked instant rice
- 1 cup frozen peas

■ In a large skillet, cook chicken, onion, carrot and garlic in butter for 5-7 minutes or until chicken is no longer pink.

■ Combine the cornstarch, broth, lemon juice and salt if desired until smooth. Gradually add to skillet; bring to a boil. Cook and stir for 2 minutes or until thickened. Stir in rice and peas. Remove from the heat; cover and let stand for 5 minutes.

Yield: 6 servings.

*Nutrition Facts: One serving (prepared with reduced-fat margarine and low-sodium broth and without salt) equals 235 calories, 5 g fat (0 saturated fat), 43 mg cholesterol, 156 mg sodium, 27 g carbohydrate, 0 fiber, 20 g protein. **Diabetic Exchanges:** 2 lean meat, 1-1/2 starch, 1 vegetable.

Christine Ecker
LINWOOD, NEW JERSEY

Our two children love chicken. Both can be finicky eaters and they're not crazy about sauces, but they adore this dish! It's so full of different flavors. It's also a great recipe to fix when company is over, because it has restaurant appeal, and can be made quickly.

Zesty Chicken with Artichokes*

PREP: 15 min. ■ COOK: 25 min.

- 2 teaspoons dried thyme
- 2 teaspoons grated lemon peel
- 1/4 teaspoon salt
- 1/4 teaspoon pepper
- 4 boneless skinless chicken breast halves (4 ounces *each*)
- 4 teaspoons olive oil, *divided*
- 1 large onion, chopped
- 2 garlic cloves, minced
- 1 can (14 ounces) water-packed artichoke hearts, rinsed, drained and halved
- 3/4 cup white wine *or* reduced-sodium chicken broth
- 1/4 cup sliced pimiento-stuffed olives, drained
- 1/4 cup sliced ripe olives, drained

■ Combine the thyme, lemon peel, salt and pepper; rub over chicken. In a large nonstick skillet, brown the chicken in 2 teaspoons oil; remove and set aside.

■ In the same skillet, saute onion and garlic in remaining oil until tender. Stir in the artichokes, wine and olives. Return chicken to the pan. Bring to a boil. Reduce heat; cover and simmer for 6-8 minutes or until a meat thermometer reads 170°.

■ Remove chicken and keep warm. Simmer artichoke mixture, uncovered, for 2-3 minutes or until liquid has evaporated; serve with chicken.

Yield: 4 servings.

✳ Nutrition Facts: 1 chicken breast half with 1/2 cup artichoke mixture equals 260 calories, 10 g fat (2 g saturated fat), 63 mg cholesterol, 706 mg sodium, 13 g carbohydrate, 2 g fiber, 26 g protein. **Diabetic Exchanges:** 3 very lean meat, 2 vegetable, 1-1/2 fat.

Buying skinned and boned chicken breasts can cut up to 15 minutes off your cooking time. Save money by buying larger size packages, then rewrap individually or in family-size portions and freeze.

Golden Chicken and Autumn Vegetables

Taste of Home Test Kitchen
GREENDALE, WISCONSIN

This comforting combination is sure to warm you up on a chilly day. Tender chicken breasts, sweet potatoes and green beans are cooked in broth seasoned with rosemary, garlic and thyme.

PREP: 10 min.
COOK: 35 min.

- 4 bone-in chicken breast halves (8 ounces *each*), skin removed
- 2 large sweet potatoes, peeled and cut into large chunks
- 2 cups fresh *or* frozen cut green beans
- 1 cup chicken broth
- 1 tablespoon minced fresh parsley
- 1/2 teaspoon garlic powder
- 1/2 teaspoon dried rosemary, crushed
- 1/4 teaspoon dried thyme

■ In a large nonstick skillet, brown chicken over medium-high heat on both sides. Add sweet potatoes and beans. In a small bowl, combine the remaining ingredients; pour over chicken and vegetables. Bring to a boil. Reduce heat; cover and cook over low heat for 20 minutes or until chicken juices run clear.

Yield: 4 servings.

Bonnie Brann
PASCO, WASHINGTON

I received the recipe for this colorful dish from my former neighbor. It's so good, for one holiday dinner, it actually replaced my traditional turkey! It's a hearty, greattasting meal-in-one.

Creole Skillet Dinner

Creole Skillet Dinner

PREP: 15 min. ■ **COOK:** 30 min.

4	cups chicken broth
2-1/2	cups uncooked long grain rice
1	cup chopped red onion
3	garlic cloves, minced, *divided*
1-1/4	teaspoons chili powder
1	teaspoon salt
1/2	teaspoon ground turmeric
1/4	teaspoon pepper
1	bay leaf
1	medium sweet red pepper, julienned
1	medium green pepper, julienned
2	green onions, sliced

1	teaspoon chopped fresh parsley
1/2	teaspoon dried basil
1/2	teaspoon dried thyme
1/4	teaspoon hot pepper sauce
2	tablespoons butter
1	cup sliced fresh mushrooms
1	medium tomato, chopped
1	cup frozen peas
1	pound boneless skinless chicken breasts, thinly sliced
2	tablespoons lemon juice
1/3	cup sliced almonds, toasted

■ In a saucepan, bring the broth, rice, onion, 1 teaspoon garlic, chili powder, salt, turmeric, pepper and bay leaf to a boil. Reduce heat; cover and simmer 20 minutes or until rice is tender. Discard bay leaf.

■ In a skillet over medium-high heat, saute the next seven ingredients and the remaining garlic in butter for 2 minutes. Add mushrooms; cook until peppers are crisp-tender. Stir in tomato and peas; heat through. Remove from the heat. Add rice; keep warm.

■ In a skillet, cook and stir chicken in lemon juice over medium-high heat until no longer pink. Add to rice mixture; toss. Top with almonds.

Yield: 6 servings.

An easy way to juice a lemon is to cut it at an angle instead of up and down. The halves are easier to squeeze and the juice flows more easily. To have lemon juice on hand, pour extra juice in ice cube trays, cover with plastic wrap and freeze. The juice will keep up to 6 months.

Harvest Chicken

Linda Hutton
HAYDEN, IDAHO

This chicken has become a Sunday-dinner standby around our house. Friends and family often comment on the fresh combination of asparagus, carrots, potatoes and chicken.

Harvest Chicken*

PREP: 10 min. ■ **COOK:** 55 min.

1/3 cup all-purpose flour
1/4 teaspoon paprika
4 boneless skinless chicken breast halves (4 ounces *each*)
1 tablespoon canola oil
2 cups chicken broth, *divided*
1 teaspoon dill weed
3/4 teaspoon salt, optional

1/4 teaspoon dried basil
1/4 teaspoon pepper
4 medium potatoes, cut into bite-size pieces
3 medium carrots, cut into 2-inch pieces
1/2 pound fresh asparagus, cut into 2-inch pieces
2 tablespoons minced fresh parsley

■ In a large resealable plastic bag, combine the flour and paprika; set aside 2 table-spoons. Add chicken; seal bag and turn to coat.

■ In a large skillet, brown the chicken in oil over medium heat. Drain and set chicken aside. In the same skillet combine 3/4 cup broth, dill, salt if desired, basil and pepper; bring to a boil. Add the potatoes and carrots. Reduce heat; cover and simmer for 10 minutes.

■ Add the chicken; cook for 10 minutes. Add asparagus; cook 15-20 minutes or until a meat thermometer reads 170° and vegetables are tender.

■ Combine the reserved flour mixture and the remaining broth; stir into skillet. Bring to a boil; cook and stir for 2 minutes or until slightly thickened. Sprinkle with parsley.

Yield: 4 servings.

*Nutrition Facts: 1/4 recipe (prepared with low-sodium chicken broth; calculated w/o added salt) equals 348 calories, 6 g fat (0 saturated fat), 68 mg cholesterol, 163 mg sodium, 68 g carbohydrate, 5 fiber, 35 g protein. **Diabetic Exchanges:** 3-1/2 lean meat, 1-1/2 starch, 1-1/2 vegetable, 1/2 fat.

Doralee Pinkerton
MILFORD, INDIANA

My interests are reading, gardening...and growing most of the ingredients I use in this dinner! My husband, daughter and son became fans of this meal from the start!

Corn and Chicken Dinner

Corn and Chicken Dinner

PREP: 10 min. ■ **COOK:** 40 min.

3 pounds chicken legs and thighs (about 8 pieces)	2 teaspoons dried tarragon, *divided*
1/2 cup butter, *divided*	1/2 teaspoon salt
3 garlic cloves, minced, *divided*	1/4 teaspoon pepper
3 ears fresh corn, husked, cleaned and cut into thirds	2 medium zucchini, sliced into 1/2-inch pieces
1/4 cup water	2 tomatoes, seeded and cut into chunks

■ In a Dutch oven or large skillet, cook chicken in butter over medium heat until browned on each side. Add two-thirds of the garlic; cook for 1-2 minutes or until garlic is tender. Reduce heat; stir in corn and water. Sprinkle with 1 teaspoon tarragon, salt and pepper. Cover; simmer for 20-25 minutes or until a thermometer inserted into chicken reads 180°.

■ Meanwhile, in a small saucepan, combine remaining garlic and tarragon; saute for 3 minutes or until garlic is tender. Layer zucchini and tomatoes over the chicken mixture. Drizzle seasoned butter over all; cover and cook for 3-5 minutes or until heated through.

Yield: 6-8 servings.

Tuxedo Pasta

PREP/TOTAL TIME: 20 min.

- 2 cups uncooked bow tie pasta
- 2 cups cubed cooked chicken
- 1 medium zucchini, sliced
- 1-1/2 cups sliced fresh mushrooms
- 1/2 cup chopped sweet red pepper
- 3 tablespoons butter, *divided*
- 1/4 cup lemon juice
- 2 tablespoons white wine *or* chicken broth
- 3/4 cup shredded Parmesan cheese
- 3 tablespoons minced fresh basil *or* 1 tablespoon dried basil

■ Cook the pasta according to package directions. Meanwhile, in a large skillet, saute the chicken, zucchini, mushrooms and red pepper in 2 tablespoons butter for 4-5 minutes or until vegetables are tender. Add the lemon juice and wine. Bring to a boil. Reduce the heat; cook and stir for 2 minutes or until heated through.

■ Drain pasta; add to skillet. Stir in the Parmesan, basil and remaining butter.

Yield: 6 servings.

To seed a tomato, cut it in half and gently squeeze each tomato half. If you don't want to lose a lot of juice, try using a small spoon to scoop out the seeds.

Jackie Hannahs
FOUNTAIN, MICHIGAN

With chicken and veggies, this pasta medley in a mild lemon and wine sauce is a complete meal-in-one that's a snap to assemble. I try to keep leftover chicken or turkey on hand so that I can fix this dish whenever I want.

Turkey Sausage with Root Vegetables

- In a Dutch oven, cook sausage, onion, rutabaga and carrots in oil for 5 minutes or until onion is tender. Add the potatoes, broth, thyme, sage, pepper and bay leaf. Bring to a boil. Place cabbage wedges on top. Reduce heat; cover and simmer for 20-25 minutes or until potatoes and cabbage are tender.

- Carefully remove cabbage to a shallow serving bowl; keep warm. Discard bay leaf. Combine the flour and water until smooth; stir into sausage mixture. Bring to a boil; cook and stir for 2 minutes or until thickened. Stir in parsley and vinegar. Spoon over cabbage.

Yield: 6 servings.

* **Nutrition Facts:** 1-1/2 cups equals 231 calories, 3 g fat (1 g saturated fat), 23 mg cholesterol, 781 mg sodium, 39 g carbohydrate, 6 g fiber, 13 g protein. **Diabetic Exchanges:** 2 starch, 1 lean meat, 1 vegetable.

Lisa Zeigler-Day
FOREST PARK, ILLINOIS

I had a delicious stew recipe but rarely prepared it because sausage can be high in fat and sodium. Now I use turkey sausage, so it tastes good and is also heart healthy.

Turkey Sausage with Root Vegetables*

PREP: 10 min. ■ **COOK:** 30 min.

- 1 package (14 ounces) smoked turkey kielbasa, cut into 1/2-inch pieces
- 1 medium onion, chopped
- 1 cup cubed peeled rutabaga
- 1 cup sliced carrots
- 1 teaspoon canola oil
- 4 cups cubed peeled potatoes
- 1 can (14-3/4 ounces) reduced-sodium chicken broth
- 1 teaspoon dried thyme
- 1/4 teaspoon rubbed sage
- 1/4 teaspoon pepper
- 1 bay leaf
- 1/2 medium head cabbage, cut into 6 wedges
- 1 teaspoon all-purpose flour
- 1 tablespoon water
- 1 tablespoon minced fresh parsley
- 2 teaspoons cider vinegar

When shopping

for rutabagas, select those that are smooth-skinned, unblemished, heavy, firm and not spongy. Look for ones no larger than 4 inches in diameter. Keep unwashed rutabagas in a plastic bag in the refrigerator's crisper drawer for up to 1 week. Just before using, wash, trim the ends and peel.

Tammy Daniels
BATAVIA, OHIO
This is so easy to toss together on a busy weeknight, and I usually have the ingredients on hand. I saute the onion and pepper first, then I prepare the rice. I like to top it with shredded cheddar cheese.

Chicken Rice Bowl

Chicken Rice Bowl

PREP/TOTAL TIME: 10 min.

1 cup uncooked instant rice
1 cup chicken broth
1/2 cup chopped frozen green pepper, thawed
1/4 cup chopped onion
2 teaspoons olive oil
1 package (9 ounces) ready-to-use grilled chicken breast strips

1/2 cup frozen corn, thawed
1/2 cup frozen peas, thawed
1 teaspoon dried basil
1 teaspoon rubbed sage
1/8 teaspoon salt
1/8 teaspoon pepper

■ Cook rice in broth according to package directions. Meanwhile, in a large skillet, saute the green pepper and onion in oil for 2-3 minutes or until crisp-tender. Stir in the chicken, corn, peas, basil and sage. Cook, uncovered, for 4-5 minutes over medium heat or until heated through. Stir in the rice, salt and pepper.

Yield: 4 servings.

To add some pizzazz to the Chicken Rice Bowl, top with chopped green onions, toasted sesame seeds or chopped roasted peanuts or cashews.

Solo Teriyaki Chicken

Bill Hilbrich
ST. CLOUD, MINNESOTA
A simple marinade flavors the chicken nicely in this meal-in-one rice dish. I try to create interesting one-serving meals for myself.

PREP: 15 min. + marinating
COOK: 15 min.

2 tablespoons plus 3/4 cup chicken broth, *divided*
1 tablespoon soy sauce
1 garlic clove, minced
1 teaspoon sugar
1 teaspoon minced fresh gingerroot
1/4 pound boneless skinless chicken breast, cubed
1 teaspoon canola oil
1/3 cup uncooked long grain rice
1 jar (4-1/2 ounces) sliced mushrooms, drained

■ In a resealable plastic bag, combine 2 tablespoons broth, soy sauce, garlic, sugar and ginger; add chicken. Seal bag and turn to coat; refrigerate for 30 minutes.

■ Drain and discard marinade. In a skillet, brown chicken in oil. Stir in the rice, mushrooms and remaining broth. Bring to a boil. Reduce heat; cover and simmer for 12-17 minutes or until the rice is tender.

Yield: 1 serving.

Pork

147

150

146

Dishes that sizzle with the bold flavor of pork are some of the tastiest around. These recipes feature hearty pork chops, smoky kielbasa, juicy tenderloin and roasts. Whether you need just the right recipe for dinner guests or a quick family meal, these dishes are sure to please.

Fruit-Topped Pork Chops and Rice

Priscilla Gilbert
INDIAN HARBOUR BEACH, FLORIDA
This is a quick and delicious meal I often serve to guests. Dried fruit adds a special touch to the dish. Served with a fast rice mix, dinner will be on the table before you know it!

Fruit-Topped Pork Chops and Rice

PREP/TOTAL TIME: 30 min.

4 bone-in center-cut pork loin chops (6 ounces *each*)	1 cup chicken broth
1/4 teaspoon pepper	1 package (8.8 ounces) ready-to-serve long grain rice
2 tablespoons plus 1 teaspoon canola oil, *divided*	4 teaspoons butter
1/3 cup chopped shallots	4 teaspoons minced fresh parsley
1 package (7 ounces) dried fruit bits	

■ Sprinkle the pork chops with pepper. In a large skillet, cook chops in 2 tablespoons oil over medium-high heat for 7-8 minutes on each side or until a meat thermometer reads 160 °. Remove and keep warm.

■ In the same skillet, saute the shallots in remaining oil for 1 minute. Add fruit and broth. Bring to a boil. Reduce heat; cover and simmer for 3-5 minutes or until mixture is slightly thickened. Return chops to the pan; cook for 1-2 minutes or until heated through.

■ Meanwhile, microwave the rice according to the package directions. Divide the rice among serving plates; dot with butter and sprinkle with parsley. Serve with pork chops and fruit.

Yield: 4 servings.

Shallots are part of the onion family and have a mild onion-garlic flavor. In place of 3 to 4 shallots, use 1 medium onion plus a pinch of garlic powder or (if you like the taste of garlic) 1 minced garlic clove.

Simone Greene,
WINCHESTER, VIRGINIA

My mom used to make these pork chops when I was still living at home. The sweetness of the apple mixture is a nice complement to the savory stuffing and chops, and makes for mouth-watering flavor.

Smothered Pork Chops

Smothered Pork Chops

PREP/TOTAL TIME: 30 min.

1 package (6 ounces) chicken stuffing mix

4 boneless pork loin chops (6 ounces *each*)

1 tablespoon butter

4 medium apples, peeled and cut into wedges

1/2 cup packed brown sugar

1/4 cup water

1/4 teaspoon salt

1/4 teaspoon ground cinnamon

■ Prepare stuffing mix according to package directions. Meanwhile, in a large skillet, cook pork chops in butter over medium heat for 2-3 minutes on each side or until lightly browned. Stir in the apples, brown sugar, water and salt. Bring to a boil. Reduce heat; cover and simmer for 8-10 minutes or until apples are tender.

■ Top with stuffing; sprinkle with cinnamon. Cook, uncovered, over medium heat for 10-12 minutes or until a meat thermometer reads 160°.

Yield: 4 servings.

To soften brown sugar, place a slice of bread or an apple wedge with the brown sugar in a covered, airtight container for a few days. Or, for a quicker method, microwave on high in 20-30 second intervals. But watch carefully, because the sugar may begin to melt.

Sweet 'n' Sour Polish Sausage

Elaine Hair
STEDMAN, NORTH CAROLINA

Since my sister shared this recipe with me, I've made it for oh-so many gatherings.

PREP: 10 min.
COOK: 35 min.

1 pound smoked kielbasa *or* Polish sausage, cut into 1/2-inch slices

1 medium onion, chopped

1 small green pepper, chopped

1 celery rib, chopped

1 tablespoon butter

1 cup packed brown sugar

3/4 cup ketchup

1/2 cup cider vinegar

1 teaspoon salt

1 can (20 ounces) pineapple chunks

3 tablespoons cornstarch

1/4 cup cold water

Hot cooked rice

■ In a large skillet, saute the sausage, onion, green pepper and chopped celery in butter over medium heat until meat is no longer pink and vegetables are tender; remove with a slotted spoon and set aside.

■ In same skillet, combine sugar, ketchup, vinegar and salt. Drain pineapple, reserving juice; set pineapple aside. Add juice to skillet; bring to a boil. Return sausage mixture to pan. Mix cornstarch and water; stir into skillet. Bring to a boil; cook and stir for 2 minutes or until thickened. Stir in pineapple; heat through. Serve over rice.

Yield: 6 servings.

- In a large skillet, saute mushrooms in butter until tender. Remove and keep warm. Sprinkle pork chops with salt and pepper. In the same skillet, brown chops in oil on both sides; drain.

- Add marinara sauce; bring to a boil. Reduce heat; simmer, uncovered, for 8-10 minutes or until a meat thermometer reads 160°, turning once. Layer pork with pepperoni, mushrooms and cheese. Remove from the heat. Cover and let stand for 2-3 minutes or until cheese is melted. Serve with noodles or pasta.

Yield: 4 servings.

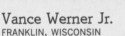
Pizza Pork Chops

Vance Werner Jr.
FRANKLIN, WISCONSIN
Pepperoni and mozzarella cheese punch up this easy skillet recipe with the flavor of pizza that everyone loves. To dress up this speedy supper, use portobello mushrooms.

Pizza Pork Chops

PREP/TOTAL TIME: 30 min.

2 cups sliced fresh mushrooms
2 tablespoons butter
4 boneless pork loin chops (1/2 inch thick and 4 ounces *each*)
1/4 teaspoon salt
1/4 teaspoon pepper

2 tablespoons olive oil
2 cups marinara *or* spaghetti sauce
16 slices pepperoni
1 cup (4 ounces) shredded part-skim mozzarella cheese
Hot cooked noodles *or* pasta

Leftover pork
chops are ideal for making an easy stir-fry dish the next day. Add strips of the cooked pork to vegetables and seasonings, and simply serve over cooked rice.

Linda Murray
ALLENSTOWN, NEW HAMPSHIRE

The sweet and savory combination of apples and raisins with pork is perfect for autumn dinners. This dish is so popular, I've passed it on to family members and friends many times! It also works well with ground pork or cubed leftover pork roast.

Apple-Spiced Pork*

PREP/TOTAL TIME: 30 min.

  2 cups uncooked yolk-free noodles
  1 pork tenderloin (1 pound), halved lengthwise and cut into 1/2-inch slices
  1/4 cup chopped celery
  2 tablespoons chopped onion
  1 tablespoon canola oil
  2 medium tart apples, chopped
  1/3 cup raisins
  1 tablespoon brown sugar
  1/2 teaspoon seasoned salt
  1/4 to 1/2 teaspoon ground cinnamon
  4-1/2 teaspoons cornstarch
  1 can (14-1/2 ounces) reduced-sodium beef broth
  2 tablespoons chopped walnuts

■ Cook noodles according to package directions; drain. Meanwhile, in a large skillet, brown pork with celery and onion in oil; drain. Add the apples, raisins, brown sugar, seasoned salt and cinnamon. Cook and stir over medium heat for 8-10 minutes or until pork is no longer pink and vegetables are tender.

■ In a small bowl, combine cornstarch and broth until smooth; gradually add to the pork mixture. Bring to a boil; cook and stir for 2 minutes or until thickened. Serve with noodles. Sprinkle with walnuts.

Yield: 4 servings.

*Nutrition Facts: 1 cup spiced pork with 1/2 cup noodles equals 376 calories, 10 g fat (2 g saturated fat), 65 mg cholesterol, 444 mg sodium, 43 g carbohydrate, 4 g fiber, 28 g protein. **Diabetic Exchanges:** 3 lean meat, 1-1/2 starch, 1 fruit, 1/2 fat.

Keep pork tenderloin in the freezer for last-minute meals since it thaws and cooks quickly. Thaw the tenderloin using the "defrost" cycle of your microwave according to the manufacturer's directions. Cut pork tenderloin while partially frozen into thin, even slices and cut slices into strips. Use in place of beef or chicken in your favorite stir-fry or fajita recipes.

Moo Shu Pork

PREP/TOTAL TIME: 20 min.

Taste of Home Test Kitchen
GREENDALE, WISCONSIN

Stir-fried vegetables make a nice accompaniment to this dish. Find hoisin sauce in the Asian aisle at your grocery store.

  1 tablespoon cornstarch
  1/4 cup cold water
  2 tablespoons reduced-sodium soy sauce
  2 teaspoons minced fresh gingerroot
  5 boneless pork loin chops (4 ounces *each*), cut into thin strips
  1 teaspoon minced garlic
  2 teaspoons sesame oil
  1/4 cup hoisin sauce
  3 cups coleslaw mix with carrots
  8 flour tortillas (8 inches), warmed

■ In a small bowl, combine the cornstarch, water, soy sauce and ginger until blended; set aside. In a large skillet, saute pork and garlic in oil for 3-5 minutes or until meat is no longer pink.

■ Stir cornstarch mixture and add to the skillet. Bring to a boil; cook and stir for 1-2 minutes or until thickened. Stir in hoisin sauce. Add coleslaw mix; stir to coat. Spoon about 1/2 cup pork mixture into the center of each tortilla; roll up tightly.

Yield: 4 servings.

- In a large nonstick skillet, cook pork in oil until no longer pink; remove and keep warm. In the same pan, saute onion and garlic until crisp-tender. Add the broth, vegetables, vinegar, sugar, tarragon and salt; bring to a boil. Reduce heat; cover and simmer for 25-30 minutes or until vegetables are tender.

- Combine the flour and milk until smooth; gradually stir into vegetable mixture. Bring to a boil; cook and stir for 2 minutes or until thickened. Add pork and heat through. Reduce heat; stir in sour cream just before serving.

Yield: 8 servings.

Pork Tenderloin Stew

Janet Alle
BELLEVILLE, ILLINOIS

This thick, creamy stew is one that my family often requests. It does an especially good job of satisfying our hunger and warming us up on cold winter days.

Pork Tenderloin Stew

PREP: 20 min. ■ COOK: 40 min.

2 pork tenderloins (1 pound *each*), cut into 1-inch cubes

1 tablespoon olive oil

1 medium onion, chopped

1 garlic clove, minced

1 can (14-1/2 ounces) reduced-sodium chicken broth

2 pounds red potatoes, peeled and cubed

1 cup sliced fresh carrots

1 cup sliced celery

1/2 pound sliced fresh mushrooms

2 tablespoons cider vinegar

2 teaspoons sugar

1-1/2 teaspoons dried tarragon

1 teaspoon salt

2 tablespoons all-purpose flour

1/2 cup fat-free milk

1/2 cup reduced-fat sour cream

Dried herbs don't spoil, but they do lose flavor and potency over time. For maximum flavor in your cooking, you may want to replace herbs that are over a year old. Store dried herbs in airtight containers and keep them away from heat and light. Don't put them in the cupboard above the stove.

Taste of Home Test Kitchen
GREENDALE, WISCONSIN

Kids and adults alike will love this dressed-up version of creamy macaroni and cheese from our Test Kitchen. It'll please even the pickiest of eaters.

Ham 'n' Cheese Pasta

Ham 'n' Cheese Pasta

PREP/TOTAL TIME: 30 min.

3 cups uncooked bow tie pasta
3/4 pound fresh asparagus, trimmed and cut into 1-inch pieces
2 tablespoons butter
1 teaspoon minced garlic
2 tablespoons all-purpose flour
1/4 teaspoon onion powder

1/4 teaspoon pepper
1/8 to 1/4 teaspoon dried thyme
2 cups milk
2 cups (8 ounces) shredded cheddar cheese
1/2 cup grated Parmesan cheese
1/2 pound sliced deli ham, chopped

■ Cook pasta according to package directions, adding asparagus during the last 3 minutes.

■ Meanwhile, in a large saucepan, melt butter; add garlic. Stir in the flour, onion powder, pepper and thyme until blended; gradually add milk. Bring to a boil; cook and stir for 2 minutes or until thickened.

■ Reduce heat. Add cheeses; stir until melted. Stir in ham; heat through. Drain pasta and asparagus; toss with cheese mixture.

Yield: 4 servings.

Pierogi Supper

PREP/TOTAL TIME: 15 min.

Holly Bosworth
OCALA, FLORIDA

My husband loves pierogies, so when I need a fast meal without a lot of cleanup, I create this all-in-one dinner. It's very filling.

1 package (16.9 ounces) frozen pierogies
2 cups cubed fully cooked ham
1 medium yellow summer squash, cut into 1/4-inch slices
1 medium zucchini, cut into 1/4-inch slices
1/2 teaspoon garlic powder
3 tablespoons butter

■ Cook pierogies according to package directions. Meanwhile, in a large skillet, cook the ham, squash, zucchini and garlic powder in butter for 4 minutes or until squash is tender. Drain pierogies and add to skillet; heat through.

Yield: 4 servings.

Summer squash,

such as zucchini, yellow and pattypan, have thin, edible skins and soft seeds. Choose summer squash that are firm, brightly colored and free from spots and bruises. Generally, smaller squash are more tender.

Mandarin Pork and Wild Rice

Melanie Gable
ROSEVILLE, MICHIGAN

Mandarin oranges add a splash of color and refreshing citrus flavor to this tasty entree. It takes only a few minutes of prep to turn a handful of ingredients into a complete meal.

Mandarin Pork and Wild Rice

PREP/TOTAL TIME: 25 min.

- 4 boneless pork loin chops (3/4 inch thick and 5 ounces *each*), cut into strips
- 1/4 teaspoon pepper
- 1/8 teaspoon salt
- 1 tablespoon canola oil

- 1 can (11 ounces) mandarin oranges
- 1-1/2 cups water
- 1 package (6.2 ounces) fast-cooking long grain and wild rice mix
- 1/4 cup thinly sliced green onions

- ■ Sprinkle pork with pepper and salt. In a large skillet, brown pork in oil. Meanwhile, drain oranges, reserving juice; set oranges aside.

- ■ Add the water, rice mix with contents of seasoning packet, onions and reserved juice to the skillet. Bring to a boil. Reduce the heat; cover and simmer for 10-12 minutes or until meat is no longer pink and liquid is absorbed. Stir in oranges; heat through.

Yield: 4 servings.

Smoky Potato Skillet

PREP: 10 min.
COOK: 25 min.

- 1 package (16 ounces) smoked sausage links, cut into 1-inch pieces
- 2 celery ribs, chopped
- 1 medium onion, chopped
- 1 tablespoon butter
- 2 cups hot water
- 2/3 cup milk
- 1 package (4.9 ounces) au gratin potatoes

- ■ In a large skillet, saute sausage, celery and onion in butter until vegetables are tender. Stir in the water, milk and contents of sauce mix from potatoes.

- ■ Bring to a boil. Stir in the potatoes. Reduce heat; cover and simmer for 20-25 minutes or until the potatoes are tender, stirring once.

Yield: 4-6 servings.

To round out the Smoky Potato Skillet, simply stir in 1/2 to 1 cup of your favorite frozen vegetable (that has been thawed first) to the skillet 3-5 minutes before the dish is done cooking. You may want to try green peas, broccoli florets or sliced carrots.

Sue Ross
CASA GRANDE, ARIZONA

This robust dish is convenient because it uses only seven ingredients, including packaged au gratin potatoes. You can change the flavor by substituting a different-flavored mix, such as scalloped potatoes with sour cream and chives.

Theresa Moore
MANCELONA, MICHIGAN

This simple dish was inspired by a few pasta recipes I use. When I didn't have the ingredients on hand, I raided the refrigerator and cupboards and came up with this perfect meal.

Smoked Sausage with Penne and Veggies

Smoked Sausage with Penne and Veggies

PREP: 20 min. ■ **COOK:** 20 min.

- 8 ounces uncooked penne pasta
- 1 cup chopped green pepper
- 1/2 cup finely chopped onion
- 2 tablespoons olive oil
- 1 pound smoked sausage, cut into 1/2-inch slices
- 2 cans (14-1/2 ounces *each*) Italian stewed tomatoes
- 2 to 3 small zucchini, quartered lengthwise and sliced 1/2 inch thick
- 1/2 cup frozen corn
- 1/2 cup water
- 1 teaspoon salt
- 1 teaspoon dried basil
- 1 teaspoon minced garlic
- 1/2 teaspoon pepper
- Shredded Parmesan cheese, optional

■ Cook pasta according to package directions. Meanwhile, in a large skillet, saute green pepper and onion in oil until crisp-tender.

■ Add the sausage, tomatoes, zucchini, corn, water, salt, basil, garlic and pepper. Bring to a boil. Reduce heat; simmer, uncovered, for 5 minutes.

■ Drain pasta; toss with sausage mixture. Garnish with cheese if desired.

Yield: *5 servings.*

One-Dish Bratwurst Dinner

Cheryl Hartwell
AMES, NEBRASKA

This recipe easily doubles and the leftovers are great. For leftovers, reheat the brats separately from the vegetable and fruit mixture. I serve this dish at least twice a month. It's easy to prepare and there is no need for side dishes.

PREP: 10 min.
COOK: 35 min.

- 2 uncooked bratwurst links
- 1 small apple, cored and cut into 1/4-inch slices
- 1 small sweet onion, halved and cut into 1/4-inch slices
- 1 medium sweet potato, peeled, halved and cut into 1/4-inch slices
- 1/4 cup apple cider *or* juice

■ In a large skillet, cook the bratwurst over medium heat until browned; drain.

■ Add the apple, onion and sweet potato; pour cider over the top. Bring to a boil. Reduce heat; cover and simmer for 25 minutes or until brats are cooked and vegetables are tender.

Yield: 2 servings.

Chinese New Year Skillet

Sherilyn West
LUBBOCK, TEXAS
This tasty stir-fry was inspired by a recipe on the back of a rice package in 1957. If you like pork, I guarantee you'll love this sweet-and-sour recipe.

Chinese New Year Skillet

PREP: 15 min. ■ COOK: 25 min.

- 1 pound boneless pork butt roast, cut into 1/2-inch cubes
- 1 tablespoon canola oil
- 1 can (20 ounces) unsweetened pineapple tidbits
- 2 tablespoons white wine vinegar
- 1 tablespoon sugar
- 3/4 teaspoon salt

- 1/4 teaspoon garlic powder
- 1 cup uncooked long grain rice
- 1 tablespoon cornstarch
- 2 tablespoons water
- 1/2 cup coarsely chopped green pepper
- 1 medium tomato, cut into wedges
- 2 tablespoons Worcestershire sauce

■ In a large skillet, cook the pork in oil over medium heat on all sides until the pork is lightly browned; drain. Drain pineapple, reserving the juice in a 2-cup measuring cup; set the pineapple aside.

■ Add enough water to juice to measure 1-1/4 cups; stir into pork. Add vinegar, sugar, salt and garlic powder. Bring to a boil, stirring constantly. Reduce heat; cover and simmer for 20 minutes or until meat is tender. Meanwhile, cook rice according to package directions.

■ In a small bowl, combine cornstarch and water until smooth; stir into pork mixture. Bring to a boil; cook and stir for 2 minutes or until thickened. Stir in the green pepper, tomato, Worcestershire sauce and reserved pineapple; heat through. Serve with rice.

Yield: 4 servings.

Vinegar should be kept in a cool dark place. Unopened, it will keep indefinitely. But once opened, it can be stored for up to 6 months.

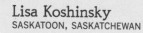

Lisa Koshinsky
SASKATOON, SASKATCHEWAN

There are loads of Asian-inspired flavors in this tasty dish. Soy sauce, fresh gingerroot, green onions and sesame oil help to create a delicious sauce. The pork tenderloin comes out tender, and the bok choy and fresh mango add a refreshing flavor.

Mango Pork Stir-Fry

PREP: 25 min. ■ COOK: 15 min.

2 tablespoons cornstarch

1/2 cup chicken broth

3 tablespoons soy sauce

1 small head bok choy

1 pound pork tenderloin, cut into thin strips

2 tablespoons canola oil, *divided*

1 garlic clove, minced

1 teaspoon minced fresh gingerroot

1/4 cup water

4 green onions, thinly sliced

1/4 teaspoon crushed red pepper flakes, optional

1 medium mango, peeled and cubed

1 teaspoon sesame oil

Hot cooked rice

■ In a small bowl, combine the cornstarch, broth and soy sauce until smooth; set aside.

■ Cut off and discard the root end of boy choy, leaving stalks with leaves. Cut enough leaves into 1-in. slices to measure 2 cups. Cut enough stalks into 1/2-in. pieces to measure 2 cups. Save the remaining bok choy for another use.

■ In a large skillet or wok, stir-fry pork in 1 tablespoon oil for 3-4 minutes or until no longer pink. Remove and keep warm.

■ Stir-fry bok choy stalks in remaining oil for 2 minutes. Add the garlic, ginger and bok choy leaves; stir-fry for 2 minutes. Add water and pepper flakes if desired; cook 2 minutes longer or until bok choy is crisp-tender.

■ Stir cornstarch mixture and add to the pan. Bring to a boil; cook and stir for 2 minutes or until thickened. Add green onions, mango and reserved pork; heat through. Stir in sesame oil. Serve with rice.

Yield: 4 servings.

To cube a mango, first wash it, then use a sharp knife to make a lengthwise cut along both sides of the long, flat seed. Remove each side of the fruit. Score each cut side of the fruit lengthwise and width- wise, without cutting through the skin. Using your hand, push the skin up, turning the fruit out. Cut the fruit off with a knife.

New England Boiled Dinner

Natalie Cook
SCARBOROUGH, MAINE

This has been a popular dinner among our family for a long time. When we moved to California in 1960, I'd make it often to remind us of New England. We're back home now and continue to enjoy this scrumptious dish.

PREP: 10 min.
COOK: 2 hours

1 smoked boneless pork shoulder butt roast (2 to 2-1/2 pounds)

1 pound fresh carrots, sliced lengthwise and halved

8 medium red potatoes. peeled and halved

2 medium onions, cut into quarters

1 large head cabbage, cut into quarters

1 large turnip, peeled and cut into quarters

1 large rutabaga, peeled, halved and sliced

■ Place pork roast in a large Dutch oven; cover with water. Bring to a boil. Reduce heat; cover and simmer for 1 hour.

■ Add the remaining ingredients; return to a boil. Reduce the heat. Cover and simmer for 1 hour or until the vegetables are tender; drain.

Yield: 8-10 servings.

Fish & Seafood

164

156

161

The beauty of creating a meal with fish and seafood is that it always cooks up fast, which is a dream come true for busy cooks! And not only are meals from this chapter a refreshing change from steak and potatoes, they offer a healthy flair, too!

- Cook the linguine according to package directions. Meanwhile, in a large nonstick skillet, saute the shrimp and mushrooms in oil for 2 minutes. Add the remaining ingredients; cook and stir for 5 minutes or until the shrimp turn pink and sauce is heated through.

- Drain the linguine; serve with the shrimp mixture.

Yield: 6 servings.

*Nutrition Facts: 1 cup shrimp mixture with 3/4 cup linguine equals 328 calories, 9 g fat (1 g saturated fat), 112 mg cholesterol, 748 mg sodium, 41 g carbohydrate, 3 g fiber, 21 g protein. **Diabetic Exchanges:** 2 starch, 2 very lean meat, 1-1/2 fat, 1 vegetable.

Mediterranean Shrimp and Linguine

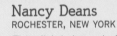

Nancy Deans
ROCHESTER, NEW YORK

This dish is lower in fat but so rich in vegetables, it looks like it came from an Italian restaurant. It's nice for a heart-healthy diet. For convenience, make ahead and reheat.

Mediterranean Shrimp and Linguine*

PREP/TOTAL TIME: 30 min.

9 ounces uncooked linguine

1 pound uncooked medium shrimp, peeled and deveined

1 cup sliced fresh mushrooms

2 tablespoons olive oil

3 medium tomatoes, chopped

1 can (14 ounces) water-packed artichoke hearts, rinsed, drained and halved

1 can (6 ounces) pitted ripe olives, drained and halved

2 garlic cloves, minced

1 teaspoon dried oregano

1/2 teaspoon dried basil

1/2 teaspoon salt

1/8 teaspoon pepper

When a recipe calls for a clove of garlic and you have no fresh bulbs, substitute 1/4 teaspoon of garlic powder for each clove. Next time you're grocery shopping, look for convenient jars of fresh minced garlic in the produce section. Use 1/2 teaspoon of minced garlic for each clove.

Norma Reynolds
OVERLAND PARK, KANSAS

One night, with shrimp already thawed, I realized there weren't enough spices in my pantry for another recipe, and created this impressive, healthy dish on the spot!

Spiced Shrimp Boil

Spiced Shrimp Boil

PREP: 20 min. ■ COOK: 1 hour

1	medium lemon, halved
2-1/2	pounds medium red potatoes (about 10), quartered
1	teaspoon ground coriander
1	teaspoon cayenne pepper
1/8	teaspoon ground allspice
1/8	teaspoon ground cloves
15	whole peppercorns
4	garlic cloves, peeled and halved
4	bay leaves
2	teaspoons mustard seed
1/2	teaspoon dill seed
4	celery ribs, halved
1	bunch parsley
2	medium onions, cut into wedges
5	quarts cold water
3	medium ears sweet corn, husked and cut into 2-inch pieces
1-1/2	pounds uncooked shell-on jumbo shrimp
1	teaspoon salt

■ Squeeze juice from lemon halves into a large bowl; add the lemon and potatoes to bowl. Sprinkle with coriander, cayenne, allspice and cloves; toss to coat. Set aside.

■ Place peppercorns, garlic, bay leaves, mustard seed and dill seed on a double thickness of cheesecloth; bring up corners of cloth and tie with string to form a bag. Place the spice bag, celery, parsley and onions in a soup kettle; add water. Bring to a boil; cover and boil for 15 minutes.

■ Strain, reserving liquid and spice bag. Discard parsley and vegetables. Return cooking liquid with spice bag to the heat; carefully add potato mixture. Bring to a boil. Reduce heat; simmer, uncovered, for 15 minutes. Add corn; simmer 15-20 minutes longer or until potatoes and corn are tender.

■ Stir in shrimp; cook for 3 minutes or until shrimp turn pink. Drain; discard spice bag and lemon. Transfer shrimp mixture to a large serving bowl. Sprinkle with salt and toss to coat.

Yield: 6 servings.

An easy way to remove the silk from corn cobs is to use a crumpled paper towel to gently brush the silk from corn. This method works better than a vegetable brush, which can be abrasive to the kernels.

Sweet-and-Sour Scallops

Tonya Michelle Burkhard
ENGLEWOOD, FLORIDA

Although it's pretty enough to be from a restaurant, this dish is filled with homemade flavor and puts a delicious twist on a classic. The tender scallops practically melt in your mouth.

Sweet-and-Sour Scallops

PREP/TOTAL TIME: 20 min.

2 cans (8 ounces *each*) pineapple chunks	1/4 cup sugar
1 pound sea scallops (about 16)	2 tablespoons cornstarch
1 tablespoon canola oil	1/2 teaspoon ground mustard
1/3 cup chopped onion	1/4 teaspoon salt
1/3 cup julienned green pepper	1/2 cup white vinegar
1/4 cup butter, cubed	2 tablespoons soy sauce
	2/3 cup cherry tomatoes, halved

■ Drain the pineapple, reserving juice; set pineapple and juice aside. In a large skillet, saute scallops in oil until firm and opaque; drain. Remove from pan and keep warm.

■ In the same pan, saute the onion and green pepper in butter for 3-4 minutes or until crisp-tender.

■ Meanwhile, in a small bowl, combine the sugar, cornstarch, ground mustard and salt. Whisk in the vinegar, soy sauce and reserved pineapple juice until smooth.

■ Gradually stir into pan. Bring to a boil; cook and stir for 2 minutes or until thickened. Stir in the tomatoes, scallops and reserved pineapple; heat through.

Yield: 4 servings.

Sea scallops are about 1-1/2 inches in diameter, whereas bay scallops are about 1/2 inch in diameter. Sea scallops are more available and affordable than bays, and come to about 30 per pound. Look for ones that are pale beige to creamy pink in color.

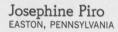

Josephine Piro
EASTON, PENNSYLVANIA

This meal-in-one is both time-saving and nutritious. The fish is deliciously seasoned with lemon-pepper, garlic powder, thyme and cayenne. The sauce, which is made with red pepper, tomatoes, olives and chives, is fresh and colorful.

Mediterranean-Style Red Snapper*

PREP/TOTAL TIME: 30 min.

1 teaspoon lemon-pepper seasoning
1/2 teaspoon garlic powder
1/2 teaspoon dried thyme
1/8 teaspoon cayenne pepper
4 red snapper fillets (6 ounces *each*)
2 teaspoons olive oil, *divided*
1/2 medium sweet red pepper, julienned
3 green onions, chopped
1 garlic clove, minced
1 can (14-1/2 ounces) diced tomatoes, undrained
1/2 cup chopped pimiento-stuffed olives
1/4 cup chopped ripe olives
1/4 cup minced fresh chives

■ Combine the lemon-pepper, garlic powder, thyme and cayenne; rub over fillets. In a large nonstick skillet coated with cooking spray, cook fillets in 1 teaspoon oil over medium heat for 4-5 minutes on each side or until fish flakes easily with a fork. Remove and keep warm.

■ In the same pan, saute the red pepper, onions and garlic in remaining oil until crisp-tender. Stir in tomatoes. Bring to a boil. Reduce heat; simmer, uncovered, for 3 minutes or until liquid has evaporated. Serve with snapper. Sprinkle with olives and chives.

Yield: 4 servings.

✳ Nutrition Facts: 1 serving (1 fillet with 1/3 cup tomato mixture and 3 tablespoons olives) equals 258 calories, 9 g fat (1 g saturated fat), 60 mg cholesterol, 754 mg sodium, 10 g carbohydrate, 3 g fiber, 35 g protein. **Diabetic Exchanges:** 5 very lean meat, 1-1/2 fat, 1 vegetable.

Overcooked fish loses its flavor and becomes tough. As a general guideline, fish is cooked 10 minutes for every inch of thickness. For fish fillets, check for doneness by inserting a fork at an angle into the thickest portion of the fish and gently parting the meat. When it is opaque and flakes into sections, it is cooked.

Skillet Fish With Spinach

PREP/TOTAL TIME: 25 min.

Taste of Home Test Kitchen
GREENDALE, WISCONSIN

Tender fish fillets get a burst of flavor from seafood seasoning and a dash of salt and pepper. Paired with dressed-up spinach, this simple main course from our Test Kitchen is sure to impress!

4 orange roughy fillets (4 ounces *each*)
1-1/2 teaspoons seafood seasoning
2 tablespoons olive oil
2 tablespoons butter
1 cup sliced fresh mushrooms
1 package (10 ounces) frozen chopped spinach, thawed and squeezed dry
1/2 cup chicken broth
Salt and pepper to taste

■ Sprinkle the fillets with the seafood seasoning. In a large skillet, cook the fillets in oil and butter over medium heat for 3-4 minutes on each side or until fish flakes easily with a fork. Remove and keep warm.

■ Add mushrooms to the skillet; cook, uncovered, for 2 minutes or until tender. Add the spinach and broth; cook 3-4 minutes longer or until the spinach is heated through. Season with salt and pepper, and serve with fish fillets.

Yield: 4 servings.

Weeknight Jambalaya

- In a large saucepan coated with cooking spray, brown chicken in 1-1/2 teaspoons oil. Add sausage and ham; cook and stir for 2 minutes or until browned and chicken is no longer pink. Remove and keep warm.

- In the same pan, saute the onion, green pepper and celery in remaining oil until tender. Add chilies and garlic; cook 1 minute longer. Stir in the tomato sauce, tomatoes, water, tomato paste, Cajun seasoning and cayenne. Bring to a boil. Reduce heat; cover and simmer for 5 minutes.

- Stir in shrimp and reserved chicken mixture; heat through. Serve with rice.

Yield: 6 servings.

Debra Marshall
SAINT LOUIS, MISSOURI

This is a great way to use up leftovers. You can mix and match any or all the meats. Feel free to leave out what you don't like and adjust the chilies and cayenne to taste.

Weeknight Jambalaya

PREP: 20 min. ■ **COOK:** 25 min.

1/4 pound boneless skinless chicken breast, cubed

3 teaspoons canola oil, *divided*

1/4 pound smoked turkey sausage, halved lengthwise and sliced

1/4 pound cubed fully cooked lean ham

1 large onion, chopped

1 medium green pepper, chopped

1 celery rib, chopped

2 tablespoons chopped green chilies

2 garlic cloves, minced

2 cans (8 ounces *each*) no-salt-added tomato sauce

1 can (14-1/2 ounces) no-salt-added diced tomatoes, undrained

1/3 cup water

3 tablespoons tomato paste

2 teaspoons Cajun seasoning

1/4 teaspoon cayenne pepper

1/2 pound deveined peeled cooked medium shrimp

3 cups hot cooked rice

Look for Cajun seasoning in the spice section of your grocery store. You can also make your own Cajun seasoning. Although there are many different blends, a typical mix includes salt, onion powder, garlic powder, cayenne pepper, ground mustard, celery seed and pepper.

Renae Rossow
UNION, KENTUCKY

This rich, creamy pasta dish with three types of seafood comes together in just a few minutes. When I serve it to guests, they say I shouldn't have worked so hard. I never tell them what a breeze it is to assemble.

Alfredo Seafood Fettuccine

Alfredo Seafood Fettuccine

PREP/TOTAL TIME: 20 min.

8 ounces uncooked fettuccine

1 envelope Alfredo sauce mix

1 package (8 ounces) imitation crabmeat

6 ounces bay scallops

6 ounces uncooked medium shrimp, peeled and deveined

1 tablespoon plus 1-1/2 teaspoons butter

1/8 to 1/4 teaspoon garlic powder

■ Cook fettuccine according to package directions. Meanwhile, prepare Alfredo sauce according to package directions.

■ In a large skillet, saute the crab, scallops and shrimp in butter for 2-3 minutes or until scallops are opaque and shrimp turn pink. Stir into Alfredo sauce. Season with garlic powder. Cook and stir for 5-6 minutes or until thickened. Drain fettuccine; top with seafood mixture.

Yield: 4 servings.

Chinese Fish*

PREP/TOTAL TIME: 15 min.

Ruth Solyntjes
WATERVILLE, MINNESOTA

A friend of Chinese descent gave me this recipe for flavorful fish. She didn't know U.S. measurements, so I'd hold up a plastic teaspoon and ask, "How much?" for each ingredient she used.

4 orange roughy fillets (6 ounces *each*)

1 tablespoon canola oil

1 cup water

1/3 cup sliced green onions

2 teaspoons cider vinegar

2 teaspoons reduced-sodium soy sauce

2 garlic cloves, minced

1/2 teaspoon Chinese five-spice powder

1/8 teaspoon crushed red pepper flakes

1/4 teaspoon salt

1/4 teaspoon ground ginger *or* 1 teaspoon minced fresh gingerroot

1/2 teaspoon sesame oil

■ In a large nonstick skillet, cook fish in canola oil for 2 minutes. Turn and cook 2 minutes longer. Add the next nine ingredients. Cover and simmer for 4 minutes or until fish flakes easily with a fork. Sprinkle with sesame oil.

Yield: 4 servings.

*Nutrition Facts: One serving equals 160 calories, 5 g fat (trace saturated fat), 34 mg cholesterol, 355 mg sodium, 2 g carbohydrate, trace fiber, 25 g protein. **Diabetic Exchange:** 3 lean meat.

Garlic-Shrimp Angel Hair

PREP/TOTAL TIME: 25 min.

Robbie Haferkamp
ENGLEWOOD, OHIO

This filling meal is sure to impress. The creamy sauce for the broccoli, pasta and seafood is delicious.

- 8 ounces uncooked angel hair pasta
- 3 tablespoons butter, *divided*
- 4-1/2 teaspoons all-purpose flour
- 2 cups half-and-half cream
- 1/4 cup grated Parmesan cheese
- 2 tablespoons prepared pesto sauce
- 2 tablespoons minced garlic, *divided*
- 1 teaspoon Worcestershire sauce
- 1 teaspoon hot pepper sauce
- 1/2 teaspoon salt
- 1/4 teaspoon pepper
- 2 cups fresh broccoli florets
- 1 pound uncooked medium shrimp, peeled and deveined

■ Cook the pasta according to the package directions. Meanwhile, in a large saucepan, melt 4-1/2 teaspoons butter over medium heat. Stir in flour until smooth. Gradually add cream. Bring to a boil; cook and stir for 2 minutes or until thickened.

■ Stir in the cheese, pesto sauce, 1 tablespoon garlic, Worcestershire sauce, hot pepper sauce, salt and pepper. Keep warm over low heat.

■ In a large skillet, saute broccoli in remaining butter for 5 minutes. Add shrimp and remaining garlic; cook and stir until shrimp turn pink. Stir in the cream sauce. Drain pasta; add to shrimp mixture and toss to coat.

Yield: 4 servings.

Broccoli comes from the Latin word "brachium," which means branch or arm. When purchasing broccoli, look for bunches that have a deep green color, tightly closed buds and crisp leaves. Store in a resealable plastic bag in the refrigerator for up to 4 days. Wash just before using. One pound of broccoli yields about 2 cups florets.

Crawfish Etouffee

PREP: 15 min.
COOK: 20 min.

- 1 medium onion, finely chopped
- 1 medium green pepper, finely chopped
- 1 celery rib, finely chopped
- 1/2 cup butter, cubed
- 4 garlic cloves, minced
- 1 can (10-3/4 ounces) condensed cream of celery soup, undiluted
- 3 teaspoons paprika
- 1 teaspoon Creole seasoning
- 1 pound frozen cooked crawfish tail meat, thawed
- 2 cups hot cooked rice

■ In a large saucepan, saute the onion, green pepper and celery in butter for 3 minutes. Add garlic. Reduce heat to medium; cook 5-7 minutes longer or until vegetables are tender.

■ Stir in the soup, paprika and Creole seasoning. Bring to a boil. Reduce heat; simmer, uncovered, for 5 minutes. Stir in crawfish; heat through. Serve with rice.

Yield: 4 servings.

Editor's Note: The following spices may be substituted for 1 teaspoon Creole seasoning: 1/4 teaspoon *each* salt, garlic powder and paprika; and a pinch *each* of dried thyme, ground cumin and cayenne pepper.

Crawdad Days Music Festival
HARRISON, ARKANSAS

Folks stand in line at the Crawdad Days festival for this hearty Cajun favorite made with aromatic vegetables and crawfish that are smothered in a buttery, savory sauce. After one bite of this classic stew, you'll feel like you're down on the Bayou.

Laurie LaClair
NORTH RICHLAND HILLS, TEXAS
Being a home-grown Texan, I love spicy foods and the fresh flavor of cilantro. I created this unique Southwestern version of shrimp scampi from my own kitchen.

Scampi Adobo

Scampi Adobo*

PREP/TOTAL TIME: 30 min.

- 2 plum tomatoes, seeded and chopped
- 1 poblano pepper, seeded and chopped
- 1 tablespoon minced chipotle pepper in adobo sauce
- 3 garlic cloves, minced
- 1 tablespoon olive oil
- 1 pound uncooked medium shrimp, peeled and deveined
- 1/2 cup white wine *or* reduced-sodium chicken broth
- 1/3 cup minced fresh cilantro
- 3 tablespoons lime juice
- 2 tablespoons reduced-fat butter
- 1/2 teaspoon salt
- 1/4 cup shredded part-skim mozzarella cheese
- Lime slices, optional

■ In a large nonstick skillet, saute the tomatoes, peppers and garlic in oil for 2 minutes. Reduce heat to medium; stir in the shrimp, wine or broth, cilantro, lime juice, butter and salt. Cook and stir for 3-4 minutes or until shrimp turn pink.

■ Remove from the heat; sprinkle with mozzarella cheese. Garnish with lime slices if desired.

Yield: 4 servings.

*Nutrition Facts: 3/4 cup equals 196 calories, 9 g fat (3 g saturated fat), 182 mg cholesterol, 562 mg sodium, 5 g carbohydrate, 1 g fiber, 21 g protein. **Diabetic Exchanges:** 3 very lean meat, 1-1/2 fat.

Editor's Note: This recipe was tested with Land O'Lakes light stick butter.

Tuna Veggie Macaroni

Al Robbins
CHANDLER, ARIZONA
After much experimenting with various versions of the same dish, it all boiled down to this super delicious recipe. My family can't get enough of it.

PREP/TOTAL TIME: 25 min.

- 1-1/4 cups uncooked elbow macaroni
- 5 ounces process cheese (Velveeta), cubed
- 1/2 cup milk
- 2 cups frozen peas and carrots, thawed
- 1 can (6 ounces) solid white tuna, drained
- 1/4 teaspoon dill weed

■ Cook the macaroni according to package directions; drain. Add the cheese and milk; stir until the cheese is melted. Stir in vegetables, tuna and dill; heat through.

Yield: 3 servings.

When stacking

non-stick skillets on cupboard shelves, place a paper towel or paper plate between each to prevent scratches. This prolongs the life of the skillets.

Shrimp 'n' Noodle Bowls

Mary Bergfeld
EUGENE, OREGON

This is a great quick meal that can be made with convenient ingredients from the grocery store. Cooked shrimp and bagged slaw reduce the time required to get it on the table.

Shrimp 'n' Noodle Bowls*

PREP/TOTAL TIME: 25 min.

8 ounces uncooked angel hair pasta
1 pound cooked small shrimp
2 cups broccoli coleslaw mix
6 green onions, thinly sliced
1/2 cup minced fresh cilantro
2/3 cup reduced-fat sesame ginger salad dressing

■ Cook pasta according to package directions; drain and rinse in cold water. Transfer to a large bowl. Add the shrimp, coleslaw mix, onions and cilantro. Drizzle with dressing; toss to coat. Cover and refrigerate until serving.

Yield: 6 servings.

*Nutrition Facts: 1-1/3 cups equals 260 calories, 3 g fat (trace saturated fat), 147 mg cholesterol, 523 mg sodium, 36 g carbohydrate, 2 g fiber, 22 g protein. Diabetic Exchanges: 2 starch, 2 very lean meat, 1/2 fat.

Trout Amandine

Bonnie Sue Greene
MESA, COLORADO

I catch wonderful trout in my town, and this recipe is a simple yet delectable way to prepare it.

PREP/TOTAL TIME: 30 min.

4 pan-dressed trout (about 1 pound *each*)
2 teaspoons salt
1/2 teaspoon pepper
2 eggs
1/2 cup half-and-half cream
1/2 cup all-purpose flour
1/2 cup slivered almonds
3 tablespoons butter, *divided*
3 to 4 tablespoons lemon juice
1/2 teaspoon dried tarragon
1/4 cup olive oil

■ In the cavity of each trout, sprinkle salt and pepper. Beat eggs and cream in a shallow bowl. Dip trout in egg mixture, then roll in flour. In a small skillet over low heat, saute the almonds in 2 tablespoons butter until lightly browned. Add lemon juice and tarragon; heat through. Remove from the heat and keep warm.

■ Meanwhile, in a skillet over medium heat, combine oil and remaining butter. Fry the trout for 8-10 minutes; carefully turn and fry 8 minutes longer or until it flakes easily with a fork. Top with almond mixture.

Yield: 4 servings.

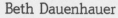

Beth Dauenhauer
PUEBLO, COLORADO

I like to serve this yummy pasta dish with a colorful vegetable side dish, such as a tomato salad or peas and carrots. The lemon juice and zest adds a refreshing flavor, and the sauce is rich and creamy. The recipe is equally good with canned salmon or tuna, too.

Tortellini with Salmon-Ricotta Sauce*

PREP/TOTAL TIME: 30 min.

- 1 package (9 ounces) refrigerated cheese tortellini
- 2 green onions, sliced
- 2 garlic cloves, minced
- 1 teaspoon butter
- 1 teaspoon cornstarch
- 1 cup fat-free milk
- 1/2 cup shredded part-skim mozzarella cheese
- 1 cup fat-free ricotta cheese
- 1 pouch (7.1 ounces) boneless skinless pink salmon
- 2 tablespoons snipped fresh dill or 2 teaspoons dill weed
- 1-1/2 teaspoons grated lemon peel
- 1-1/2 teaspoons lemon juice
- 1/4 teaspoon salt

■ Cook tortellini according to package directions. Meanwhile, in a large saucepan, saute onions and garlic in butter until tender. Combine cornstarch and milk until smooth; gradually stir into the pan. Bring to a boil; cook and stir for 2 minutes or until slightly thickened.

■ Stir in mozzarella cheese until melted. Stir in the ricotta cheese, salmon, dill, lemon peel, lemon juice and salt.

■ Drain tortellini; add to ricotta sauce. Cook and stir until heated through.

Yield: 4 servings.

*Nutrition Facts: 1 cup equals 373 calories, 11 g fat (6 g saturated fat), 67 mg cholesterol, 797 mg sodium, 40 g carbohydrate, 2 g fiber, 28 g protein. Diabetic Exchanges: 3 lean meat, 2-1/2 starch, 1/2 fat.

If you have fresh herbs, to prevent from wasting any extras, just freeze. Place the chopped herbs in freezer containers or bags, freeze and use the amount you need directly from the freezer.

Fish with Florentine Rice

Margrit Eagen
CRESTWOOD, MISSOURI

A handful of ingredients is all you'll need to prepare this speedy skillet supper. The entire dinner conveniently cooks in one pan and eliminates the hassle of breading and frying the fish.

PREP/TOTAL TIME: 25 min.

- 1 package (6.9 ounces) chicken-flavored rice mix
- 2 tablespoons butter
- 2-3/4 cups water
- 1 package (10 ounces) frozen chopped spinach
- 1 pound orange roughy or tilapia fillets
- 1/4 cup slivered almonds, toasted

■ Set the rice seasoning packet aside. In a large skillet, saute rice mix in butter. Add the water, spinach and contents of seasoning packet. Bring to a boil. Reduce heat; cover and simmer for 10 minutes. Top with the fish fillets.

■ Cover and simmer for 5-10 minutes or until the fish flakes easily with a fork. Sprinkle with the almonds.

Yield: 4 servings.

OVEN ENTREES

Beef & Ground Beef

183

175

172

Hearty beef entrees are a must in a busy cook's recipe collection because of their reliability. You'll find tasty new twists on classics such as pot roast and beefy baked pasta dishes, plus robust, family-friendly casseroles that make cooking oh-so easy!

Supreme Pizza Casserole

- Cook fettuccine according to package directions. Meanwhile, in a Dutch oven, cook beef and onion over medium heat until meat is no longer pink; drain. Stir in the mushrooms, tomato sauce, pizza sauce, tomato paste, sugar and seasonings. Drain the pasta and stir into meat sauce.

- Divide half of the mixture between two greased 2-qt. baking dishes; sprinkle each with 1 cup mozzarella cheese. Repeat layers. Top each with pepperoni and Parmesan cheese.

- Cover casseroles and bake at 350° for 20 minutes. Uncover; bake 10-15 minutes longer or until heated through.

Yield: 2 casseroles (8 servings each).

Nancy Foust
STONEBORO, PENNSYLVANIA

I like to take these hearty casseroles to busy potlucks, where they are always popular. The flavor tastes like a pizza, but with a lot less work.

Supreme Pizza Casserole

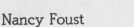

PREP: 20 min. ■ BAKE: 30 min.

8 ounces uncooked fettuccine	1/2 teaspoon sugar
2 pounds ground beef	1/2 teaspoon garlic powder
1 medium onion, chopped	1/2 teaspoon onion powder
2 cans (8 ounces *each*) mushroom stems and pieces, drained	1/2 teaspoon dried oregano
	4 cups (16 ounces) shredded part-skim mozzarella cheese, *divided*
1 can (15 ounces) tomato sauce	1 package (3-1/2 ounces) sliced pepperoni
1 jar (14 ounces) pizza sauce	1/2 cup grated Parmesan cheese
1 can (6 ounces) tomato paste	

To transport a casserole dish to a potluck dinner, put the dish inside a clear plastic oven bag. Just slide the dish in and seal with a twist tie. The bag won't melt, it catches spills and organizers can see what's inside.

Brenda Hlivyak
LA CENTER, WASHINGTON

This tender and juicy roast looks beautiful when I serve it to guests. It also creates a wonderful aroma as it cooks. I usually serve it with warm French bread and a salad topped with buttermilk dressing, but hot dinner rolls and your favorite vegetable works fine, too.

Rosemary-Garlic Roast Beef

PREP: 15 min. ■ **BAKE:** 40 min.

- 4 garlic cloves, minced
- 1 tablespoon dried rosemary, crushed
- 1 teaspoon salt
- 1/2 teaspoon pepper
- 1 beef tri-tip roast (2 to 3 pounds)
- 4-1/2 teaspoons olive oil
- 12 small red potatoes, quartered
- 2 medium sweet yellow peppers, cut into 1-inch pieces
- 1 large sweet onion, cut into 1-inch slices

■ Combine the garlic, rosemary, salt and pepper; set aside 4 teaspoons. Rub the remaining mixture over roast and place in a greased shallow roasting pan.

■ In a small bowl, whisk reserved herb mixture with oil. In a large resealable plastic bag, combine the potatoes, yellow peppers and onion; add oil mixture. Seal bag and toss to coat. Arrange vegetables around roast.

■ Bake, uncovered, at 425° for 30-60 minutes or until meat reaches desired doneness (for medium-rare, a meat thermometer should read 145°; medium, 160°; well-done, 170°).

■ Transfer roast and peppers to a warm serving platter. Let stand for 10-15 minutes before slicing. Meanwhile, return potatoes and onion to the oven; bake 10 minutes longer or until potatoes are tender.

Yield: 6 servings.

To reheat leftover pot roast, slice the meat and place it in a baking dish. Then pour the leftover pan juices over the meat, adding extra beef broth if needed to cover. Cover the pan with aluminum foil and bake at 325° only until heated through. This helps retain any moisture without overcooking or drying out the meat.

Cheeseburger And Fries Casserole

Karen Owen
RISING SUN, INDIANA

Kids love this dish because it combines burger and fries, two of their favorite fast foods. And I like the fact that I can whip it up with just four ingredients.

PREP: 10 min.
BAKE: 50 min.

- 2 pounds lean ground beef
- 1 can (10-3/4 ounces) condensed golden mushroom soup, undiluted
- 1 can (10-3/4 ounces) condensed cheddar cheese soup, undiluted
- 1 package (20 ounces) frozen crinkle-cut French fries

■ In a large skillet, cook the beef over medium heat until no longer pink; drain. Stir in the soups. Pour into a greased 13-in. x 9-in. baking dish.

■ Arrange French fries on top. Bake, uncovered, at 350° for 50-55 minutes or until the fries are golden brown.

Yield: 6-8 servings.

Beef 'n' Sausage Lasagna

- In a large skillet, cook the beef, sausage, green pepper and onion over medium heat until the meat is no longer pink; drain. Set aside 1 cup spaghetti sauce; stir remaining sauce into meat mixture. Simmer the meat sauce, uncovered, for 10 minutes or until thickened.

- In a small saucepan, melt cream cheese over medium heat. Remove from the heat. Stir in cottage cheese, eggs and minced parsley.

- Spread the meat sauce in a greased 13-in. x 9-in. baking dish. Top with three noodles, cheddar cheese, 1-1/2 teaspoons Italian seasoning and cream cheese mixture. Layer with remaining noodles and reserved spaghetti sauce; sprinkle with the mozzarella and remaining Italian seasoning.

- Cover and bake at 350° for 35 minutes. Uncover; bake 10-15 minutes more or until bubbly. Let lasagna stand 15 minutes before serving.

Yield: 12 servings.

Eydee Bernier
LOUISVILLE, KENTUCKY

Here's a traditional lasagna with a dash of imagination. I make it unique by using cream cheese and white cheddar, and by layering the meat on the bottom and cheese on top.

Beef 'n' Sausage Lasagna

PREP: 45 min. ■ **BAKE:** 45 min. + standing

- 1 pound ground beef
- 1 pound bulk Italian sausage
- 1 medium green pepper, chopped
- 1 medium onion, chopped
- 1 jar (26 ounces) spaghetti sauce
- 1 package (8 ounces) cream cheese, cubed
- 1 cup (8 ounces) 4% cottage cheese
- 2 eggs, lightly beaten
- 1 tablespoon minced fresh parsley
- 6 lasagna noodles, cooked and drained
- 2 cups (8 ounces) shredded white cheddar cheese
- 3 teaspoons Italian seasoning, *divided*
- 2 cups (8 ounces) shredded part-skim mozzarella cheese

When a recipe in a Taste of Home publication calls for Italian sausage, it is referring to sweet Italian sausage. Recipes using hot Italian sausage call for that type of sausage.

Quick Tater Tot Bake

Jean Ferguson
ELVERTA, CALIFORNIA

I like to make this dish when time before supper is short. It serves two to three people, but if we have unexpected company I double the ingredients and use a 9-in. x 13-in. pan. I call it my "Please Stay Casserole!"

PREP: 10 min.
BAKE: 30 min.

- 3/4 to 1 pound ground beef *or* turkey
- 1 small onion, chopped

Salt and pepper to taste

- 1 package (16 ounces) frozen Tater Tot potatoes
- 1 can (10-3/4 ounces) condensed cream of mushroom soup, undiluted
- 2/3 cup milk *or* water
- 1 cup (4 ounces) shredded cheddar cheese

- ■ In a large skillet, cook beef and onion over medium heat until no longer pink; drain. Season with salt and pepper.

- ■ Transfer to a greased 2-qt. baking dish. Top with potatoes. Combine soup and milk; pour over potatoes. Sprinkle with cheese. Bake, uncovered, at 350° for 30-40 minutes or until heated through.

Yield: 2-3 servings.

Rhonda Hampton
COOKEVILLE, TENNESSEE

My family loves garlic, so the more there is in a dish, the better. This mouthwatering recipe is requested for Sunday dinner every other week.

Garlic Pot Roast

Garlic Pot Roast

PREP: 20 min. ■ **BAKE:** 2-1/2 hours

- 1 boneless beef chuck roast (3 pounds)
- 4 garlic cloves, peeled and halved
- 3 teaspoons garlic powder
- 3 teaspoons Italian salad dressing mix
- 1/2 teaspoon pepper
- 1 tablespoon canola oil
- 3 cups water
- 1 envelope onion soup mix
- 1 teaspoon reduced-sodium beef bouillon granules
- 5 medium potatoes, peeled and quartered
- 1 pound fresh baby carrots
- 1 large onion, cut into 1-inch pieces

- ■ Using the point of a sharp knife, make eight slits in the roast. Insert garlic into slits. Combine the garlic powder, salad dressing mix and pepper; rub over roast. In a Dutch oven, brown roast in oil on all sides; drain.

- ■ Combine the water, onion soup mix and bouillon; pour over roast. Cover and bake at 325° for 1-1/2 hours.

- ■ Add the potatoes, carrots and onion. Cover and bake 1 hour longer or until meat and vegetables are tender. Thicken pan juices if desired.

Yield: 8 servings.

Winter Day Dinner

Linda Hagedorn
ROCKVILLE, MARYLAND

In the middle of winter, I often rely on this recipe to warm us up! My husband doesn't care much for noodles, so I look for different ways to serve potatoes.

PREP: 25 min. ■ **BAKE:** 30 min.

1-1/2 pounds ground beef	**CHEESE SAUCE:**
1 medium onion, chopped	1/4 cup butter, cubed
2 tablespoons Worcestershire sauce	1/3 cup all-purpose flour
1 teaspoon salt	1/2 teaspoon salt
1/2 teaspoon pepper	1/4 teaspoon pepper
8 medium potatoes, sliced	2 cups milk
1 package (16 ounces) frozen peas, thawed	4 ounces process cheese (Velveeta), cubed

■ In a large skillet, cook the beef and onion over medium heat until the beef is no longer pink; drain. Stir in the Worcestershire sauce, salt and pepper.

■ In a greased 13-in. x 9-in. baking dish, layer with half of the potatoes, meat mixture, peas and remaining potatoes; set aside.

■ For sauce, in a large saucepan, melt butter over medium heat. Stir in the flour, salt and pepper until smooth. Gradually stir in milk. Bring to a boil; cook and stir for 2 minutes or until thickened. Stir in cheese until melted. Pour over potatoes.

■ Cover and bake at 350° for 1-1/2 hours or until the potatoes are tender.

Yield: 8 servings.

When buying potatoes, look for those that are firm and free of blemishes. Avoid potatoes that are wrinkled, cracked or sprouting. If kept in a well-ventilated, cool, dark place, potatoes will keep for up to 2 weeks.

Broccoli Beef Braids

PREP/TOTAL TIME: 30 min.

1 pound ground beef
1/2 cup chopped onion
3 cups frozen chopped broccoli
1 cup (4 ounces) shredded part-skim mozzarella cheese
1/2 cup sour cream
1/4 teaspoon salt
1/4 teaspoon pepper
2 tubes (8 ounces *each*) refrigerated crescent rolls

■ In a large skillet, cook the beef and onion over medium heat until meat is no longer pink; drain. Add the broccoli, cheese, sour cream, salt and pepper; heat through.

■ Unroll one tube of dough on a greased baking sheet; seal the seams and perforations, forming a 12-in. x 8-in. rectangle. Spread half of beef mixture lengthwise down the center. On each side, cut 1-in.-wide strips 3 in. into center.

■ Starting at one end, fold alternating strips at an angle across filling; seal ends. Repeat. Bake at 350° for 15-20 minutes or until golden brown.

Yield: 2 loaves (8 servings each).

Penny Lapp
NORTH ROYALTON, OHIO

Each slice of this fast-to-fix and golden bread is like a hot sandwich packed with beef, mozzarella and broccoli. Served with a green salad, the braid-shaped loaf makes a great lunch or dinner. If you want something easy to make for football game parties, this recipe fits the bill.

Meat and Potato Pie

Helen Ellingson
SWAN RIVER, MANITOBA

When I was working full-time, this hearty beef pie was always a favorite of my family. Now that I'm retired, I still rely on this sure-to-please recipe.

Meat and Potato Pie

PREP: 35 min. ■ BAKE: 30 min.

2 tablespoons shortening
1-1/2 cups biscuit/baking mix
3 to 4 tablespoons cold water

FILLING:

1-1/2 pounds ground beef
1 medium onion, chopped
1 can (10-3/4 ounces) condensed cream of mushroom soup, undiluted
1/2 teaspoon salt
1/2 teaspoon dried rosemary, crushed
1/2 teaspoon dried thyme
1 can (15 ounces) sliced carrots, drained
1 can (8 ounces) mushroom stems and pieces, drained
2 cups hot mashed potatoes (prepared with milk and butter)
1/2 cup sour cream
1/2 cup shredded cheddar cheese

■ In a small bowl, cut shortening into biscuit mix until the mixture resembles coarse crumbs. Add the water, 1 tablespoon at a time, tossing lightly with a fork until dough forms a ball.

■ On a lightly floured surface, roll out the pastry to fit a 9-in. pie plate. Line ungreased pie plate with pastry; trim and flute edges or make a decorative edge. Set aside.

■ For filling, in a large skillet, cook beef and onion over medium heat until meat is no longer pink; drain. Stir in soup and seasonings; bring to a boil. Reduce heat; simmer, uncovered, for 5 minutes.

■ Pour into pie shell. Top with carrots and mushrooms. Combine potatoes and sour cream; spread over pie. Bake, uncovered, at 425° for 15 minutes. Reduce heat to 350°. Bake 15 minutes longer or until golden brown. Sprinkle with cheese; let stand for 5-10 minutes.

Yield: 6 servings.

Shortening is

100% vegetable oil that is solid at room temperature. It's commonly sold under the brand names Crisco and Spree. When making biscuits or pie crusts, use a grid-style potato masher to easily cut the shortening into the dry ingredients.

Linda McGinty
PARMA, OHIO

This fork-tender steak with rich gravy was often requested when I was growing up. Mom took pride in preparing scrumptious, hearty meals like this for family and guests.

So-Tender Swiss Steak

So-Tender Swiss Steak

PREP: 30 min. ■ **BAKE:** 2 hours

1/4 cup all-purpose flour
1/2 teaspoon salt
1/4 teaspoon pepper
  2 pounds beef top round steak, cut into serving-size pieces
  2 tablespoons canola oil
  1 medium onion, thinly sliced
  2 cups water
  2 tablespoons Worcestershire sauce

GRAVY:
  1/4 cup all-purpose flour
  1/4 teaspoon salt
  1/8 teaspoon pepper
1-1/4 cups beef broth *or* water

Hot cooked noodles *or* mashed potatoes, optional

■ In a large resealable plastic bag, combine the flour, salt and pepper. Add steak, a few pieces at a time and shake to coat. Remove meat from bag and pound with a mallet to tenderize.

■ In a Dutch oven, brown the steak in oil on both sides. Arrange onion slices between layers of meat. Add water and Worcestershire sauce.

■ Cover and bake at 325° for 2 to 2-1/2 hours or until meat is very tender. Remove to a serving platter and keep warm.

■ For gravy, in a small bowl, combine the flour, salt, pepper and broth until smooth; stir into pan juices. Bring to a boil over medium heat; cook and stir for 2 minutes. Serve steak and gravy with noodles or mashed potatoes if desired.

Yield: **8 servings.**

The process of "swissing" does not refer to Switzerland, but rather a method of preparing a tough cut of meat, usually beef, by pounding it out and tenderizing it. The term originally came from the fabric industry, where the term "swissing" refers to placing rough fabric through rollers in order to soften it.

Debra Sanders
BREVARD, NORTH CAROLINA

If your gang likes the homespun flavor of stuffed cabbage rolls, then they'll love this satisfying, beefy recipe. You'll love that it has all the hearty taste of traditional stuffed cabbage, but with a lot less work! This recipe is a delicious way to sneak nutritious cabbage into a recipe.

Italian Cabbage Casserole*

PREP: 35 min. ■ BAKE: 15 min.

1 medium head cabbage, coarsely shredded
1 pound lean ground beef
1 large green pepper, chopped
1 medium onion, chopped
1 can (14-1/2 ounces) diced tomatoes, undrained
1 can (8 ounces) tomato sauce
3 tablespoons tomato paste
1-1/2 teaspoons dried oregano
1/2 teaspoon garlic powder
1/2 teaspoon pepper
1/8 teaspoon salt
1/2 cup shredded part-skim mozzarella cheese

■ Place cabbage in a steamer basket; place in a large saucepan over 1 in. of water. Bring to a boil; cover and steam for 6-8 minutes or until tender. Drain and set aside.

■ In a large nonstick skillet over medium heat, cook and stir the beef, green pepper and onion until meat is no longer pink; drain. Stir in the tomatoes, tomato sauce, tomato paste and seasonings. Bring to a boil. Reduce heat; simmer, uncovered, for 10 minutes.

■ Place half of the cabbage in an 11-in. x 7-in. baking dish coated with cooking spray; top with half of beef mixture. Repeat layers (dish will be full). Sprinkle with cheese. Bake, uncovered, at 350° for 15-20 minutes or until heated through.

Yield: 6 servings.

*Nutrition Facts: 1-1/3 cups equals 223 calories, 7 g fat (3 g saturated fat), 42 mg cholesterol, 438 mg sodium, 20 g carbohydrate, 7 g fiber, 21 g protein. **Diabetic Exchanges:** 2 lean meat, 1 starch.

To shred cabbage by hand, first cut the head of cabbage in half or quarters. To remove the tough core, make a V-shaped cut around the core and remove it. Place the cut side down of each wedge on a cutting board. With a large, sharp knife, cut into thin slices.

Baked Ziti With Fresh Tomatoes

Barbara Johnson
DECKER, INDIANA

When making this simple dish, I prepare the sauce ahead of time to save time after we come in after working out in the fields!

PREP: 70 min.
BAKE: 30 min.

1 pound ground beef
1 cup chopped onion
3 pounds plum tomatoes, peeled, seeded and chopped (about 15 tomatoes)
1-1/2 teaspoons salt
1 teaspoon dried basil
1/4 teaspoon pepper
8 ounces uncooked ziti
2 cups (8 ounces) shredded part-skim mozzarella cheese, *divided*
2 tablespoons grated Parmesan cheese

■ In a Dutch oven, cook the beef and onion over medium heat until meat is no longer pink; drain. Stir in the tomatoes, salt, basil and pepper. Reduce heat to low; cover and cook for 45 minutes, stirring occasionally.

■ Cook ziti according to package directions; drain. Stir in the sauce and 1 cup mozzarella cheese. Transfer to a greased 3-qt. baking dish; sprinkle with the Parmesan and remaining mozzarella cheese.

■ Cover; bake at 350° for 15 minutes. Uncover; bake 15 minutes longer or until heated through.

Yield: 6 servings.

Nacho Cheese Beef Bake

- Cook noodles according to package directions; drain. Meanwhile, in a large saucepan, cook beef over medium heat until no longer pink; drain. Stir in the tomatoes, soup, olives and chilies. Bring to a boil. Reduce heat; simmer, uncovered, for 10 minutes. Stir in the noodles.

- Transfer to a greased 11-in. x 7-in. baking dish. Sprinkle with the cheese. Bake at 350° for 15-20 minutes or until heated through. Top with tortilla chips; drizzle with salad dressing. Serve with lettuce, sour cream and/or salsa if desired.

Yield: 4 servings.

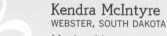

Kendra McIntyre
WEBSTER, SOUTH DAKOTA

My daughter came up with this recipe when she was visiting her fiance's family. Her future father-in-law thought she was a great cook after sampling it!

Nacho Cheese Beef Bake

PREP: 25 min. ■ **BAKE:** 15 min.

- 2 cups uncooked egg noodles
- 1 pound ground beef
- 1 can (14-1/2 ounces) diced tomatoes
- 1 can (10-3/4 ounces) condensed nacho cheese soup, undiluted
- 1 jar (5-3/4 ounces) sliced pimiento-stuffed olives, drained
- 1 can (4 ounces) chopped green chilies
- 1-1/2 cups (6 ounces) shredded cheddar cheese
- 2 cups crushed tortilla chips
- 1/3 cup prepared ranch salad dressing

Shredded lettuce, sour cream *and/or* salsa, optional

For a lighter

version of Nacho Cheese Beef Bake, use ground turkey instead of ground beef. To spice things up a little, substitute half of the shredded cheddar with shredded Pepper Jack cheese.

Zucchini Garden Casserole

Dordana Mason
IOWA CITY, IOWA

This tasty recipe is a great way to use up extra zucchini from your garden. I think that zucchini is best picked when it's small and tender. To keep the squash fresh, store in your shed or garage. When the temperature is below freezing, keep zucchini in a cool room in your basement.

PREP: 20 min. ■ **BAKE:** 1-1/4 hours

4 medium zucchini (about 1-1/2 pounds), sliced	1 teaspoon salt
1 tablespoon olive oil	1/4 teaspoon ground cinnamon
1 can (28 ounces) diced tomatoes, drained	1/4 teaspoon ground allspice
1 cup uncooked instant rice	1/4 teaspoon pepper
1/4 cup chopped green pepper	1-1/2 pounds lean ground beef
1/4 cup chopped onion	1 can (8 ounces) tomato sauce
2 tablespoons chopped fresh parsley	1 cup (4 ounces) shredded Colby cheese

■ In a large skillet, saute zucchini in oil until crisp-tender. Arrange half of the zucchini in a greased 13-in. x 9-in. baking dish. Layer with half of the tomatoes.

■ In a large bowl, combine the rice, green pepper, onion, parsley, and seasonings. Crumble beef over mixture and mix well. Stir in tomato sauce. Spoon over tomato layer. Top with remaining tomatoes and zucchini.

■ Cover and bake at 375° for 1 hour or until a meat thermometer reads 160°. Uncover and sprinkle with cheese. Bake 15 minutes longer or until cheese is melted.

Yield: 8 servings.

To peel tomatoes, first wash and core them. Using a slotted spoon, carefully drop the tomatoes in boiling water and blanch for 30 seconds, then transfer to a bowl of ice water to cool. The skins should come off easily.

Corn Bread Taco Bake

Vicki Good
OSCODA, MICHIGAN

The corn bread mix makes this entree convenient. It's packed with south-of-the-border flavor. Everyone who tries it likes it!

PREP: 20 min.
BAKE: 25 min.

1-1/2 pounds ground beef
   1 can (15-1/4 ounces) whole kernel corn, drained
   1 can (8 ounces) tomato sauce
  1/2 cup water
  1/2 cup chopped green pepper
   1 envelope taco seasoning
   1 package (8-1/2 ounces) corn bread/muffin mix
   1 can (2.8 ounces) french-fried onions, *divided*
  1/3 cup shredded cheddar cheese

■ In a large skillet, cook the beef over medium heat until no longer pink; drain. Stir in the corn, tomato sauce, water, green pepper and taco seasoning. Spoon into a greased 2-qt. baking dish.

■ Prepare the corn bread mix according to package directions for corn bread. Stir in half of the onions. Spread over beef mixture. Bake, uncovered, at 400° for 20 minutes.

■ Sprinkle with the cheese and remaining onions. Bake 3-5 minutes longer or until the cheese is melted and a toothpick inserted into corn bread layer comes out clean.

Yield: 6 servings.

Baked Flank Steak*

Susan Tannahill
WESTFORD, MASSACHUSETTS

I've been making this wonderfully satisfying dish for my family for some 15 years now. It's low in calories, full of flavor and healthy vegetables, and it always receives rave reviews.

PREP: 15 min. ■ BAKE: 50 min.

1 beef flank steak
   (1-1/2 pounds)
2 medium tomatoes, cut into
   eighths
1 medium green pepper,
   sliced into rings
1 large onion, thinly sliced
   and separated into rings
2 cups sliced fresh
   mushrooms

3 tablespoons chili sauce
3 tablespoons ketchup
1 tablespoon Worcestershire
   sauce
1/2 teaspoon salt
1/2 teaspoon pepper
2 tablespoons cornstarch
3 tablespoons cold water

■ Score the surface of the steak, making shallow diagonal cuts. Place in a 13-in. x 9-in. baking pan coated with cooking spray. Place tomatoes, green pepper, onion and mushrooms around meat. Combine the chili sauce, ketchup, Worcestershire sauce, salt and pepper; drizzle over the meat and vegetables.

■ Cover and bake at 350° for 50-60 minutes or until meat and vegetables are tender. Remove and keep warm. Pour pan juices into a measuring cup; skim fat.

■ In a small saucepan, combine cornstarch and water until smooth. Gradually stir in 1-1/2 cups pan juices. Bring to a boil; cook and stir for 2 minutes or until thickened. Thinly slice steak across the grain; serve with vegetables and gravy.

Yield: 6 servings.

*Nutrition Facts: 3 ounces cooked beef with vegetables and 1/4 cup gravy equals 233 calories, 9 g fat (4 g saturated fat), 54 mg cholesterol, 628 mg sodium, 15 g carbohydrate, 2 g fiber, 24 g protein. Diabetic Exchanges: 3 lean meat, 1 vegetable, 1/2 starch.

There's a good reason the recipe for Baked Flank Steak states to score the surface of the steak in the method. This is to keep the steak from curling. The cuts keep the steak flat as it bakes in the oven.

Chili Mac Casserole*

PREP: 20 min.
BAKE: 25 min.

1 cup uncooked wagon
   wheel pasta
1 pound lean ground beef
1/2 cup chopped onion
1/2 cup chopped green
   pepper
1 can (15 ounces) turkey
   chili with beans
1 can (14-1/2 ounces)
   stewed tomatoes,
   undrained
1 cup crushed baked tortilla
   chip scoops
1 cup (4 ounces) shredded
   reduced-fat cheddar
   cheese, *divided*
1/4 cup uncooked instant rice
1 teaspoon chili powder
1/4 teaspoon salt
1/8 teaspoon pepper

■ Cook pasta according to package directions. Meanwhile, in a large nonstick skillet, cook the beef, onion and green pepper over medium heat until meat is no longer pink; drain. Stir in the chili, tomatoes, chips, 1/2 cup cheese, rice, chili powder, salt and pepper. Drain pasta; add to beef mixture.

■ Transfer to a 2-qt. baking dish coated with cooking spray. Sprinkle with the remaining cheese. Bake, uncovered, at 350° for 25-30 minutes or until cheese is melted.

Yield: 6 servings.

*Nutrition Facts: 1 cup equals 358 calories, 11 g fat (5 g saturated fat), 60 mg cholesterol, 847 mg sodium, 36 g carbohydrate, 4 g fiber, 28 g protein. Diabetic Exchanges: 3 lean meat, 2 starch, 1 vegetable.

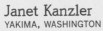

Janet Kanzler
YAKIMA, WASHINGTON

With wagon wheel pasta, store-bought convenience items and popular Tex-Mex ingredients, this beefy main dish is a sure family-pleaser. It's always a favorite at my house. Simply add light dressing to a mixed green salad for a complete dinner.

Lois Gallup
Edwards
WOODLAND,
CALIFORNIA

My husband, a meat loaf lover, and I have five grown children and eight grandchildren. I'm retired, but my days are still busy. So easy dishes like this still are a blessing to me.

Meat Loaf Potato Surprise

Meat Loaf Potato Surprise

PREP: 20 min. ■ **BAKE:** 50 min.

1 cup soft bread crumbs
1/2 cup beef broth
1 egg, lightly beaten
4 teaspoons dried minced onion
1 teaspoon salt
1/4 teaspoon Italian seasoning
1/4 teaspoon pepper
1-1/2 pounds ground beef
4 cups frozen shredded hash brown potatoes, thawed
1/3 cup grated Parmesan cheese
1/4 cup minced fresh parsley
1 teaspoon onion salt

SAUCE:
1 can (8 ounces) tomato sauce
1/4 cup beef broth
2 teaspoons prepared mustard

Additional Parmesan cheese, optional

■ In a large bowl, combine the crumbs, broth, egg and seasonings; let stand for 2 minutes. Sprinkle beef over mixture and mix well.

■ On a piece of waxed paper, pat meat mixture into a 10-in. square. Combine hash browns, cheese, parsley and onion salt; spoon over meat.

■ Roll up, jelly-roll style, removing waxed paper as you roll. Pinch edges and ends to seal; place with seam side down in an ungreased shallow baking pan.

■ Bake at 375° for 40 minutes. Combine the first three sauce ingredients; spoon over meat loaf. Return to the oven for 10 minutes. Sprinkle with Parmesan if desired.

Yield: 8 servings.

Cheesy Beef Spirals

Brenda Marschall
POPLAR BLUFF, MISSOURI

My mom shared this recipe with me years ago. You can also use large shells or ziti noodles.

PREP: 25 min.
BAKE: 30 min.

2 cups uncooked spiral pasta
2 pounds ground beef
2 small onions, chopped
1 garlic clove, minced
1 jar (26 ounces) spaghetti sauce
1 jar (4-1/2 ounces) sliced mushrooms, drained
1/2 cup sour cream
1/2 pound process cheese (Velveeta), cubed
2 cups (8 ounces) shredded part-skim mozzarella cheese

■ Cook pasta according to package directions. Meanwhile, in a large saucepan, cook the beef, onions and garlic over medium heat until meat is no longer pink; drain. Stir in spaghetti sauce and mushrooms; bring to a boil. Reduce heat; cover and simmer for 20 minutes.

■ Place 1/2 cup meat sauce in a greased shallow 2-1/2-qt. baking dish. Drain pasta; place half over sauce. Top with half of the remaining meat sauce; spread with sour cream. Top with process cheese and remaining pasta and meat sauce. Sprinkle with mozzarella cheese.

■ Cover; bake at 350° for 25-30 minutes. Uncover; bake 5-10 minutes longer or until bubbly.

Yield: 8-10 servings.

Sicilian Supper

Gloria Warczak
CEDARBURG, WISCONSIN
Ground beef, tomato and a tasty cream cheese sauce come together in this hot, hearty casserole. I recently took it to a banquet, and requests for the recipe came from every table.

Sicilian Supper

PREP: 30 min. ■ BAKE: 20 min.

2 cups uncooked egg noodles
1 pound ground beef
1/2 cup chopped onion
1/4 cup chopped green pepper
1 can (6 ounces) tomato paste
3/4 cup water
1-1/2 teaspoons sugar, *divided*
1/2 teaspoon salt
1/2 teaspoon dried basil
1/4 teaspoon garlic powder

1/4 teaspoon chili powder
1/4 teaspoon pepper, *divided*
1 tablespoon finely chopped green onion
1 tablespoon olive oil
1 package (8 ounces) cream cheese, cubed
3/4 cup milk
1/3 cup plus 2 tablespoons grated Parmesan cheese, *divided*

■ Cook noodles according to package directions. Meanwhile, in a large skillet, cook the ground beef, onion and green pepper over medium heat until the meat is no longer pink; drain. Stir in tomato paste, water, 1 teaspoon sugar, salt, basil, garlic powder, chili powder and 1/8 teaspoon pepper.

■ In a large saucepan, saute green onion in oil until tender. Add cream cheese and milk; stir until blended. Stir in 1/3 cup Parmesan cheese, and remaining sugar and pepper. Drain the noodles; stir into cheese mixture.

■ In a greased 8-in. square baking dish, arrange alternate rows of beef and noodle mixtures. Sprinkle with remaining Parmesan cheese. Cover and bake at 350° for 20-25 minutes or until bubbly.

Yield: 4 servings.

Garlic and onion powders tend to absorb moisture, which causes clumping. Store them in airtight spice jars to keep them dry.

Poultry

198

197

195

Home-style cooking has never been easier with the comforting casseroles and other oven-baked dinners in this chapter. Chock-full of chicken or turkey and other wholesome ingredients, these recipes are perfect for family gatherings, potlucks and weeknight dinners alike.

- In several large bowls, combine the chicken, macaroni, mushrooms, pimientos, onions and peppers. In another large bowl, combine the soups, cheese, milk, basil and lemon-pepper; add to chicken mixture.

- Place about 12 cups of mixture in each of four greased 13-in. x 9-in. baking dishes. Cover and refrigerate overnight.

- Remove from the refrigerator 30 minutes before baking. Combine the cornflakes and butter; sprinkle over casseroles. Cover; bake at 350° for 45 minutes. Uncover and bake 15-20 minutes longer or until bubbly.

Yield: 4 casseroles (12 servings each).

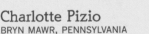

Chicken Church Casserole

Charlotte Pizio
BRYN MAWR, PENNSYLVANIA

This chicken and pasta hot dish is a creamy and down-home treasure that's become a favorite at my church's luncheons. Try it the next time you're cooking for a crowd.

Chicken Church Casserole

PREP: 35 min. + chilling ■ BAKE: 1 hour

20 cups cubed cooked chicken
1 package (2 pounds) elbow macaroni, cooked and drained
6 jars (6 ounces *each*) sliced mushrooms, drained
2 jars (4 ounces *each*) diced pimientos, drained
2 large onions, chopped
2 large green peppers, chopped
4 cans (10-3/4 ounces *each*) condensed cream of celery soup, undiluted

4 cans (10-3/4 ounces *each*) condensed cream of mushroom soup, undiluted
2 pounds process cheese (Velveeta), cubed
1-1/3 cups milk
4 teaspoons dried basil
2 teaspoons lemon-pepper seasoning
2 cups crushed cornflakes
1/4 cup butter, melted

Watch rummage

sales and thrift stores for pretty casserole dishes, bowls or platters that are priced very inexpensively. You can use them when baking or presenting your recipes when going to a potluck. Just let your host keep the dish, so you won't lose a cherished baking dish or plate.

Krista Davis-Keith
NEW CASTLE, INDIANA

I'm usually in the kitchen before dinner, making some kind of hearty dish for my family, neighbors or the local fire department to pass around and try. My husband is a firefighter in our town, and this satisfying casserole is a favorite there.

Firefighter's Chicken Spaghetti

PREP: 20 min. ■ BAKE: 45 min.

- 12 ounces uncooked spaghetti, broken in half
- 1 can (10-3/4 ounces) condensed cream of chicken soup, undiluted
- 1 can (10-3/4 ounces) condensed cream of mushroom soup, undiluted
- 1 cup (8 ounces) sour cream
- 1/2 cup milk
- 1/4 cup butter, melted, *divided*
- 2 tablespoons dried parsley flakes
- 1/2 teaspoon garlic powder
- 1/2 teaspoon salt
- 1/4 teaspoon pepper
- 2 cups (8 ounces) shredded part-skim mozzarella cheese
- 1 cup grated Parmesan cheese
- 2 to 3 celery ribs, chopped
- 1 medium onion, chopped
- 1 can (4 ounces) mushroom stems and pieces, drained
- 5 cups cubed cooked chicken
- 1-1/2 cups crushed cornflakes

■ Cook spaghetti according to package directions; drain. In a large bowl, combine the soups, sour cream, milk, 2 tablespoons butter and seasonings. Add the cheeses, celery, onion and mushrooms. Stir in the chicken and spaghetti.

■ Transfer to a greased 3-qt. baking dish (dish will be full). Combine the cornflakes and remaining butter; sprinkle over the top.

■ Bake, uncovered, at 350° for 45-50 minutes or until bubbly.

Yield: 12-14 servings.

When a recipe calls for cooked chicken, an easy and fast way to cook it is in a pressure cooker. From start to finish, it takes about 15 minutes to cook a whole chicken. It's a great way to save time when making casseroles or even chicken salad.

Fiesta Chicken

Teresa Peterson
KASSON, MINNESOTA

Chili powder and picante sauce add just the right dash of zip to this hearty main dish. It's a snap to assemble because it utilizes convenience foods.

PREP: 15 min.
BAKE: 40 min.

- 1 can (10-3/4 ounces) condensed cream of chicken soup, undiluted
- 1 can (10-3/4 ounces) condensed cream of mushroom soup, undiluted
- 2 small tomatoes, chopped
- 1/3 cup picante sauce
- 1 medium green pepper, chopped
- 1 small onion, chopped
- 2 to 3 teaspoons chili powder
- 12 corn tortillas (6 inches), cut into 1-inch strips
- 3 cups cubed cooked chicken
- 1 cup (4 ounces) shredded Colby cheese

■ In a large bowl, combine the soups, chopped tomatoes, picante sauce, green pepper, onion and chili powder. In a greased 13-in. x 9-in. baking dish, layer half of the tortilla strips, chicken, soup mixture and cheese. Repeat layers.

■ Cover and bake at 350° for 40-50 minutes or until bubbly.

Yield: 6-8 servings.

Melanie Kennedy
BATTLE GROUND, WASHINGTON

Mushrooms, bacon and cheese top marinated chicken for a family favorite that always receives rave reviews when I serve it.

Bacon-Cheese Topped Chicken

Bacon-Cheese Topped Chicken

PREP: 40 min. + marinating ■ BAKE: 20 min.

1/2 cup Dijon mustard
1/2 cup honey
4-1/2 teaspoons canola oil, *divided*
1/2 teaspoon lemon juice
4 boneless skinless chicken breast halves
1/4 teaspoon salt
1/8 teaspoon pepper
Dash paprika

2 cups sliced fresh mushrooms
2 tablespoons butter
1 cup (4 ounces) shredded Monterey Jack cheese
1 cup (4 ounces) shredded cheddar cheese
8 bacon strips, partially cooked
2 teaspoons minced fresh parsley

■ In a small bowl, combine the mustard, honey, 1-1/2 teaspoons oil and lemon juice. Pour 1/2 cup into a large resealable plastic bag; add the chicken. Seal the bag and turn to coat; refrigerate for 2 hours. Cover and refrigerate the remaining marinade.

■ Drain and discard marinade from chicken. In a large skillet over medium heat, brown chicken in remaining oil on all sides. Sprinkle with salt, pepper and paprika. Transfer to a greased 11-in. x 7-in. baking dish.

■ In the same skillet, saute mushrooms in butter until tender. Spoon reserved marinade over chicken. Top with cheeses and mushrooms. Place bacon strips in a crisscross pattern over chicken.

■ Bake, uncovered, at 375° for 20-25 minutes or until a meat thermometer reads 170°. Sprinkle with parsley.

Yield: 4 servings.

Love Me Tender Chicken Bake

Alcy Thorne
LOS MOLINOS, CALIFORNIA

This dish lives up to its name. Basking in a rich, creamy broth and topped with buttery cracker crumbs, the chicken breast pieces melt in your mouth. Elvis himself could not have resisted this heart-warming dish.

PREP: 25 min.
BAKE: 20 min.

2 medium onions, chopped
6 celery ribs, chopped
1/2 cup butter, cubed
5 cups cubed cooked chicken
3/4 cup water
2 cans (10-3/4 ounces *each*) condensed cream of mushroom soup, undiluted
1 cup (8 ounces) sour cream
2 cans (8 ounces *each*) sliced water chestnuts, drained
1 cup sliced almonds, toasted
1 cup crushed butter-flavored crackers

■ In a large skillet, saute onions and celery in butter until tender. Add chicken and water; heat through. Remove from the heat. Stir in the soup, sour cream, water chestnuts and sliced almonds.

■ Pour into eight greased 1-1/2-cup baking dishes. Sprinkle with cracker crumbs. Bake, uncovered, at 400° for 20-25 minutes or until bubbly.

Yield: 8 servings.

Biscuit-Topped Lemon Chicken

Pattie Ishee
STRINGER, MISSISSIPPI
This homey recipe combines two of my favorite things: hot biscuits and a lemon-pepper sauce. I often take it to potlucks and even give it as a gift with potatoes and carrots baked in.

Biscuit-Topped Lemon Chicken

PREP: 40 min. ■ **BAKE:** 35 min.

2	large onions, finely chopped
4	celery ribs, finely chopped
2	garlic cloves, minced
1	cup butter, cubed
8	green onions, thinly sliced
2/3	cup all-purpose flour
8	cups milk
12	cups cubed cooked chicken
2	cans (10-3/4 ounces *each*) condensed cream of chicken soup, undiluted

1/2	cup lemon juice
2	tablespoons grated lemon peel
2	teaspoons pepper
1	teaspoon salt

CHEDDAR BISCUITS:

5	cups self-rising flour
2	cups milk
2	cups (8 ounces) shredded cheddar cheese
1/4	cup butter, melted

- In a Dutch oven, saute the onions, celery and garlic in butter. Add green onions. Stir in flour until blended; gradually add the milk. Bring to a boil; cook and stir for 2 minutes or until thickened.

- Add the chicken, soup, lemon juice and peel, pepper and salt; heat through. Pour into two greased 13-in. x 9-in. baking dishes; set aside.

- In a large bowl, combine the biscuit ingredients just until moistened. Turn onto a lightly floured surface; knead 8-10 times. Pat or roll out to 3/4-in. thickness. With a well floured 2-1/2-in. biscuit cutter, cut out 30 biscuits.

- Place biscuits over the chicken mixture. Bake, uncovered, at 350° for 35-40 minutes or until golden brown.

Yield: 15 servings (30 biscuits).

As a substitute

for each cup of self-rising flour, place 1-1/2 teaspoons baking powder and 1/2 teaspoon salt in a measuring cup. Add all-purpose flour to measure 1 cup.

Chicken with Cranberry Stuffing

PREP: 1 hour ■ **BAKE:** 30 min.

JoAnne Cloughly
EAST WORCESTER, NEW YORK

This delicious chicken entree is easy to prepare, but looks as if you slaved all day. The dried cranberries add a tartness to the stuffing, which turns ordinary chicken breasts into an extraordinary all-in-one meal.

1/4 cup chopped onion	1/4 teaspoon pepper
2 garlic cloves, minced	8 bacon strips
2 tablespoons butter	4 boneless skinless chicken breast halves (4 ounces *each*)
3-1/2 cups chicken broth	
1/2 cup uncooked brown rice	
1/2 cup uncooked wild rice	1/4 cup honey
1/2 cup dried cranberries	CREAMY MUSTARD SAUCE:
1 tablespoon minced fresh parsley	1 cup heavy whipping cream
	3 tablespoons spicy brown mustard
1/4 teaspoon dried thyme	

■ In a large saucepan, saute onion and garlic in butter until tender. Add the broth, brown rice and wild rice; bring to a boil. Reduce heat; cover and cook for 55-65 minutes or until rice is tender. Drain any excess liquid if necessary. Stir in the cranberries, parsley, thyme and pepper.

■ In a large skillet, cook bacon over medium heat until cooked but not crisp; drain on paper towels.

■ Flatten chicken to 1/4-in. thickness. Top each with 1/4 cup rice mixture; roll up from one end. Wrap two strips of bacon around each roll-up and secure with toothpicks. Place remaining rice mixture in a greased 11-in. x 7-in. baking dish; place roll-ups over rice.

■ In a microwave-safe bowl, heat the honey, uncovered, on high for 30 seconds; spoon over chicken. Bake, uncovered, at 325° for 28-30 minutes or until chicken is no longer pink. Discard toothpicks.

■ For sauce, in a small saucepan, combine cream and mustard. Cook over medium-low heat until mixture is reduced and begins to thicken, stirring constantly. Serve warm with chicken.

Yield: 4 servings.

Chicken Angelo*

PREP: 15 min.
BAKE: 30 min.

- 1/2 pound medium fresh mushrooms, sliced, *divided*
- 1/2 cup egg substitute
- 1 cup bread crumbs
- 4 bone-in chicken breast halves (7 ounces *each*), skinned and boned
- 2 tablespoons butter
- 6 slices part-skim mozzarella cheese
- 3/4 cup chicken broth

Hot cooked rice *or* noodles

Fresh parsley, chopped

■ Place half the mushrooms in a 13-in. x 9-in. baking dish; set aside. Place the egg substitute and bread crumbs in separate shallow bowls. Dip chicken in the egg substitute, then roll in bread crumbs.

■ In large skillet, brown both sides of chicken in butter; place chicken on top of mushrooms. Arrange remaining mushrooms on chicken; top with cheese. Add chicken broth to pan.

■ Bake at 350° for 30-35 minutes or until a meat thermometer reads 170°. Serve chicken with hot cooked rice or noodles. Sprinkle with parsley.

Yield: 4 servings.

✱Nutrition Facts: 1/4 recipe (calculated without noodles) equals 482 calories, 26 g fat (0 saturated fat), 178 mg cholesterol, 695 mg sodium, 25 g carbohydrate, 0 fiber, 45 g protein. **Diabetic Exchanges:** 6 lean meat, 1-1/2 starch, 1 vegetable.

Carol Oswald
SCHNECKSVILLE, PENNSYLVANIA

While growing up, my grandmother always made this dish when we came over for Sunday dinner. I still enjoy it today because it's quick and simple, and I can garden while it cooks! It always makes a satisfying dinner, and leftovers make a great lunch the next day.

Wild Rice Chicken Dinner

- Heat rice according to package directions. Meanwhile, in a Dutch oven, combine the green beans, soup, water chestnuts, onion, pimientos, mayonnaise, milk and pepper. Bring to a boil. Reduce heat; cover and simmer for 5 minutes. Stir in chicken and rice; cook 3-4 minutes longer or until chicken is heated through.

- Transfer half of the mixture to a serving dish; sprinkle with 1/2 cup almonds. Serve immediately. Pour remaining mixture into a greased 13-in. x 9-in. baking dish; cool. Sprinkle with remaining almonds. Cover and freeze for up to 3 months.

- **TO USE FROZEN CASSEROLE:** Thaw in the refrigerator overnight. Cover and bake at 350° for 40-45 minutes or until heated through.

Yield: 2 casseroles (6-8 servings each).

Editor's Note: Reduced-fat or fat-free mayonnaise is not recommended for this recipe.

Lorraine Hanson
INDEPENDENCE, IOWA

Chicken, green beans and the crunchy water chestnuts and almonds help to create this delicious casserole. The ready-to-serve wild rice mix makes putting it together a breeze.

Wild Rice Chicken Dinner

PREP/TOTAL TIME: 30 min.

- 2 packages (8.8 ounces *each*) ready-to-serve long grain and wild rice
- 2 packages (16 ounces *each*) frozen French-style green beans, thawed
- 2 cans (10-3/4 ounces *each*) condensed cream of celery soup, undiluted
- 2 cans (8 ounces *each*) sliced water chestnuts, drained
- 2/3 cup chopped onion
- 2 jars (4 ounces *each*) sliced pimientos, drained
- 1 cup mayonnaise
- 1/2 cup milk
- 1 teaspoon pepper
- 6 cups cubed cooked chicken
- 1 cup slivered almonds, *divided*

To prevent nuts, such as almonds and peanuts, from turning rancid and to keep them fresh, place in a freezer bag, label and store in the freezer. Use only what you need for a recipe and keep the rest stored in the freezer for up to 1 year.

Taste of Home
Test Kitchen
GREENDALE,
WISCONSIN
*Ribbons of buttery
phyllo dough make
a crispy topping for
this impressive
chicken entree. The
rich, creamy sauce
is flavored with
thyme and sherry.*

Phyllo Chicken Potpie

Phyllo Chicken Potpie*

PREP: 35 min. ■ **BAKE:** 10 min.

6 cups water	3 tablespoons sherry *or* additional reduced-sodium chicken broth
2 cups fresh pearl onions	
1-1/2 pounds boneless skinless chicken breasts, cubed	3 tablespoons cornstarch
2 tablespoons canola oil, *divided*	1/2 cup fat-free milk
2 medium red potatoes, peeled and chopped	1-1/2 teaspoons minced fresh thyme
1 cup sliced fresh mushrooms	1/2 teaspoon salt
	1/4 teaspoon pepper
1 can (14-1/2 ounces) reduced-sodium chicken broth	10 sheets phyllo dough (14 inches x 9 inches)
1/2 pound fresh asparagus, trimmed and cut into 1-inch pieces	Refrigerated butter-flavored spray

■ In a Dutch oven, bring the water to a boil. Add pearl onions; boil for 3 minutes. Drain and rinse in cold water; peel and set aside.

■ In a large skillet, cook chicken in 1 tablespoon oil over medium heat until no longer pink; remove and keep warm. In the same pan, saute potatoes in remaining oil for 5 minutes. Add onions and mushrooms; saute 3 minutes longer. Add the broth, asparagus and sherry or additional broth. Bring to a boil. Reduce heat; cover and simmer for 5 minutes or until the potatoes are tender.

■ Combine cornstarch and milk until smooth; stir into skillet. Bring to a boil; cook and stir for 2 minutes or until thickened. Drain chicken; add to onion mixture. Stir in the thyme, salt and pepper. Transfer to an 8-in. square baking dish coated with cooking spray.

■ Stack all 10 phyllo sheets. Roll up, starting at a long side; cut into 1/2-in. strips. Place in a large bowl and toss to separate strips. Spritz with the butter-flavored spray. Arrange over chicken mixture; spritz again.

■ Bake the potpie, uncovered, at 425° for 10-15 minutes or until golden brown.

Yield: 6 servings.

To prepare asparagus for cooking, rinse the stalks well in cold water. Snap off the stalk ends as far down as they will easily break when gently bent, or cut off the tough white portion. If stalks are large, use a vegetable peeler to gently peel the tough area of the stalk from the end to just below the tip. If the tips are large, scrape off scales with a knife.

*Nutritional Facts: 1 serving equals 325 calories, 8 g fat (1 g saturated fat), 63 mg cholesterol, 542 mg sodium, 33 g carbohydrate, 2 g fiber, 29 g protein. **Diabetic Exchanges:** 3 very lean meat, 2 vegetable, 1-1/2 starch, 1 fat.

Ruth
Andrewson
LEAVENWORTH,
WASHINGTON

This wonderful casserole is sure to chase away chilly evenings. It's full of chicken, ham, broccoli and rice. You won't believe that it's made with reduced-fat ingredients!

Company Casserole

Company Casserole

PREP: 35 min. ■ **BAKE:** 40 min.

1 package (6 ounces) long grain and wild rice mix

4 cups frozen broccoli florets, thawed and drained

1-1/2 cups cubed cooked chicken breast

1 cup cubed fully cooked lean ham

1/2 cup shredded reduced-fat cheddar cheese

1 cup sliced fresh mushrooms

1 can (10-3/4 ounces) reduced-fat reduced-sodium condensed cream of mushroom soup, undiluted

2/3 cup reduced-fat plain yogurt

1/3 cup reduced-fat mayonnaise

1 teaspoon prepared mustard

1/4 teaspoon curry powder

2 tablespoons grated Parmesan cheese

■ Prepare rice according to package directions, omitting the butter. In a 13-in. x 9-in. baking dish coated with cooking spray, layer the rice, broccoli, chicken, ham, cheddar cheese and mushrooms.

■ In a small bowl, combine the soup, yogurt, mayonnaise, mustard and curry powder. Spread evenly over top of casserole; sprinkle with Parmesan cheese.

■ Bake, uncovered, at 350° for 40-45 minutes or until heated through.

Yield: *6 servings.*

Roasted Chicken with Rosemary

PREP: 20 min.
BAKE: 2 hours + standing

1/2 cup butter

4 tablespoons minced fresh *or* 2 tablespoons dried rosemary, crushed

2 tablespoons minced fresh parsley

3 garlic cloves, minced

1 teaspoon salt

1/2 teaspoon pepper

1 whole roasting chicken (5 to 6 pounds)

6 small red potatoes, halved

6 medium carrots, halved lengthwise and cut into 2-inch pieces

2 medium onions, quartered

■ In a small saucepan, melt butter and stir in the seasonings. Place chicken breast side up on a rack in a roasting pan; tie the drumsticks together with kitchen string. Spoon half of the butter mixture over the chicken. Place potatoes, carrots and onions around chicken. Drizzle remaining butter mixture over vegetables.

■ Cover and bake at 350° for 1-1/2 hours, basting every 30 minutes. Uncover; bake 30-60 minutes longer or until a meat thermometer reaches 180° and vegetables are tender, basting occasionally.

■ Cover with foil and let stand for 10-15 minutes before carving. Serve vegetables with roast.

Yield: *9 servings.*

Isabel Zienkosky
SALT LAKE CITY, UTAH

This supper is similar to a pot roast, only it uses chicken instead of beef. The rosemary adds flavor and blends well with the garlic, butter and parsley. With the addition of potatoes, carrots and onions, this recipe makes a mouthwatering meal-in-one.

Marvelous Chicken Enchiladas

Rebekah Sabo
ROCHESTER, NEW YORK

I love Mexican food, and this is one of my favorites. Try using Monterey Jack cheese in place of the cheddar for a slightly milder flavor.

Marvelous Chicken Enchiladas*

PREP: 30 min. ■ **BAKE:** 25 min.

1	pound boneless skinless chicken breasts, cut into thin strips
4	teaspoons chili powder
2	teaspoons olive oil
2	tablespoons all-purpose flour
1-1/2	teaspoons ground coriander
1	teaspoon baking cocoa
1	cup fat-free milk
1	cup frozen corn, thawed
4	green onions, chopped

1	can (4 ounces) chopped green chilies, drained
1/2	teaspoon salt
1/2	cup minced fresh cilantro, *divided*
6	whole wheat tortillas (8 inches)
1/2	cup salsa
1/2	cup tomato sauce
1/2	cup shredded reduced-fat cheddar cheese

■ Sprinkle the chicken with chili powder. In a large nonstick skillet coated with cooking spray, cook the chicken in olive oil over medium heat until no longer pink. Sprinkle with the flour, coriander and cocoa; stir until blended.

■ Gradually stir in milk. Bring to a boil; cook and stir for 2 minutes or until thickened.

■ Add the corn, onions, chilies and salt; cook and stir 2 minutes longer or until heated through. Remove from the heat. Stir in 1/4 cup cilantro.

■ Spread 2/3 cup filling down the center of each tortilla. Roll up and place seam side down in a 13-in. x 9-in. baking dish coated with cooking spray.

■ In a small bowl, combine the salsa, tomato sauce and remaining cilantro; pour over enchiladas. Sprinkle with cheese.

■ Cover; bake at 375° for 25 minutes or until heated through.

Yield: 6 enchiladas.

*Nutrition Facts: 1 enchilada equals 270 calories, 7 g fat (2 g saturated fat), 49 mg cholesterol, 768 mg sodium, 35 g carbohydrate, 4 g fiber, 24 g protein. **Diabetic Exchanges:** 2 starch, 2 very lean meat, 1 fat.

Tastes Like Thanksgiving Casserole

Mary Lou Timpson
COLORADO CITY, ARIZONA

This hearty, rich-tasting main dish is sure to be a hit with your family. It's a delicious way to use up leftover turkey. You can substitute 5-1/2 cups mashed potatoes for the 6 potatoes.

Tastes Like Thanksgiving Casserole

PREP: 30 min. ■ BAKE: 30 min.

6	medium potatoes, peeled and cut into chunks
1-1/4	cups chopped celery
3/4	cup chopped onion
1/2	cup butter, cubed
6	cups unseasoned stuffing cubes
1	teaspoon poultry seasoning
1/4	teaspoon rubbed sage
1	cup chicken broth
4	cups cubed cooked turkey
2	cans (10-3/4 ounces *each*) condensed cream of chicken soup, undiluted
1	teaspoon garlic powder
3/4	cup sour cream, *divided*
4	ounces cream cheese, softened
1/2	teaspoon pepper
1/4	teaspoon salt
1-1/2	cups (6 ounces) shredded cheddar cheese

■ Place the potatoes in a Dutch oven and cover with water. Bring to a boil. Reduce the heat; cover and cook for 15-20 minutes or until tender.

■ Meanwhile, in a large skillet, saute the celery and onion in butter until tender. Remove from the heat. In a large bowl, combine the stuffing cubes, poultry seasoning and sage. Stir in the broth and celery mixture. Transfer to a greased 13-in. x 9-in. baking dish.

■ In another large bowl, combine the turkey, soup, garlic powder and 1/4 cup sour cream; spoon over stuffing mixture. Drain the potatoes; mash in a large bowl. Beat in cream cheese, pepper, salt and remaining sour cream; spread over turkey mixture. Sprinkle with cheese.

■ Bake, uncovered, at 350° for 30-35 minutes or until heated through.

Yield: 8 servings.

When you have extra time, chop a few stalks of celery or a few onions. After sauteing them in oil or butter, spoon them into ice cube trays, freeze, then pop the frozen "veggie cubes" into a labeled freezer bag to store. The cubes come in handy when making soups or casseroles.

Linda Howe
LISLE, ILLINOIS

This creamy, comforting casserole is a fantastic way to use up that leftover Thanksgiving turkey. And it's a real family pleaser! It contains a lot of flavorful ingredients, such as Parmesan cheese and sherry, but fat-free evaporated milk keeps the calories in check.

Mushroom Turkey Tetrazzini*

PREP: 35 min. ■ BAKE: 25 min.

12 ounces uncooked spaghetti, broken into 2-inch pieces
2 teaspoons chicken bouillon granules
1/2 pound sliced fresh mushrooms
2 tablespoons butter
2 tablespoons all-purpose flour
1/4 cup sherry or reduced-sodium chicken broth
3/4 teaspoon salt-free lemon-pepper seasoning
1/2 teaspoon salt
1/8 teaspoon ground nutmeg
1 cup fat-free evaporated milk
2/3 cup grated Parmesan cheese, *divided*
4 cups cubed cooked turkey breast
1/4 teaspoon paprika

■ Cook the spaghetti according to package directions. Drain, reserving 2-1/2 cups cooking liquid. Stir bouillon into cooking liquid and set aside. Place the spaghetti in a 13-in. x 9-in. baking dish coated with cooking spray; set aside.

■ In a large nonstick skillet, saute mushrooms in butter until tender. Stir in flour until blended. Gradually stir in sherry or broth and reserved cooking liquid. Add the lemon-pepper, salt and nutmeg. Bring to a boil; cook and stir for 2 minutes or until thickened.

■ Reduce heat to low; stir in milk and 1/3 cup Parmesan cheese until blended. Add turkey; cook and stir until heated through. Pour turkey mixture over spaghetti and toss to combine. Sprinkle with paprika and remaining Parmesan cheese.

■ Cover and bake at 375° for 25-30 minutes or until bubbly.

Yield: 8 servings.

*Nutrition Facts: 1 cup equals 362 calories, 7 g fat (3 g saturated fat), 75 mg cholesterol, 592 mg sodium, 40 g carbohydrate, 2 g fiber, 33 g protein. Diabetic Exchanges: 3 starch, 3 very lean meat, 1/2 fat.

To use the frozen Chicken Manicotti casserole, first thaw it in the refrigerator. After letting it stand at room temperature for at least 30 minutes, continue to bake as directed in the recipe.

Chicken Manicotti

Jamie Valocchi
MESA, ARIZONA

I gave this dish to a girlfriend when she came home from the hospital with her newborn.

PREP: 25 min.
BAKE: 65 min.

1 tablespoon garlic powder
1-1/2 pounds boneless skinless chicken breast
16 uncooked manicotti shells
2 jars (26 ounces *each*) spaghetti sauce, *divided*
1 pound bulk Italian sausage, cooked and drained
1/2 pound fresh mushrooms, sliced
4 cups (16 ounces) shredded part-skim mozzarella cheese
2/3 cup water

■ Rub the garlic powder over chicken; cut into 1-in. strips. Stuff chicken into manicotti shells. Spread 1 cup spaghetti sauce in each of two greased 13-in. x 9-in. baking dishes.

■ Place eight stuffed manicotti shells in each dish. Sprinkle with sausage and mushrooms. Pour remaining spaghetti sauce over the top. Sprinkle with cheese.

■ Drizzle water around the edge of each dish. Cover and bake one casserole at 375° for 65-70 minutes or until chicken juices run clear and pasta is tender. Cover and freeze remaining casserole for up to 1 month.

Yield: 2 casseroles (4 servings each).

Chicken Lasagna

Dena Stapelman
LAUREL, NEBRASKA

For a cooking class several years ago, I lightened up a classic lasagna and created this chicken version. It was preferred over the traditional dish by my family, friends and students.

Chicken Lasagna*

PREP: 50 min. ■ BAKE: 30 min. + standing

10	uncooked lasagna noodles
1	pound boneless skinless chicken breasts
1	can (14-1/2 ounces) diced tomatoes, undrained
1	can (12 ounces) tomato paste
1-1/2	cups sliced fresh mushrooms
1/4	cup chopped onion
1	tablespoon dried basil
1-3/4	teaspoons salt, *divided*
1/8	teaspoon garlic powder
3	cups (24 ounces) 2% cottage cheese
1/2	cup egg substitute
1/2	cup grated Parmesan cheese
1/3	cup minced fresh parsley
1/2	teaspoon pepper
2	cups (8 ounces) shredded part-skim mozzarella cheese

- Cook noodles according to package directions. Meanwhile, broil chicken 6 in. from the heat until juices run clear; let stand for 15 minutes or until cool enough to handle. Shred the chicken with two forks. Drain noodles; set aside.

- In a large nonstick skillet, combine the shredded chicken, tomatoes, tomato paste, mushrooms, onion, basil, 3/4 teaspoon salt and garlic powder. Bring to a boil. Reduce heat; cover and simmer for 25-30 minutes. In a bowl, combine the cottage cheese, egg substitute, Parmesan cheese, parsley, pepper and remaining salt.

- In a 13-in. x 9-in. baking dish coated with cooking spray, place half of the noodles, overlapping them. Layer with half of the cheese mixture, chicken mixture and mozzarella. Repeat layers. Cover and bake at 375° for 25-30 minutes or until bubbly. Uncover; bake 5 minutes longer. Let stand for 15 minutes before cutting.

Yield: 12 servings.

*Nutrition Facts: One serving (1 piece) equals 240 calories, 7 g fat (4 g saturated fat), 43 mg cholesterol, 1,038 mg sodium, 17 g carbohydrate, 2 g fiber, 28 g protein. **Diabetic Exchanges:** 2 lean meat, 1 starch, 1 fat.

Michelle Krzmarczick
REDONDO BEACH, CALIFORNIA

This mouthwatering casserole makes an excellent potluck dish. It's creamy, and has a golden cornflake and almond topping.

Almond Chicken Casserole

Almond Chicken Casserole

PREP: 15 min. ■ BAKE: 25 min.

2 cups cubed cooked chicken
1 can (10-3/4 ounces) condensed cream of chicken soup, undiluted
1 cup (8 ounces) sour cream
3/4 cup mayonnaise
2 celery ribs, chopped
3 hard-cooked eggs, chopped
1 can (4 ounces) mushroom stems and pieces, drained
1 can (8 ounces) water chestnuts, drained and chopped

1 tablespoon finely chopped onion
2 teaspoons lemon juice
1/2 teaspoon salt
1/4 teaspoon pepper
1 cup (4 ounces) shredded cheddar cheese
1/2 cup crushed cornflakes
2 tablespoons butter, melted
1/4 cup sliced almonds

■ In a large bowl, combine the first 12 ingredients. Transfer to a greased 13-in. x 9-in. baking dish; sprinkle with cheese.

■ Toss cornflakes with butter; sprinkle over cheese. Top with almonds. Bake, uncovered, at 350° for 25-30 minutes or until heated through.

Yield: 6-8 servings.

If you find it difficult to peel hard-cooked eggs, it may be because they are too fresh! The American Egg Board suggests storing eggs in the refrigerator for a week to 10 days before cooking them.

Artichoke Chicken

Kathy Peters
NORTH VERSAILLES, PENNSYLVANIA

This elegant, no-fuss entree is ideal for everyday or company.

PREP: 25 min.
BAKE: 25 min.

1/2 teaspoon paprika
1/2 teaspoon salt
1/4 teaspoon pepper
4 boneless skinless chicken breast halves (4 ounces *each*)
2 tablespoons butter, *divided*
1 can (14 ounces) water-packed artichoke hearts, rinsed, drained and halved
1/2 pound sliced fresh mushrooms
1 cup reduced-sodium chicken broth
1/8 teaspoon dried tarragon
2 tablespoons flour
1/2 cup sherry *or* additional chicken broth

■ Combine paprika, salt and pepper; sprinkle over both sides of chicken. Cook chicken in large nonstick skillet in 1 tablespoon butter until browned on both sides. Transfer to a greased 2-qt. baking dish; top with artichokes.

■ In same skillet, saute mushrooms in remaining butter until tender. Stir in broth and tarragon; bring to a boil. Combine flour and sherry until smooth; stir into skillet. Bring to a boil; stir for 2 minutes or until thickened. Pour over chicken.

■ Cover and bake at 350° for 25-30 minutes or until a meat thermometer reads 170°.

Yield: 4 servings.

Pork

214

212

207

It's hard to resist the flavor of pork, whether you're savoring Italian sausage, relishing the smoky flavor of ham, or enjoying tenderloin, roasts or chops. From a fast-to-fix stir-fry to elegant stuffed pork loin, there's a meal for every occasion in this chapter.

Upside-Down Pizza Bake

Sandy Bastian
TINLEY PARK, ILLINOIS

This easy, but exceptionally delicious recipe is one I've been preparing and serving to my children and now to my grand-children for over 30 years! It has all the fun flavor of pizza.

Upside-Down Pizza Bake

PREP: 20 min. ■ **BAKE:** 25 min.

1/2 pound Italian sausage links, cut into 1/4-inch slices

1 cup spaghetti sauce

1/2 cup sliced fresh mushrooms

1/2 cup julienned green pepper

1 cup (4 ounces) shredded part-skim mozzarella cheese, *divided*

1 cup biscuit/baking mix

1 egg

1/2 cup milk

■ In a large skillet, cook sausage over medium heat until meat is no longer pink; drain.

■ Pour spaghetti sauce into a greased 8-in. square baking dish. Top with the mushrooms, green pepper, sausage and 1/2 cup cheese.

■ In a small bowl, combine the biscuit mix, egg and milk until blended. Pour over top. Sprinkle with remaining cheese.

■ Bake, uncovered, at 400° for 25-30 minutes or until golden brown.

Yield: 4 servings.

Scalloped Potatoes And Pork Chops

Susan Chavez
VANCOUVER, WASHINGTON

I truly enjoy trying new recipes and baking hearty casseroles, like this one, for my family. This dish is easy to prepare, and baking the chops with the potatoes creates great flavor.

PREP: 10 min.
BAKE: 1-1/4 hours

5 cups thinly sliced peeled potatoes

1 cup chopped onion

Salt and pepper to taste

1 can (10-3/4 ounces) condensed cream of mushroom soup, undiluted

1/2 cup sour cream

6 pork loin chops (1 inch thick)

Chopped fresh parsley

■ In a greased 13-in. x 9-in. baking dish, layer half of the potatoes and onion; sprinkle with salt and pepper. Repeat layers. Combine the soup and sour cream; pour over the potato mixture. Cover and bake at 375° for 30 minutes.

■ Meanwhile in a nonstick skillet, brown pork chops on both sides. Place chops on top of casserole. Cover and bake for 30 minutes. Uncover and bake 15 minutes longer or until chops are tender. Sprinkle with chopped parsley.

Yield: 6 servings.

Monterey Sausage Pie

Pork Noodle Casserole

PREP: 25 min.
BAKE: 45 min.

>   2   cups uncooked egg
>   noodles
>   2   pounds boneless pork, cut
>   into 3/4-inch cubes
>   2   medium onions, chopped
>   2   cans (15-1/4 ounces *each*)
>   whole kernel corn, drained
>   2   cans (10-3/4 ounces *each*)
>   condensed cream of
>   mushroom soup,
>   undiluted
>   1/2   teaspoon salt
>   1/2   teaspoon pepper

■ Cook the noodles according to package directions. In a large skillet, cook the pork and onions over medium heat until meat is no longer pink. Drain noodles. Stir the noodles, corn, soup, salt and pepper into the pork mixture.

■ Transfer to a greased 3-qt. baking dish. Cover and bake at 350° for 30 minutes. Uncover; bake 15 minutes longer.

Yield: 8 servings.

For quick and easy accompaniments to the Pork Noodle Casserole, try making biscuits from a mix or store-bought dough. Add a refreshing salad made from mixed greens and bottled dressing for a well-rounded meal.

Bonnie Marlow
OTTOVILLE, OHIO

It's a snap to make this dish using baking mix. I got the idea from a similar recipe with hamburger and cheddar cheese. After a few changes for my family's taste, this was a hit!

Monterey Sausage Pie

PREP: 15 min. ■ **BAKE:** 25 min. + standing

>   1   pound bulk pork sausage
>   1   cup chopped onion
>   1   cup chopped sweet red
>   pepper
>   1/2   cup chopped fresh
>   mushrooms
>   3   teaspoons minced garlic

>   2-1/2   cups (10 ounces) shredded
>   Monterey Jack cheese,
>   *divided*
>   1-1/3   cups milk
>   3   eggs
>   3/4   cup biscuit/baking mix
>   3/4   teaspoon rubbed sage
>   1/4   teaspoon pepper

■ In a large skillet, cook the sausage, onion, red pepper, mushrooms and garlic over medium heat until meat is no longer pink; drain. Stir in 2 cups cheese. Transfer to a greased 9-in. deep-dish pie plate.

■ In a small bowl, combine the milk, eggs, biscuit mix, sage and pepper. Pour over sausage mixture.

■ Bake at 400° for 20-25 minutes or until a knife inserted near the center comes out clean. Sprinkle with the remaining cheese; bake 1-2 minutes longer or until cheese is melted. Let stand for 10 minutes before cutting.

Yield: 8 servings.

Bernice Morris
MARSHFIELD, MISSOURI

Less expensive cuts of pork become tender and tasty in this creamy, meal-in-one casserole. It's an all around great supper, because it's tasty and affordable. And to make things easier, the recipe only uses 5 ingredients plus salt and pepper.

1. Prepare rice mixes according to package directions. Meanwhile, in a large skillet, cook the sausage, celery and carrots over medium heat until meat is no longer pink; drain.

2. In a large bowl, combine the sausage mixture, rice, soups, onion powder, garlic powder and pepper. Transfer to two greased 11-in. x 7-in. baking dishes.

3. Cover and freeze one casserole for up to 3 months. Cover and bake the remaining casserole at 350° for 40-45 minutes or until vegetables are tender.

4. **To use frozen casserole:** Thaw in the refrigerator overnight. Remove from the refrigerator 30 minutes before baking. Bake as directed.

Yield: 2 casseroles (6-8 servings each).

Sausage Rice Casserole

Jennifer Trost
WEST LINN, OREGON

I fiddled around with this dish, trying to adjust it to my family's tastes. When my pickiest child cleaned her plate, I knew I'd found the right flavor combination.

Sausage Rice Casserole

PREP: 30 min. ■ **BAKE:** 40 min.

2 packages (7.2 ounces *each*) rice pilaf
2 pounds bulk pork sausage
6 celery ribs, chopped
4 medium carrots, sliced
1 can (10-3/4 ounces) condensed cream of chicken soup, undiluted
1 can (10-3/4 ounces) condensed cream of mushroom soup, undiluted
2 teaspoons onion powder
1/2 teaspoon garlic powder
1/4 teaspoon pepper

Here's a great way to utilize the leaves from a bunch of celery. First, cut the leaves off, wash, drain and dry with paper towels. Arrange on a cookie sheet and place in a 250° oven. When dry, allow to cool. Crush the leaves and store in a jar. The dried leaves add a nice flavor to food when fresh celery isn't on hand.

Pork Chop Supper

Edie DeSpain
LOGAN, UTAH

Here's a casserole supper that is so delicious and satisfying, there's no need for side dishes or extras. I found this wonderful, stick-to-the-ribs recipe in an old cookbook.

PREP: 20 min. ■ **BAKE:** 25 min.

1 medium tart apple, cored	2 tablespoons chopped onion
2 bone-in pork loin chops (about 3/4 inch thick and 8 ounces *each*)	3/4 cup water
	1 teaspoon chicken bouillon granules
3/4 teaspoon salt, *divided*	2 teaspoons butter, melted
1/4 teaspoon pepper	2 teaspoons brown sugar
2 teaspoons canola oil	1/8 teaspoon ground cinnamon
1/3 cup uncooked long grain rice	

■ Cut apple widthwise in half. Peel and chop half of apple; set aside. Cut remaining half into three rings; set aside.

■ Sprinkle chops with 1/2 teaspoon salt and pepper. In a large skillet, brown chops in oil for 3-4 minutes on each side. Transfer to a greased 11-in. x 7-in. baking dish; keep warm.

■ In same skillet, cook and stir rice and onion in drippings until rice is lightly browned. Stir in the water, bouillon and remaining salt. Stir in chopped apple. Bring to a boil. Reduce heat; cover and simmer for 10 minutes.

■ Spoon rice mixture around pork chops. In a small bowl, combine the butter, brown sugar and cinnamon; brush over apple slices. Arrange apple slices on top of chops.

■ Cover and bake at 350° for 25-30 minutes or until meat juices run clear and rice is tender.

Yield: 2 servings.

The amount of pork you need varies with the cut selected. Follow these guidelines: 2 to 2-1/2 servings per 1 pound of bone-in chops and roasts; 3 to 4 servings per 1 pound of boneless chops and roasts; about 1 serving per 1 pound of spareribs.

Creamy Ham And Macaroni

Christy Looper
COLORADO SPRINGS, COLORADO

The original American comfort food, macaroni and cheese, gets a makeover with the addition of cubed ham and grated Parmesan. Kids will love it!

PREP: 20 min.
BAKE: 20 min.

- 2 cups uncooked elbow macaroni
- 1/4 cup butter, cubed
- 1/4 cup all-purpose flour
- 2 cups milk
- 4 teaspoons chicken bouillon granules
- 1/4 teaspoon pepper
- 2 cups (8 ounces) shredded cheddar cheese, *divided*
- 1-1/2 cups cubed fully cooked ham
- 1/4 cup grated Parmesan cheese

■ Cook macaroni according to package directions; drain and set aside. In a large saucepan, melt butter over low heat; whisk in flour until smooth. Whisk in the milk, bouillon and pepper. Bring to a boil; cook and stir for 2 minutes or until thickened. Remove from the heat. Stir in 1 cup cheddar cheese, ham, Parmesan cheese and macaroni.

■ Transfer macaroni mixture to a greased 2-qt. baking dish. Sprinkle with the remaining cheddar cheese. Bake, uncovered, at 350° for 20-25 minutes or until bubbly. Let stand for 5 minutes before serving.

Yield: 6 servings.

Julie Jackman
BOUNTIFUL, UTAH

Here's a delightfully rich and creamy, all-in-one meal. My family just loves the easy-to-fix sauce. Plus, the dish is a great way to use up leftover ham.

Ham and Swiss Casserole

Ham and Swiss Casserole

PREP: 15 min. ■ BAKE: 30 min.

- 8 ounces uncooked penne pasta
- 2 envelopes country gravy mix
- 1 package (10 ounces) frozen chopped spinach, thawed and squeezed dry
- 2 cups (8 ounces) shredded Swiss cheese
- 2 cups cubed fully cooked ham
- 4-1/2 teaspoons ground mustard

- ■ Cook the pasta according to package directions. Meanwhile, in a large saucepan, cook the gravy mix according to package directions. Stir in the spinach, Swiss cheese, ham and ground mustard. Drain the pasta; stir into ham mixture.

- ■ Transfer pasta mixture to a greased 13-in. x 9-in. baking dish. Cover and bake at 350° for 20 minutes. Uncover; bake 10-15 minutes longer or until heated through.

Yield: 8 servings.

It's usually less expensive to buy cheese in blocks than in shredded form. To save money, purchase large quantities of cheese such as cheddar, Monterey Jack and Swiss, then shred in a food processor. Store the shredded cheese in heavy-duty resealable plastic bags and freeze, so you have it readily available whenever it's needed.

Sweet Potato Sausage Casserole

PREP: 20 min.
BAKE: 25 min.

- 8 ounces uncooked spiral pasta
- 8 ounces smoked sausage, cut into 1/4-inch slices
- 2 medium sweet potatoes, peeled and cut into 1/2-inch cubes
- 1 cup chopped green pepper
- 1/2 cup chopped onion
- 1 teaspoon minced garlic
- 2 tablespoons olive oil
- 1 can (14-1/2 ounces) diced tomatoes, undrained
- 1 cup heavy whipping cream
- 1/4 teaspoon salt
- 1/4 teaspoon pepper
- 1 cup (4 ounces) shredded cheddar cheese

- ■ Cook the pasta according to package directions. Meanwhile, in a large skillet, cook the sausage, sweet potatoes, green pepper, onion and garlic in olive oil over medium heat for 5 minutes or until the vegetables are tender; drain.

- ■ Add the tomatoes, cream, salt and pepper. Bring to a boil; remove from the heat. Drain the pasta; stir into the sausage mixture. Transfer to a greased 13-in. x 9-in. baking dish. Sprinkle with cheese.

- ■ Bake, uncovered, at 350° for 25-30 minutes or until bubbly. Let casserole stand for about 5 minutes before serving.

Yield: 8 servings.

Rickey Madden
CLINTON, SOUTH CAROLINA

Most people never consider combining sweet potatoes with pasta and kielbasa, but after adapting this recipe from several others, I've received several compliments on it. You can add more sausage or cheese, or use different varieties, to suit your taste.

- In a large skillet, saute the first five ingredients in butter for 5 minutes or until the red pepper and onion are tender. Remove from the heat; stir in the bread cubes, broth, apple juice, sage and basil.

- Meanwhile, in another large skillet, brown the chops in oil. Place the stuffing in a greased 11-in. x 7-in. baking dish. Place the chops on top; sprinkle with salt and pepper. Arrange the sweet potato around the edges of the dish.

- Cover and bake at 350° for 35-40 minutes or until a meat thermometer reads 160°.

Yield: 2 servings.

Winter Pork Chop Bake

Virginia Ricks
ROY, UTAH

Pork has always been a family favorite, and this recipe is a winner. All the work is done in the preparation, so there is very little cleanup after the meal.

Winter Pork Chop Bake

PREP: 20 min. ■ **BAKE:** 35 min.

1 medium tart apple, diced	3 tablespoons apple juice
1 small sweet red pepper, diced	1/2 teaspoon rubbed sage
1 small onion, chopped	1/4 teaspoon dried basil
1/4 cup golden raisins	2 bone-in pork chops (1/2 inch thick)
1/4 cup chopped walnuts	1 tablespoon canola oil
1 tablespoon butter	Salt and pepper to taste
3 slices rye bread, toasted and cubed	1 medium sweet potato, peeled and cut into 1/2-inch pieces
1/4 cup chicken broth	

Two varieties of sweet potato are readily available: one with pale skin and light yellow flesh, and another with dark skin and orange flesh. Both can be used in recipes interchangeably. The dark orange variety is commonly known as a yam, although true yams are not readily available in this country and are seldom grown here.

Wild Rice-Stuffed Pork Loin

Kim Rubner
WORTHINGTON, IOWA

This recipe features a flavorful stuffing made with wild rice, apricots and dried herbs tucked inside a tender pork roast. Topped with bacon strips, it's an impressive entree.

Wild Rice-Stuffed Pork Loin

PREP: 20 min. ■ **BAKE:** 2 hours + standing

- 1 whole boneless pork loin roast (4 pounds), trimmed
- 1 teaspoon salt
- 1/2 teaspoon garlic powder
- 1/4 teaspoon pepper
- 2 cups wild rice, cooked and drained
- 1-1/2 cups coarsely chopped dried apricots
- 1 cup chopped onion
- 3/4 cup finely chopped celery
- 3/4 cup minced fresh parsley
- 1/2 teaspoon rubbed sage
- 1/2 teaspoon dried thyme
- 1/2 cup chicken broth
- 5 bacon strips, cut in half

■ Cut roast down the center lengthwise to within 1/2 in. of bottom. Open roast so it lies flat. On each half, make a lengthwise slit down the center to within 1/2 in. of bottom. Sprinkle with salt, garlic powder and pepper.

■ In a large bowl, combine the rice, apricots, onion, celery, parsley, sage, thyme and broth. Divide half of the stuffing among the three slits. Roll up roast from a long side; tie with kitchen string at 2-in. intervals. Place the remaining stuffing in a greased shallow 2-qt. baking dish; set aside.

■ Bake roast, uncovered, at 350° for 2 hours. Carefully remove string. Place bacon strips over top. Bake 30-45 minutes longer or until a meat thermometer reads 160°.

■ Cover and bake reserved stuffing for 30 minutes or until heated through. Let roast stand for 10 minutes before slicing.

Yield: 8-10 servings.

A dark-hulled, aquatic grass native to North America, wild rice has a chewy texture and nutty flavor. Grains expand 3 to 4 times their original size and some of the kernels may pop, allowing you to see the white insides. Wild rice should be rinsed before cooking.

Kimberly Andresen
CHIEFLAND, FLORIDA

Here's a main course that's impressive enough for guests but simple enough for weeknights. The moist stuffing only takes a few moments to prepare. If it's summer when you make the recipe, try using fresh corn instead of frozen—it'll make the dish even more special.

Corn-Stuffed Pork Chops

PREP: 15 min. ■ **BAKE:** 35 min.

1/4 cup chopped onion	1/4 teaspoon salt
1/4 cup chopped green pepper	1/8 teaspoon ground cumin
1 tablespoon butter	1/8 teaspoon pepper
3/4 cup corn bread stuffing mix	4 bone-in pork loin chops (7 ounces *each*)
1/2 cup frozen corn, thawed	
2 tablespoons diced pimientos	

■ In a large skillet, saute the onion and green pepper in butter for 3-4 minutes or until tender. Stir in the stuffing mix, corn, pimientos, salt, cumin and pepper.

■ Cut a pocket in each chop by slicing almost to the bone. Stuff each chop with the mixture. Secure with toothpicks if necessary.

■ Place in an 11-in. x 7-in. baking dish coated with cooking spray. Bake, uncovered, at 375° for 35-40 minutes or until meat thermometer in the meat reads 160°. Discard toothpicks.

Yield: 4 servings.

Making a pocket in a pork chop is much easier than it seems. Keeping the chop flat on the cutting board, use a small, sharp knife, or the pointed end of a large, sharp knife to make a horizontal slit in the middle of the chop. Slice almost to the bone.

Kielbasa And Pepper Casserole

Sara Wilson
MIDDLEBOURNE, WEST VIRGINIA

This hearty, well-rounded casserole has a wonderful smoky flavor from the kielbasa. It's a meal-in-one that always goes over well at dinnertime. Cream adds just the right touch of richness.

PREP: 15 min.
BAKE: 55 min.

- 1/2 pound smoked kielbasa *or* Polish sausage, cut into 1/2-inch slices
- 4 small red potatoes, halved
- 1 medium onion, halved and sliced
- 1 medium sweet red pepper, cut into 1-inch pieces
- 2 tablespoons olive oil
- 1/8 teaspoon salt
- 1/8 teaspoon pepper
- 1/4 cup heavy whipping cream

Minced fresh parsley

■ In a small bowl, combine the sausage, potatoes, onion and red pepper. Drizzle with oil; sprinkle with salt and pepper. Toss to coat. Transfer to a greased 1-qt. baking dish.

■ Cover and bake at 375° for 45 minutes. Stir in cream; cover and bake 10-15 minutes longer or until vegetables are tender and the cream has thickened. Sprinkle with parsley.

Yield: 2 servings.

Penne and Smoked Sausage

Au Gratin Ham Potpie

PREP: 15 min.
BAKE: 40 min.

- 1 package (4.9 ounces) au gratin potatoes
- 1-1/2 cups boiling water
- 2 cups frozen peas and carrots
- 1-1/2 cups cubed fully cooked ham
- 1 can (10-3/4 ounces) condensed cream of chicken soup, undiluted
- 1 can (4 ounces) mushroom stems and pieces, drained
- 1/2 cup milk
- 1/2 cup sour cream
- 1 jar (2 ounces) diced pimientos, drained
- 1 sheet refrigerated pie pastry

■ In a large bowl, combine potatoes, contents of sauce mix and water. Stir in peas and carrots, ham, soup, mushrooms, milk, sour cream and pimientos. Transfer to an ungreased 2-qt. round baking dish.

■ Roll out pastry to fit top of dish; place over potato mixture. Flute edges; cut slits in pastry. Bake at 400° for 40-45 minutes or until golden brown. Let stand for 5 minutes before serving.

Yield: 4-6 servings.

Margaret Wilson
SUN CITY, CALIFORNIA

This must-try casserole tastes so good when it's fresh, hot and bubbly from the oven. The cheddar french-fried onions lend a cheesy, crunchy touch.

Penne and Smoked Sausage

PREP: 15 min. ■ **BAKE:** 30 min.

- 2 cups uncooked penne pasta
- 1 pound smoked sausage, cut into 1/4-inch slices
- 1-1/2 cups milk
- 1 can (10-3/4 ounces) condensed cream of celery soup, undiluted
- 1-1/2 cups cheddar french-fried onions, *divided*
- 1 cup (4 ounces) shredded part-skim mozzarella cheese, *divided*
- 1 cup frozen peas

■ Cook pasta according to package directions. Meanwhile, in a large skillet, brown sausage over medium heat for 5 minutes; drain. In a large bowl, combine milk and soup. Stir in 1/2 cup onions, 1/2 cup cheese, peas and sausage. Drain pasta; stir into sausage mixture.

■ Transfer to a greased 13-in. x 9-in. baking dish. Cover and bake at 375° for 25-30 minutes or until bubbly. Sprinkle with remaining onions and cheese. Bake, uncovered, 3-5 minutes longer or until cheese is melted.

Yield: 6 servings.

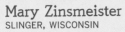

Mary Zinsmeister
SLINGER, WISCONSIN

We first had Aunt Dolly's potpie at a family get-together. We loved it and were so happy when she shared the recipe with us. Now, we make it almost every time we bake a ham. It's easy to double the recipe and create two potpies for a potluck.

Pantry Pork Dish

- Combine pork, half of the onion, allspice, oregano, 1/4 teaspoon salt and 1/4 teaspoon pepper. Press into the bottom of a greased 9-in. square baking dish. Top with potatoes and the remaining onion. Combine flour and remaining salt; sprinkle over potatoes.

- Cover with foil. Bake at 350° for 40 minutes; drain.

- Layer the squash, nutmeg, remaining pepper and beans on top of potatoes. Cover and bake 30 minutes longer or until vegetables are tender. Sprinkle with almonds; return to the oven for 5 minutes or until bubbly.

Yield: 4 servings.

Julia Trachsel
VICTORIA, BRITISH COLUMBIA

I put this dish together one day when we had unexpected company for dinner. I used ingredients from my pantry and tossed in some ground pork. Our guests raved about the flavor.

Pantry Pork Dish

PREP: 10 min. ■ BAKE: 1-1/4 hours

1 pound ground pork	2 tablespoons all-purpose flour
1 small onion, chopped, *divided*	2-1/2 cups julienned peeled butternut squash
1/2 teaspoon ground allspice	1/4 teaspoon ground nutmeg
1/2 teaspoon dried oregano	1-1/2 cups frozen green beans
1/2 teaspoon salt, *divided*	1/4 cup sliced almonds, toasted
1/2 teaspoon pepper, *divided*	
3 medium potatoes, peeled and sliced 1/4 inch thick	

Preparing winter squash for a recipe can be challenging because of the tough skin and flesh. To make peeling butternut squash easier, microwave the raw whole squash on high in 30-second increments. In 2-4 minutes, the squash's peel will become easier to remove and the flesh easier to cut.

Kate Collins
AUBURN, WASHINGTON

This recipe is wonderful because it's not only tasty, but the potatoes are a built-in side dish! We made it for our anniversary party, and our guests were more than impressed.

Herbed Pork and Potatoes

Herbed Pork and Potatoes*

PREP: 25 min. ■ BAKE: 1-1/2 hours + standing

3 tablespoons minced fresh rosemary	2 teaspoons salt
2 tablespoons minced fresh marjoram	2 teaspoons pepper
8 garlic cloves, minced	1 boneless whole pork loin roast (3 pounds)
4 teaspoons minced fresh sage	4 pounds medium red potatoes, quartered
4 teaspoons olive oil, *divided*	

■ Combine the rosemary, marjoram, garlic, sage, 3 teaspoons oil, salt and pepper. Rub roast with 2 tablespoons herb mixture.

■ In a Dutch oven over medium-high heat, brown roast in remaining oil on all sides. Place in a roasting pan coated with cooking spray. Toss potatoes with remaining herb mixture; arrange around roast.

■ Cover and bake at 350° for 1-1/2 to 2 hours or until a meat thermometer reads 160°. Let stand for 10 minutes before slicing.

Yield: 9 servings.

✱Nutrition Facts: 4 ounces cooked pork with 3/4 cup potatoes equals 358 calories, 9 g fat (3 g saturated fat), 75 mg cholesterol, 581 mg sodium, 34 g carbohydrate, 4 g fiber, 33 g protein. **Diabetic Exchanges:** 4 lean meat, 2 starch, 1/2 fat.

One-Pot Pork And Rice*

Duna Stephens
PALISADE, COLORADO

No one will guess that this filling entree goes easy on fat and calories. Green pepper and onion enhance the Spanish-style rice and tender chops, which are covered with diced tomatoes and gravy.

PREP: 20 min.
BAKE: 1 hour

    6 boneless pork loin chops
      (5 ounces *each*)
    2 teaspoons canola oil
    1 cup uncooked long grain
      rice
    1 large onion, sliced
    1 large green pepper, sliced
    1 envelope pork gravy mix
    1 can (28 ounces) diced
      tomatoes, undrained
1-1/2 cups water

■ In a Dutch oven, brown pork chops in oil on both sides; drain. Remove chops. Layer rice, onion and green pepper in Dutch oven; top with pork chops. Combine the gravy mix, tomatoes and water; pour over chops. Cover; bake at 350° for 1 hour or until a meat thermometer reads 160°.

Yield: 6 servings.

✱Nutrition Facts: 1 pork chop with 1/2 cup rice equals 391 calories, 10 g fat (3 g saturated fat), 83 mg cholesterol, 545 mg sodium, 40 g carbohydrate, 3 g fiber, 33 g protein. **Diabetic Exchanges:** 3-1/2 lean meat, 2 starch, 2 vegetable.

4

Bobbie Keefer
BYERS, COLORADO

These tasty shish kabobs are baked instead of grilled, so you can enjoy them even when the weather doesn't cooperate. The sweet glaze, made with apricot preserves, brown sugar, pineapple juice and spices, mixes with the pan drippings for a delicious sauce.

Baked Pineapple-Pork Kabobs

PREP: 30 min. ■ BAKE: 25 min.

2 pounds boneless pork loin roast, cubed

1 large green pepper, cut into 1-inch pieces

1 sweet onion, cut into 1-inch pieces

18 medium fresh mushrooms

18 fresh sweet cherries, pitted

18 pineapple chunks

1/2 cup apricot preserves

1/2 cup packed brown sugar

2 tablespoons butter, melted

1 tablespoon unsweetened pineapple juice

1/4 to 1/2 teaspoon ground cloves

Hot cooked rice

■ Line a 15-in. x 10-in. x 1-in. baking pan with aluminum foil and grease the foil. On six metal or soaked wooden skewers, alternately thread the pork, green pepper, onion, mushrooms, cherries and pineapple. Place in the prepared pan.

■ In a small bowl, combine the preserves, brown sugar, butter, pineapple juice and cloves. Spoon half of the sauce over kabobs.

■ Bake at 375° for 15 minutes on each side, or until meat is no longer pink, basting occasionally with remaining sauce. Serve with rice.

Yield: 6 servings.

While pitting cherries, place your hands and the pitter inside a large, clear plastic bag. When being pitted, cherries tend to splatter, staining your clothes and anything else in the vicinity. The plastic bag helps to contain the juice, and to prevent you from doing an extra load of laundry!

Ham-Noodle Bake

Mary Richards
ELLENDALE, MINNESOTA

My husband and I build up quite an appetite after a long day doing chores on the farm. So I've come to rely on this creamy, comforting casserole. Horseradish and mustard add a little zip.

PREP: 10 min.
BAKE: 30 min.

1/4 cup butter, cubed

1/4 cup all-purpose flour

1/2 teaspoon salt

1/8 teaspoon pepper

2-1/2 cups milk

3 to 4 teaspoons prepared horseradish

1 tablespoon prepared mustard

6 cups cooked wide egg noodles

2 cups cubed fully cooked ham

1 cup cubed cheddar cheese

1/2 cup soft bread crumbs, toasted

■ In a large saucepan over medium heat, melt butter. Stir in flour, salt and pepper until smooth. Gradually add milk. Bring to a boil. Cook and stir for 2 minutes or until thickened and bubbly. Add horseradish and mustard; mix well. Stir in the noodles, ham and cheese.

■ Pour into a greased 2-1/2-qt. baking dish. Cover and bake at 350° for 20 minutes. Uncover; sprinkle with bread crumbs. Bake 10-15 minutes longer or until bubbly and heated through.

Yield: 4-6 servings.

Janet Ware
Novotny
GRAND ISLAND,
NEBRASKA

This economical dish is comforting. If you know time will be short, boil the potatoes a day ahead and refrigerate. That way you can just assemble and bake the day you serve it.

Penny Casserole

Penny Casserole

PREP: 25 min. ■ BAKE: 25 min.

1-1/4 pounds red potatoes, cubed
10 hot dogs (1 pound), sliced
2 tablespoons diced onion
1 cup frozen peas, thawed
1 can (10-3/4 ounces) condensed cream of mushroom soup, undiluted
3 tablespoons butter, melted
1 tablespoon prepared mustard
1/8 teaspoon pepper

■ Place potatoes in a large saucepan and cover with water. Bring to a boil. Reduce heat; cover and simmer for 15-20 minutes or until tender. Drain.

■ In a greased 2-1/2-qt. baking dish, combine the potatoes, hot dogs, onion and peas. Combine the soup, butter, mustard and pepper; gently stir into potato mixture.

■ Bake, uncovered, at 350° for 25 minutes or until heated through.

Yield: 6-8 servings.

Remember to preheat your oven before baking or roasting. Baked items depend on the correct oven temperature to help them cook properly. This takes 15 to 20 minutes and can be done while preparing the recipe.

Pork Tenderloin With Glazed Onions*

PREP: 20 min.
BAKE: 40 min.

4 large sweet onions, sliced (about 8 cups)
1/4 cup butter, cubed
1 cup chopped dried apricots *or* golden raisins
1/4 cup packed brown sugar
1/4 cup balsamic vinegar
1/2 teaspoon salt
1/2 teaspoon pepper
2 pork tenderloins (1 pound *each*)

■ In large skillet, saute onions in butter for 2 minutes. Stir in the apricots, brown sugar, vinegar, salt and pepper; cook until onions are tender.

■ Place pork tenderloins on a rack coated with cooking spray in a shallow roasting pan; top with onion mixture.

■ Bake, uncovered, at 375° for 40-45 minutes or until a meat thermometer reads 160°. Let the tenderloins stand for 5-10 minutes before slicing. Serve with onion mixture.

Yield: 8 servings.

*Nutrition Facts: 4 ounces of cooked pork with 1/4 cup onion mixture equals 284 calories, 10 g fat (5 g saturated fat), 78 mg cholesterol, 252 mg sodium, 26 g carbohydrate, 2 g fiber, 24 g protein. **Diabetic Exchanges:** 3 lean meat, 1 vegetable, 1 fruit, 1 fat, 1/2 starch.

Janice Christofferson
EAGLE RIVER, WISCONSIN

My husband and I love pork, especially when it's dressed up like this. Dried apricots and glazed sweet onions go beautifully with the juicy meat. It's a great dish to serve company, but also for everyday. Any leftover pork makes a great sandwich the next day.

Fish & Seafood

236

233

226

For a refreshing change of pace, try a hearty oven entree made with seafood. You'll find healthy twists on traditional one-dish meals like lasagna, stuffed peppers, hot dishes and pizza. What a great way to take a break from meat and potatoes!

Delightful Tuna Casserole

- Cook macaroni according to package directions. Meanwhile, in a large bowl, combine the soup, mushrooms, cheese, milk, tuna, pimientos, onion, mustard and salt. Drain macaroni; add to tuna mixture and mix well.

- Transfer to a 2-qt. baking dish coated with cooking spray. Sprinkle with cornflakes. Bake, uncovered, at 350° for 25-30 minutes or until bubbly.

Yield: 5 servings.

To make Delightful Tuna Casserole even more appealing to kids, try using different shapes of pasta instead of the macaroni called for in the recipe. Give these fun pasta shapes a try: fusilli (corkscrew shape), rotelle (wagon wheels), farfalle (butterflies) or small shell-shaped pasta.

Colleen Willey
HAMBURG, NEW YORK
This mild, homemade tuna casserole will truly satisfy your family's craving for heartwarming comfort food! It's a great way to get kids to eat fish, too.

Delightful Tuna Casserole

PREP: 15 min. ■ BAKE: 25 min.

1 package (7 ounces) elbow macaroni

1 can (10-3/4 ounces) reduced-fat reduced-sodium condensed cream of mushroom soup, undiluted

1 cup sliced fresh mushrooms

1 cup (4 ounces) shredded reduced-fat cheddar cheese

1 cup fat-free milk

1 can (6 ounces) light water-packed tuna, drained and flaked

2 tablespoons diced pimientos

3 teaspoons dried minced onion

1 teaspoon ground mustard

1/4 teaspoon salt

1/3 cup crushed cornflakes

Carole Lynn Derifield
VALDEZ, ALASKA

North meets south of the border in this versatile hot dish, where I roll our local Alaskan halibut into flour tortillas. It's one of my most requested recipes and a mainstay for potlucks and wedding buffets. If you are unable to find halibut, it's okay to use any firm white fish, such as cod or haddock.

Halibut Enchiladas

PREP: 45 min. ■ BAKE: 40 min.

3 pounds halibut fillets
1/2 teaspoon salt
1/8 teaspoon pepper
1/8 teaspoon cayenne pepper
1 medium onion, finely chopped
1 medium green pepper, finely chopped
1 tablespoon canola oil
2 garlic cloves, minced
1 can (10 ounces) hot enchilada sauce
1 can (10 ounces) green enchilada sauce

1 cup (8 ounces) sour cream
1 cup mayonnaise
2 cans (4 ounces each) chopped green chilies
2 cans (10 ounces each) mild enchilada sauce
4 cups (16 ounces) shredded Colby-Monterey Jack cheese
24 flour tortillas (6 inches), warmed
1 bunch green onions, thinly sliced
2 tablespoons chopped ripe olives

■ Place fillets on a greased baking sheet. Sprinkle with salt, pepper and cayenne. Bake, uncovered, at 350° for 15-20 minutes or until fish flakes easily with a fork.

■ Meanwhile, in a large skillet, saute onion and green pepper in oil until tender. Add garlic; saute 1-2 minutes longer.

■ Flake the fish with two forks and set aside. In a large bowl, combine the hot enchilada sauce, green enchilada sauce, sour cream, mayonnaise, chilies, onion mixture and fish. Spread 1/2 cup mild enchilada sauce into each of two greased 13-in. x 9-in. baking dishes. Sprinkle each with 1 cup cheese.

■ Place a heaping 1/3 cup halibut mixture down the center of each tortilla. Roll up each and place seam side down over cheese. Pour remaining sauce over top.

■ Cover and bake at 350° for 30 minutes. Sprinkle with the green onions, olives and remaining cheese. Bake, uncovered, for 10-15 minutes longer or until cheese is melted.

Yield: 12 servings.

Fish Stick Supper

Ruth Andrewson
LEAVENWORTH, WASHINGTON

Dill adds fresh flavor to this comforting combination of foods you likely keep in your freezer. When our children were growing up, they loved this meal.

PREP: 10 min.
BAKE: 50 min.

1 package (12 ounces) frozen shredded hash brown potatoes, thawed
4 eggs
2 cups milk
1 tablespoon dried minced onion
1 tablespoon snipped fresh dill *or* 1 teaspoon dill weed
1-1/4 teaspoons seasoned salt
1/8 teaspoon pepper
1 cup (4 ounces) shredded cheddar cheese
1 package (12 ounces) frozen breaded fish sticks (about 18)

■ Break apart the hash browns with a fork; set aside. In a large bowl, beat eggs and milk. Add minced onion, dill, seasoned salt and pepper. Stir in the hash browns and cheese. Transfer to a greased 11-in. x 7-in. baking dish; arrange the fish sticks over the top.

■ Bake, uncovered, at 350° for 50 minutes or until top is golden brown and fish flakes with a fork. Let casserole stand for 5 minutes before cutting.

Yield: 6 servings.

Hazel McMullin
AMHERST,
NOVA SCOTIA

My father was a fisherman, so we ate fish almost every day. Over the years, I've tasted many seafood dishes, but none better than this one.

Seafood Au Gratin

Seafood Au Gratin

PREP: 30 min. ■ BAKE: 15 min.

4 tablespoons butter, *divided*
2 tablespoons all-purpose flour
1/8 teaspoon pepper
1 cup chicken broth
1/2 cup milk
1/2 cup grated Parmesan cheese, *divided*
1/2 pound sea scallops

1 pound haddock *or* cod fillets, cut into six pieces
1-1/2 cups sliced fresh mushrooms
1/2 cup shredded part-skim mozzarella cheese
1/2 cup shredded cheddar cheese

■ In a large saucepan, melt 2 tablespoons butter. Stir in flour and pepper until smooth; gradually add broth and milk. Bring to a boil; cook and stir for 2 minutes or until thickened. Stir in 1/4 cup Parmesan cheese; set aside.

■ Place scallops in another saucepan; cover with water. Simmer, uncovered, for 4-5 minutes or until firm and opaque. Meanwhile, place fillets in a shallow 2-qt. microwave-safe dish. Cover and microwave on high for 2-4 minutes or until fish flakes easily with a fork. Drain scallops. Arrange fish and scallops in a greased 11-in. x 7-in. baking dish.

■ In a small skillet, saute mushrooms in remaining butter until tender; stir into cheese sauce. Spoon over seafood. Sprinkle with the mozzarella, cheddar and remaining Parmesan cheese.

■ Cover and bake at 350° for 15-20 minutes or until bubbly and the cheeses are melted.

Yield: 6 servings.

Baked Fish And Rice

Jo Groth
PLAINFIELD, IOWA

The first time I tried this meal-in-one dish, it was an instant hit at our house. Fish and rice are a tasty change of pace from traditional meat-and-potato fare.

PREP: 5 min.
BAKE: 35 min.

1-1/2 cups boiling chicken broth
1/2 cup uncooked long grain rice
1/4 teaspoon Italian seasoning
1/4 teaspoon garlic powder
3 cups frozen chopped broccoli, thawed and drained
1 tablespoon grated Parmesan cheese
1 can (2.8 ounces) french-fried onions, *divided*
1 pound fresh *or* frozen fish fillets, thawed

Dash paprika
1/2 cup shredded cheddar cheese

■ In a greased 11-in. x 7-in. baking dish, combine the broth, rice, Italian seasoning and garlic powder. Cover and bake at 375° for 10 minutes. Add the broccoli, Parmesan cheese and half of the onions. Top with fish fillets; sprinkle with paprika.

■ Cover and bake 20-25 minutes longer or until the fish flakes easily with a fork. Uncover; sprinkle with cheddar cheese and remaining onions. Return to the oven for 3 minutes or until cheese is melted.

Yield: 4 servings.

Cheesy Fish Fillets with Spinach

Marla Brenneman
GOSHEN, INDIANA

If you have trouble coaxing children to eat their greens, such as spinach, this fast-to-fix dish might be the solution. The cheese sauce works for me every time!

Cheesy Fish Fillets With Spinach*

PREP: 20 min. ■ **BAKE:** 25 min.

- 2 tablespoons butter
- 2 tablespoons all-purpose flour
- 1 teaspoon chicken bouillon granules
- Dash nutmeg
- Dash cayenne pepper
- Dash white pepper
- 1 cup milk
- 2/3 cup shredded cheddar *or* shredded Swiss cheese

- 1 package (10 ounces) frozen chopped spinach, thawed and well-drained
- 1 tablespoon lemon juice
- 1 pound cod fillet *or* haddock fillets, cut into serving-size pieces
- 1/2 teaspoon salt
- 2 tablespoons grated Parmesan cheese
- Paprika

■ In a large skillet, melt butter. Stir in the flour, bouillon, nutmeg, cayenne and white pepper until smooth. Gradually stir in milk. Bring to a boil; cook and stir for 1-2 minutes or until thickened. Stir in the cheddar cheese until melted; set aside.

■ Place spinach in an ungreased 8-in. square baking dish. Sprinkle with lemon juice. Arrange fish on spinach; sprinkle with salt. Spoon sauce over top.

■ Bake, uncovered, at 350° for 20-25 minutes or until fish flakes easily with a fork. Sprinkle with Parmesan cheese and paprika; bake 5 minutes longer or until lightly browned.

Yield: 4 servings.

*Nutrition Facts: 1 sole fillet equals 307 calories, 16 g fat (0 saturated fat), 108 mg cholesterol, 860 mg sodium, 10 g carbohydrate, 0 fiber, 31 g protein. **Diabetic Exchanges:** 2 vegetable, 1 fat.

One pound of fresh spinach will yield 10-12 cups of torn leaves, which will cook down to about 1 cup. You can substitute 1-1/2 pounds of fresh spinach that are cooked for one package of frozen chopped spinach (which yields about 1-1/2 cups).

Salmon Stuffed Peppers

Kathleen Bowman
SUN VALLEY, NEVADA

These colorful stuffed peppers are a nice change from the usual ground beef versions. The dried herbs and fresh cilantro really complement the fresh salmon.

Salmon Stuffed Peppers

PREP: 35 min. ■ BAKE: 25 min.

6 medium green, sweet yellow *or* red peppers

1-1/4 pounds salmon fillets *or* salmon steaks

3/4 cup chicken broth

1 medium leek (white portion only), chopped *or* 1/2 cup chopped green onions

1 to 3 medium jalapeno peppers, minced

2 tablespoons minced fresh cilantro

1 teaspoon Worcestershire sauce

1/2 teaspoon dried tarragon

1/2 teaspoon dried oregano

1/4 teaspoon salt

1/8 teaspoon pepper

2 cups hot cooked rice

1/2 cup tartar sauce

1/2 cup sour cream

2 tablespoons shredded Parmesan cheese

■ Cut tops off peppers and remove seeds. Cook peppers in boiling water for 3-5 minutes or until crisp-tender. Drain and rinse in cold water; set aside.

■ Broil salmon 4-6 in. from the heat for 4-5 minutes on each side or until fish flakes easily with a fork. Discard the bones and skin. Flake fish with a fork; set aside.

■ In a large skillet, combine the broth, leek, jalapenos, cilantro, Worcestershire sauce, tarragon, oregano, salt and pepper. Bring to a boil. Reduce heat; simmer, uncovered, for 10 minutes or until the liquid has evaporated.

■ Stir in the hot rice, tartar sauce and sour cream. Fold in the cooked salmon. Spoon into the peppers. Place in an ungreased shallow baking dish. Sprinkle with Parmesan cheese.

■ Cover and bake at 350° for 25-30 minutes or until peppers are tender and filling is hot.

Yield: 6 servings.

Editor's Note: When cutting hot peppers, disposable gloves are recommended. Avoid touching your face.

An excellent substitute for rice in stuffed peppers is cooked barley or whole kernel corn. Adding a tablespoon or two of quick-cooking oats will help keep the dishes from getting too saucy after baking.

Jeanne Holt
MENDOTA HEIGHTS,
MINNESOTA
*I serve this dish with
rice or biscuits. You
can use frozen
asparagus instead
of artichokes and
cream of asparagus
soup instead of
cream of shrimp.*

Artichoke Shrimp Bake

Artichoke Shrimp Bake

PREP: 20 min. ■ BAKE: 20 min.

- 1 pound cooked medium shrimp, peeled and deveined
- 1 can (14 ounces) water-packed quartered artichoke hearts, rinsed, drained and quartered
- 2/3 cup frozen pearl onions, thawed
- 2 cups sliced fresh mushrooms
- 1 small sweet red pepper, chopped
- 2 tablespoons butter
- 1 can (10-3/4 ounces) condensed cream of shrimp soup, undiluted
- 1/2 cup sour cream
- 1/4 cup sherry *or* chicken broth
- 2 teaspoons Worcestershire sauce
- 1 teaspoon grated lemon peel
- 1/8 teaspoon white pepper

TOPPING:
- 1/2 cup soft bread crumbs
- 1/3 cup grated Parmesan cheese
- 1 tablespoon minced fresh parsley
- 1 tablespoon butter, melted

Hot cooked rice, optional

■ Place the shrimp, artichokes and onions in a greased 11-in. x 7-in. baking dish; set aside. In a large skillet, saute mushrooms and red pepper in butter until tender. Stir in the soup, sour cream, sherry or broth, Worcestershire sauce, lemon peel and white pepper; heat through. Pour over shrimp mixture.

■ For topping, combine the bread crumbs, Parmesan, parsley and butter; sprinkle over top. Bake, uncovered, at 375° for 20-25 minutes or until bubbly and topping is golden brown. Serve with rice if desired.

Yield: 4 servings.

Broccoli Tuna Bake

Pamela Tesoriero
ETIWANDA, CALIFORNIA
*I remember the day I rushed
home from my home economics
class at school with this recipe in
hand. My parents loved it then,
and my husband and son do now.
This recipe comes in handy on a
busy evening, when I need a good,
quick meal.*

PREP: 10 min.
BAKE: 30 min.

- 1 can (10-3/4 ounces) condensed cream of chicken soup, undiluted
- 1/3 cup milk
- 1 tablespoon lemon juice
- 1 can (12 ounces) albacore tuna, drained and flaked
- 1-1/2 cups cooked rice
- 1/4 teaspoon pepper
- 6 cups frozen broccoli florets, cooked and drained
- 1/2 cup shredded cheddar cheese

■ In a large bowl, combine the soup, milk and lemon juice. Stir in tuna, rice and pepper.

■ Transfer to a greased 10-in. pie plate or quiche dish. Bake, uncovered, at 375° for 25 minutes. Top with the broccoli; sprinkle with the cheese. Bake 5-10 minutes longer or until cheese is melted.

Yield: 4-6 servings.

Susan LeBrun
SULPHUR, LOUISIANA

Topped with fresh shrimp and melted cheese, the delicious main dish makes a timely supper with a special touch. A pre-baked pizza crust takes the fuss out of this recipe.

Shrimp Pizza

Shrimp Pizza*

PREP/TOTAL TIME: 30 min.

1 tablespoon butter

4-1/2 teaspoons all-purpose flour

1/4 to 1/2 teaspoon ground mustard

1/8 to 1/4 teaspoon cayenne pepper

1/8 teaspoon salt

1 cup 2% milk

1 small onion, chopped

1 pound uncooked medium shrimp, peeled and deveined

1 prebaked Italian bread shell crust (14 ounces)

3/4 cup shredded part-skim mozzarella cheese

■ For white sauce, in a small nonstick saucepan, melt butter. Stir in the flour, mustard, cayenne and salt until smooth; gradually add milk. Bring to a boil; cook and stir for 2 minutes or until thickened. Remove from the heat; set aside.

■ In a large nonstick skillet coated with cooking spray, cook onion over medium heat for 2 minutes. Add shrimp; cook and stir 2-3 minutes longer. Drain.

■ Place crust on a pizza pan or baking sheet; spread with white sauce. Top with shrimp mixture and cheese. Bake at 425° for 8-12 minutes or until shrimp turn pink and cheese is melted.

Yield: 6 slices.

*Nutrition Facts: 1 slice equals 317 calories, 9 g fat (3 g saturated fat), 128 mg cholesterol, 633 mg sodium, 34 g carbohydrate, trace fiber, 24 g protein. **Diabetic Exchanges:** 2 starch, 2 lean meat, 1 fat.

Crab Cake-Stuffed Portobellos

PREP/TOTAL TIME: 30 min.

6 large portobello mushrooms

3/4 cup finely chopped sweet onion

2 tablespoons olive oil, *divided*

1 package (8 ounces) cream cheese, softened

1 egg

1/2 cup seasoned bread crumbs

1/2 cup plus 1 teaspoon grated Parmesan cheese, *divided*

1 teaspoon seafood seasoning

2 cans (6-1/2 ounces *each*) lump crabmeat, drained

1/4 teaspoon paprika

■ Remove stems from mushrooms (discard or save for another use); set caps aside. In a small skillet, saute onion in 1 tablespoon oil until tender. In a small bowl, combine the cream cheese, egg, bread crumbs, 1/2 cup Parmesan cheese and seafood seasoning. Gently stir in crab and onion.

■ Spoon 1/2 cup crab mixture into each mushroom cap; drizzle with the remaining olive oil. Sprinkle with paprika and the remaining Parmesan cheese. Place in a greased 15-in. x 10-in. x 1-in. baking pan.

■ Bake, uncovered, at 400° for 15-20 minutes or until mushrooms are tender.

Yield: 6 servings.

Jennifer Coduto
KENT, OHIO

These stuffed mushrooms are delicious, and the canned crabmeat transforms them into something absolutely elegant and impressive. This recipe is also versatile because it can be served as an hors d'oeuvre or a light main dish.

Elena Hansen
RUIDOSO,
NEW MEXICO

This comforting dish is loaded with scallops, shrimp and crab. The creamy sauce helps make it the "crown jewel" in my repertoire of recipes.

Seafood Lasagna

Seafood Lasagna

PREP: 35 min. ■ **BAKE:** 35 min. + standing

- 1 green onion, finely chopped
- 2 tablespoons canola oil
- 2 tablespoons plus 1/2 cup butter, *divided*
- 1/2 cup chicken broth
- 1 bottle (8 ounces) clam juice
- 1 pound bay scallops
- 1 pound uncooked small shrimp, peeled and deveined
- 1 package (8 ounces) imitation crabmeat, chopped

- 1/4 teaspoon white pepper, *divided*
- 1/2 cup all-purpose flour
- 1-1/2 cups milk
- 1/2 teaspoon salt
- 1 cup heavy whipping cream
- 1/2 cup shredded Parmesan cheese, *divided*
- 9 lasagna noodles, cooked and drained

To peel and devein shrimp, start on the underside, by the head area, and pull the legs and first section of shell to one side. Continue to pull the remainder of the shell off (remove the shell by tail if desired). Use a small knife to make a shallow slit down the back of the shrimp, then remove the vein by rinsing the shrimp under cold water.

■ In a large skillet, saute onion in oil and 2 tablespoons butter until tender. Stir in broth and clam juice; bring to a boil. Add the scallops, shrimp, crab and 1/8 teaspoon pepper; return to a boil. Reduce heat; simmer, uncovered, for 4-5 minutes or until shrimp turn pink and the scallops are firm and opaque, stirring gently. Drain, reserving cooking liquid; set the seafood mixture aside.

■ In a large saucepan, melt the remaining butter; stir in flour until smooth. Combine milk and reserved cooking liquid; gradually add to the saucepan. Add salt and remaining pepper. Bring to a boil; cook and stir for 2 minutes or until thickened. Remove from the heat; stir in cream and 1/4 cup Parmesan cheese. Stir 3/4 cup white sauce into the seafood mixture.

■ Spread 1/2 cup white sauce in a greased 13-in. x 9-in. baking dish. Top with three noodles; spread with half of the seafood mixture and 1-1/4 cups sauce. Repeat layers. Top with the remaining noodles, sauce and Parmesan cheese.

■ Bake, uncovered, at 350° for 35-40 minutes or until golden brown. Let stand for 15 minutes before cutting.

Yield: 12 servings.

Mango Couscous with Salmon

- In a small bowl, combine the oil, minced garlic, salt, pepper and 2 tablespoons parsley. Rub over salmon. Broil 4 in. from the heat for 6-8 minutes on each side or until fish flakes easily with a fork.

- Meanwhile, in a large saucepan, bring the broth and butter to a boil. Stir in couscous. Cover and remove from the heat; let stand for 5 minutes. Stir in the tomatoes, mango and remaining parsley.

- In a blender, combine the sauce ingredients; cover and puree for 1-2 minutes or until smooth. Serve with the salmon and couscous.

Yield: 4 servings.

Tammy Strange
STATHAM, GEORGIA
This elegant meal-in-one features a hearty portion of salmon served on flavorful couscous and topped with an amazing mango sauce featuring basil, honey and Dijon mustard.

Mango Couscous with Salmon

PREP/TOTAL TIME: 30 min.

1/4 cup canola oil
2-1/2 teaspoons minced garlic
1/4 teaspoon salt
1/4 teaspoon pepper
1/4 cup minced fresh parsley, *divided*
4 salmon fillets (6 ounces *each*)
2 cups chicken broth
1 tablespoon butter
1 package (10 ounces) plain couscous
2 medium tomatoes, chopped
1 medium mango, peeled and chopped

MANGO SAUCE:
1 medium mango, peeled and cut into chunks
2 tablespoons lemon juice
2 tablespoons honey
2 fresh basil leaves
1 tablespoon minced fresh parsley
1 tablespoon water
1 tablespoon Dijon mustard

When buying

fresh fish fillets or steaks, look for firm flesh that has a moist look. Don't purchase fish that looks dried out. Fresh fish should have a mild smell, not a strong odor.

Cynthia Kolberg
SYRACUSE, INDIANA

I make this pie a lot because it's quick and easy to prepare. I teach during the day, so my cooking time is limited, and this is one of my husband's favorites. I like the combination of potato flakes and french-fried onions in this pastry crust.

Tater Crust Tuna Pie

PREP: 15 min. ■ **BAKE:** 30 min.

1 cup all-purpose flour

1-1/4 cups mashed potato flakes, *divided*

1/2 cup cold butter

3 to 4 tablespoons ice water

1 can (2.8 ounces) french-fried onions, *divided*

1 egg

1 can (10-3/4 ounces) reduced-fat reduced-sodium condensed cream of mushroom soup, undiluted

1 cup (4 ounces) shredded cheddar cheese, *divided*

1 can (6-1/2 ounces) light water-packed tuna, drained and flaked

2 tablespoons chopped pimiento-stuffed green olives

■ In a small bowl, combine flour and 1/2 cup potato flakes; cut in butter until crumbly. Add water, 1 tablespoon at a time, until dough is moist enough to hold together. Press pastry over bottom and up sides of an ungreased 9-in. pie plate. Flute edge. Set aside 1/2 cup onions for the topping. Sprinkle remaining onions into pastry shell.

■ In a large bowl, combine the egg, soup, 1/2 cup cheese, remaining potato flakes, tuna and olives. Spoon into pastry crust.

■ Bake at 350° for 25 minutes or until crust is golden. Sprinkle with remaining cheese and reserved onions; bake 5-10 minutes longer or until cheese is melted. Let stand for 5 minutes before serving.

Yield: 6-8 servings.

To flute a pie crust, the pastry should be trimmed to 1/2 in. beyond the rim of the pie plate for a single-crust pie and 1 in. for a double-crust pie. This overhang is then turned under to form the built-up edge. Position your index finger on the edge of the crust, pointing out. Place the thumb and index finger of your other hand on the outside edge and pinch dough around the index finger to form a V shape. Continue around the edge.

Broccoli-Stuffed Sole*

Edna Lee
GREELEY, COLORADO
Lemon enhances the mild-tasting sole, and the stuffing makes this fish special enough for company.

PREP: 15 min.
BAKE: 25 min.

2 tablespoons butter, melted

1 to 2 tablespoons lemon juice

1 teaspoon salt

1/4 teaspoon pepper

3 cups frozen chopped broccoli, thawed and drained

1 cup cooked rice

1 cup (4 ounces) shredded reduced-fat cheddar cheese

8 sole *or* whitefish fillets (4 ounces *each*)

■ In a small bowl, combine the butter, lemon juice, salt and pepper. In another bowl, combine the broccoli, rice, cheese and half of the butter mixture.

■ Spoon 1/2 cup onto each fillet. Roll up; place seam side down in a baking dish coated with cooking spray. Pour remaining butter mixture over roll-ups.

■ Bake, uncovered, at 350° for 25 minutes or until fish flakes easily with a fork. Baste with pan drippings; sprinkle with paprika.

Yield: 8 servings.

＊**Nutrition Facts:** 1 stuffed fillet equals 190 calories, 6 g fat (3 g saturated fat), 64 mg cholesterol, 478 mg sodium, 8 g carbohydrate, 1 g fiber, 26 g protein. **Diabetic Exchanges:** 3 lean meat, 1 vegetable.

Shirley Gever
TOMS RIVER,
NEW JERSEY

Ideal for anyone counting calories, this meal is super tasty, easy and quick. I recommend serving it with baked potatoes.

Dilled Fish and Vegetable Packet

Dilled Fish and Vegetable Packet*

PREP: 15 min. ■ **BAKE:** 20 min.

4 tilapia fillets (4 ounces *each*)

Refrigerated butter-flavored spray

1/2 teaspoon salt, *divided*

1/4 teaspoon pepper, *divided*

2 cups fresh snow peas

2 cups fresh baby carrots, halved lengthwise

1 green onion, thinly sliced

2 tablespoons minced fresh dill

2 garlic cloves, minced

1/2 cup white wine *or* reduced-sodium chicken broth

■ Place an 18-in. x 12-in. piece of heavy-duty foil on a large baking sheet. Arrange fillets in a single layer on foil; spritz with butter-flavored spray. Sprinkle with 1/4 teaspoon salt and 1/8 teaspoon pepper.

■ Combine the peas, carrots, onion, dill, garlic and remaining salt and pepper; spoon over fish. Drizzle with wine or broth. Top with a second large piece of foil. Bring edges of foil pieces together; crimp to seal, forming a large packet.

■ Bake at 400° for 20-25 minutes or until fish flakes easily with a fork and vegetables are crisp-tender. Open foil carefully to allow steam to escape.

Yield: 4 servings.

*Nutrition Facts: 1 fillet with 3/4 cup vegetables equals 178 calories, 2 g fat (1 g saturated fat), 55 mg cholesterol, 396 mg sodium, 13 g carbohydrate, 4 g fiber, 24 g protein. **Diabetic Exchanges:** 3 very lean meat, 2 vegetable.

New England Fish Bake

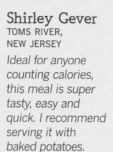

Norma DesRoches
WARWICK, RHODE ISLAND

I've lived in Rhode Island for 36 years, and this fresh seafood dish is a favorite of mine.

PREP: 25 min.
BAKE: 20 min.

4 medium potatoes, peeled

1 teaspoon all-purpose flour

1 small onion, sliced into rings

1/2 teaspoon salt

1/4 teaspoon pepper

3/4 cup milk, *divided*

1-1/2 pounds cod fillets *or* freshwater fish (trout, catfish *or* pike)

3 tablespoons grated Parmesan cheese, optional

2 tablespoons minced fresh parsley *or* 2 teaspoons dried parsley flakes

1/4 teaspoon paprika

■ Place potatoes in a saucepan and cover with water. Bring to a boil. Reduce heat; cover and simmer for 15-20 minutes or until tender. Drain; cool slightly.

■ Slice the potatoes 1/8 in. thick; place in a greased shallow 2-qt. baking dish. Sprinkle with flour. Top with onion; sprinkle with salt and pepper. Pour half of milk over potatoes. Place fish on top; pour remaining milk over fish. Sprinkle with Parmesan.

■ Cover; bake at 375° for 20-30 minutes or until fish flakes with a fork. Sprinkle with parsley and paprika.

Yield: 3-4 servings.

In a nonstick skillet, saute the leeks and garlic in olive oil until tender; set aside. Coat a 13-in. x 9-in. baking dish with cooking spray. Arrange the basil in a single layer in dish; top with fish fillets. Sprinkle with salt. Top with leek mixture.

Arrange the tomatoes and olives over the fish. Thinly slice half of the lemon; place over the top. Squeeze juice from the remaining lemon over all. Sprinkle with pepper.

Cover; bake at 425 for 15-20 minutes or until the fish flakes easily with a fork. Garnish with rosemary.

Yield: 4 servings.

*Nutrition Facts: One serving equals 186 calories, 6 g fat (1 g saturated fat), 34 mg cholesterol, 857 mg sodium, 9 g carbohydrate, 3 g fiber, 26 g protein. **Diabetic Exchanges:** 3 lean meat, 1 vegetable.

Mediterranean Baked Fish

Ellen De Munnik
CHESTERFIELD, MICHIGAN

The mouthwatering aroma of this herbed dish baking is sure to lure guests to your kitchen. It makes a lovely and colorful presentation for company.

Mediterranean Baked Fish*

PREP/TOTAL TIME: 30 min.

1 cup thinly sliced leeks (white portion only)	2 plum tomatoes, sliced
2 garlic cloves, minced	1 can (2-1/4 ounces) sliced ripe olives, drained
2 teaspoons olive oil	1 medium lemon
12 large fresh basil leaves	1/8 teaspoon pepper
1-1/2 pounds orange roughy fillets	4 fresh rosemary sprigs
1 teaspoon salt	

To prepare leeks for slicing or chopping, remove withered outer leaves, trim the root end and cut off the green upper leaves at the point where the pale green becomes dark green. Leeks often contain sand between their many layers, so cut the leek lengthwise and rinse each half under cold running water, separating the leaves as they are rinsed.

Slow Cooking 101

43

60

102

The original slow cooker, called a Crock-Pot®, was introduced in 1971 by Rival®. Today, the term "slow cooker" and the name Crock-Pot® are frequently used interchangeably when referring to this appliance.

Most slow cookers have two or more settings. Foods will cook faster on the high setting, however, the low setting is ideal for all-day cooking or for less tender cuts of meat. If your slow cooker has a "warm" setting, use it to keep food warm until it's ready to serve. All the recipes in this cookbook refer to cooking on either "high" or "low."

Some newer slow cookers seem to heat up more quickly than older ones. If you have an older model and your recipe directs to cook on low, you may want to set it on the highest setting for the first hour of cooking to ensure food safety.

When a range in cooking time is provided, this accounts for variables such as thickness of meat, how full the slow cooker is or the temperature of the food going into the cooker. As you become more familiar with your slow cooker, you'll be better able to judge which end of the range to use.

When Using Your Slow Cooker...

Slow cookers come in a range of sizes, from 1-1/2 to 7 quarts. It's important to use the right size for the amount of food you're making. In general, to serve a dip from a buffet, the smallest slow cookers are ideal. To entertain or cook for a potluck dinner, the larger cookers work best.

To cook properly and safely, manufacturers and the USDA recommend slow cookers be filled at least half full but no more than two-thirds full. Check the chart below to find a useful size for your household.

With many slow cooker recipes, all of the ingredients are added at once and are cooked all day. For convenience, place the ingredients in the crock the night before, then cover and refrigerate overnight (a removable stoneware insert makes this an easy task). In the morning, place the crock in the slow cooker and select the temperature.

Do not preheat your slow cooker. An insert that has been in the refrigerator overnight should always be put into a cold base unit. Stoneware is sensitive to dramatic temperature changes, and cracking or breakage could occur if the base is preheated.

When the recipe has cooked for the required amount of time, cool leftovers and store in the refrigerator. Slow cookers should not be used to reheat leftovers. Use a microwave, stovetop burner, or conventional oven to reheat foods to 165° to ensure that the food is safe to eat.

Following a power outage of less than two hours, you can finish cooking your food with your stovetop or microwave. If it's been more than two hours or you are unsure how long the power has been out, discard the food.

Slow Cooker Size

Household Size	Slow Cooker Capacity
1 person	1-1/2 quarts
2 people	2 to 3-1/2 quarts
3 or 4 people	3-1/2 to 4-1/2 quarts
4 or 5 people	4-1/2 to 5 quarts
6 or more people	5 to 7 quarts

Tips for Tasty Outcomes

- No peeking! Refrain from lifting the lid while the food cooks in the slow cooker, unless you're instructed in a recipe to stir or add ingredients. The loss of steam can mean an additional 20 to 30 minutes of cooking time each time you lift the lid.

- Be sure the lid is placed on the ceramic insert properly, not tilted or askew. The steam during cooking creates a seal.

- When food is finished cooking, remove it from the slow cooker within 1 hour and promptly refrigerate any leftovers.

- Slow cooking may take longer at higher altitudes.

- Don't forget your slow cooker when you go camping, provided electricity is available. It's a handy appliance when space is limited and you want "set-it-and-forget-it" meals.

- Reheating foods in a slow cooker is not recommended. Cooked food can be heated on the stovetop or in the microwave and then put into a slow cooker to keep hot for serving.

- Use a slow cooker on a buffet table to keep soups, stews, warm dips or mashed potatoes hot.

Converting Recipes for the Slow Cooker

Almost any recipe that bakes in the oven or simmers on the stovetop can be converted for the slow cooker. Here are some guidelines.

Before converting recipes, check the manufacturer's guidelines for your particular slow cooker. Locate a recipe similar to the one you want to convert. Use it as a guide. Note the quantity and size of meat and vegetable pieces, heat setting, cooking time and amount of liquid.

Since there is no evaporation, adjusting the amount of liquid in your recipe may be necessary. If a recipe calls for 6 to 8 cups of water, try starting with 5 cups. Conversely, recipes should include some liquid. If a recipe does not include liquid, add a 1/2 cup of water or broth.

In general, 1 hour of simmering on the range or baking at 350°F in the oven is equal to 6-8 hours on low or 3-4 hours on high in a slow cooker. Check the chart below.

Flour and cornstarch are often used to thicken foods (such as soup and stew) that are cooked in a slow cooker.

Cooking Times

Conventional Recipe	Slow Cooker
15 to 30 minutes	Low: 4 to 6 hours High: 1-1/2 to 2 hours
35 to 45 minutes	Low: 6 to 8 hours High: 3 to 4 hours
50 minutes or more	Low: 8 to 10 hours High 4 to 6 hours

Helpful Foil Handles

Layered dishes or meat loaves, such as Mushroom Meat Loaf (p. 55), are easier to get out of the slow cooker using foil handles. Here's how:

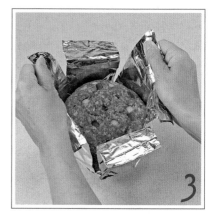

Cut three 20- x 3-inch strips of heavy-duty aluminum foil or create them by folding wider strips of regular foil. Crisscross the strips so they resemble the spokes of a wheel.

Place the meat loaf in the center of the strips, and pull them up and bend the edges to form handles.

Grasp the foil handles to lift the loaf and lower it into the slow cooker. Leave the foil in while you cook so you can easily lift the meat out to serve.

*Note: For a layered dish, place the strips in the cooker and up the sides before putting in the food. Leave them in. Once the food is cooked, pull the strips together as a handle to neatly remove the food in one piece.

A Melting Pot of Ingredients

Beans. Dried beans can be tricky to work with in the slow cooker. Minerals in the water and variations in voltage affect different types of beans in different ways. As a result, dried beans should always be soaked before adding to a slow cooker recipe. To soak beans for use in a slow cooker, place them in a Dutch oven or stockpot and add water to cover by 2 inches. Bring to a boil, and boil for 2 minutes. Remove from the heat, cover and let stand for 1 hour. Drain and rinse the beans, discarding the liquid. Sugar, salt and acidic ingredients, such as vinegar, have a hardening effect on beans and will prevent them from becoming tender. So it's best not to cook beans with these flavorings, but to add them only after the beans are fully cooked. Lentils and split peas do not need to be soaked.

Dairy. Milk-based products tend to break down during slow cooking. If possible, add items like milk, sour cream, cream cheese or cream during the last hour of cooking. Cheeses don't generally hold up over extended periods of cooking, so they should be added near the end of cooking. Condensed cream soups can be cooked in slow cookers for extended periods of time with minimal curdling concerns.

Fish & Seafood. Since fish and seafood cooks quickly in a slow cooker and can break down if cooked too long, it is often added toward the end of the cooking time.

Meats. For enhanced flavor and appearance, meat may be browned before going into the slow cooker, but it's not necessary. However, browning may improve the color of the meat and create an overall richer flavor. When cooking a roast over 3 pounds, be sure to cut it in half before placing it in the slow cooker. This ensures thorough cooking. Frozen meats should be completely thawed before placing in a slow cooker. When preparing meat or poultry for the slow cooker, trim off excess fat. It retains heat, and large amounts of fat could raise the temperature of the cooking liquid, causing the meat to overcook.

Oats. Quick-cooking and old-fashioned oats are often interchangeable in recipes. However, old-fashioned oats hold up better when cooked in a slow cooker.

Pasta & Couscous. If added to a slow cooker when dry, pasta tends to become very sticky. It is better to cook it according to the package directions and stir it into the slow cooker just before serving. Small pastas, such as orzo and ditalini, may be cooked in the slow cooker. To keep them from becoming mushy, add during the last hour of cooking. For the best results when using couscous, cook on a stovetop instead of a slow cooker.

Rice. Converted rice is ideal for all-day cooking. If using instant rice, add it during the last 30 minutes of cooking.

Vegetables. Vegetables, especially potatoes and root vegetables (such as carrots), tend to cook slower than meat. Place these vegetables on the bottom and around the sides of the slow cooker and put meat on top of the vegetables. Add tender vegetables, like peas and zucchini, or those you'd prefer to be crisp-tender, during the last 15 to 60 minutes.

Hints for Cleaning Slow Cookers

Removable stoneware inserts make cleanup a breeze. Be sure to cool the insert before rinsing or cleaning with water to avoid cracking. Do not immerse the metal base unit in water. Clean it with a damp sponge.

Wash the insert in the dishwasher or in warm soapy water. Avoid using abrasive cleansers since they may scratch the stoneware.

To remove mineral stains on a crockery insert, fill the cooker with hot water and 1 cup white vinegar; cover. Turn heat control to high for 2 hours. Then empty. When cool, wash with hot sudsy water and a cloth or sponge. Rinse well and dry with a towel.

To remove water marks from a highly glazed crockery insert, rub the surface with vegetable oil and allow to stand for 2 hours before washing with hot sudsy water.

Substitutions & Equivalents

Equivalent Measures

3 teaspoons	=	1 tablespoon	16 tablespoons	=	1 cup
4 tablespoons	=	1/4 cup	2 cups	=	1 pint
5-1/3 tablespoons	=	1/3 cup	4 cups	=	1 quart
8 tablespoons	=	1/2 cup	4 quarts	=	1 gallon

Food Equivalents

Grains

Macaroni	1 cup (3-1/2 ounces) uncooked	=	2-1/2 cups cooked
Noodles, Medium	3 cups (4 ounces) uncooked	=	4 cups cooked
Popcorn	1/3 to 1/2 cup unpopped	=	8 cups popped
Rice, Long Grain	1 cup uncooked	=	3 cups cooked
Rice, Quick-Cooking	1 cup uncooked	=	2 cups cooked
Spaghetti	8 ounces uncooked	=	4 cups cooked

Crumbs

Bread	1 slice	=	3/4 cup soft crumbs, 1/4 cup fine dry crumbs
Graham Crackers	7 squares	=	1/2 cup finely crushed
Buttery Round Crackers	12 crackers	=	1/2 cup finely crushed
Saltine Crackers	14 crackers	=	1/2 cup finely crushed

Fruits

Bananas	1 medium	=	1/3 cup mashed
Lemons	1 medium	=	3 tablespoons juice, 2 teaspoons grated peel
Limes	1 medium	=	2 tablespoons juice, 1-1/2 teaspoons grated peel
Oranges	1 medium	=	1/4 to 1/3 cup juice, 4 teaspoons grated peel

Vegetables

Cabbage	1 head	=	5 cups shredded	Green Pepper	1 large	=	1 cup chopped
Carrots	1 pound	=	3 cups shredded	Mushrooms	1/2 pound	=	3 cups sliced
Celery	1 rib	=	1/2 cup chopped	Onions	1 medium	=	1/2 cup chopped
Corn	1 ear fresh	=	2/3 cup kernels	Potatoes	3 medium	=	2 cups cubed

Nuts

Almonds	1 pound	=	3 cups chopped	Pecan Halves	1 pound	=	4-1/2 cups chopped
Ground Nuts	3-3/4 ounces	=	1 cup	Walnuts	1 pound	=	3-3/4 cups chopped

Easy Substitutions

When you need...		Use...
Baking Powder	1 teaspoon	1/2 teaspoon cream of tartar + 1/4 teaspoon baking soda
Buttermilk	1 cup	1 tablespoon lemon juice or vinegar + enough milk to measure 1 cup (let stand 5 minutes before using)
Cornstarch	1 tablespoon	2 tablespoons all-purpose flour
Honey	1 cup	1-1/4 cups sugar + 1/4 cup water
Half-and-Half Cream	1 cup	1 tablespoon melted butter + enough whole milk to measure 1 cup
Onion	1 small, chopped (1/3 cup)	1 teaspoon onion powder or 1 tablespoon dried minced onion
Tomato Juice	1 cup	1/2 cup tomato sauce + 1/2 cup water
Tomato Sauce	2 cups	3/4 cup tomato paste + 1 cup water
Unsweetened Chocolate	1 square (1 ounce)	3 tablespoons baking cocoa + 1 tablespoon shortening or oil
Whole Milk	1 cup	1/2 cup evaporated milk + 1/2 cup water

Cooking Terms

Here's a quick reference for some of the cooking terms used in *Taste of Home* recipes:

Baste—To moisten food with melted butter, pan drippings, marinades or other liquid to add more flavor and juiciness.

Beat—A rapid movement to combine ingredients using a fork, spoon, wire whisk or electric mixer.

Blend—To combine ingredients until just mixed.

Boil—To heat liquids until bubbles form that cannot be "stirred down." In the case of water, the temperature will reach 212°.

Bone—To remove all meat from the bone before cooking.

Cream—To beat ingredients together to a smooth consistency, usually in the case of butter and sugar for baking.

Dash—A small amount of seasoning, less than 1/8 teaspoon. If using a shaker, a dash would comprise a quick flip of the container.

Dredge—To coat foods with flour or other dry ingredients. Most often done with pot roasts and stew meat before browning.

Fold—To incorporate several ingredients by careful and gentle turning with a spatula. Used generally with beaten egg whites or whipped cream when mixing into the rest of the ingredients to keep the batter light.

Julienne—To cut foods into long thin strips much like matchsticks. Used most often for salads and stir-fry dishes.

Mince—To cut into very fine pieces. Used often for garlic or fresh herbs.

Parboil—To cook partially, usually used in the case of chicken, sausages and vegetables.

Partially Set—Describes the consistency of gelatin after it has been chilled for a small amount of time. Mixture should resemble the consistency of egg whites.

Puree—To process foods to a smooth mixture. Can be prepared in an electric blender, food processor, food mill or sieve.

Saute—To fry quickly in a small amount of fat, stirring almost constantly. Most often done with onions, mushrooms and other chopped vegetables.

Score—To cut slits partway through the outer surface of foods. Often used with ham or flank steak.

Stir-Fry—To cook meats and/or vegetables with a constant stirring motion in a small amount of oil in a wok or skillet over high heat.

General Recipe Index

Alphabetical Recipe Index